Reading Romans as Lament

Reading Romans as Lament

Paul's Use of Old Testament Lament
in His Most Famous Letter

CHANNING L. CRISLER

Foreword by
MARK A. SEIFRID

☙PICKWICK *Publications* · Eugene, Oregon

READING ROMANS AS LAMENT
Paul's Use of Old Testament Lament in His Most Famous Letter

Copyright © 2016 Channing L. Crisler. All rights reserved. Except for brief quotations in critical publications or reviews, no part of this book may be reproduced in any manner without prior written permission from the publisher. Write: Permissions, Wipf and Stock Publishers, 199 W. 8th Ave., Suite 3, Eugene, OR 97401.

Pickwick Publications
An Imprint of Wipf and Stock Publishers
199 W. 8th Ave., Suite 3
Eugene, OR 97401

www.wipfandstock.com

PAPERBACK ISBN 13: 978-1-4982-3216-6
HARDCOVER ISBN 13: 978-1-4982-3218-0

Cataloguing-in-Publication Data

Crisler, Channing L.

Romans as lament : Paul's use of Old Testament lament in his most famous letter / Channing L. Crisler, with a foreword by Mark A. Seifrid

x + 242 p. ; 23 cm. Includes bibliographical references.

ISBN: 978-1-4982-3216-6 (paperback) | ISBN: 978-1-4982-3218-0 (hardback)

1. Bible. Romans—Criticism, interpretation, etc. 2. Laments in the Bible. 3. Suffering—Biblical teaching. I. Seifrid, Mark A. II. Title.

BS2665.52 C84 2016

Manufactured in the U.S.A.   04/11/2016

To Kelley, my greatest help and precious wife, and to those whose suffering was never far from my heart—Taylee, my daughter who had a "bad day"; Kimberly, my strong sister; Edie, who lost so much; the late Donald Moore, whose smile I can still see; and the late Dwight Ball, whom I am honored to have called a friend.

Contents

Foreword by Mark A. Seifrid | ix

1 Introduction | 1
2 The Literary Form and Theological Message of Old Testament Lament | 16
3 The Gospel as the Answer to the Righteous Lamenter (Romans 1:16–17) | 45
4 The Gospel as the Answer to the Unrighteous Lamenter (Romans 3:1–26) | 66
5 The Gospel as the Answer to the Lamenting "I" (Romans 7:7—8:4) | 94
6 The Gospel as the Answer to Groans and Inexplicable Rejection (Romans 8:18–39) | 119
7 The Gospel as the Answer to Israel's Intercessory Lamenter (Romans 9:1—11:36) | 151
8 The Gospel as the Answer to the Church's Lament (Romans 15:1–6) | 189
9 Lament and Paul's Theology of Suffering in Romans | 202

Bibliography | 219
Ancient Documents Index | 227

Foreword

CHANNING CRISLER'S THOROUGH STUDY of the way biblical lament resounds within Paul's argument in Romans has the potential of revolutionizing the way in which we read the letter. If God's righteousness is nothing other than God's fulfillment of God's saving promises in the resurrected Jesus in the face of human lament, all our calculations of how the world works are turned upside down. "Justice" is then not finally a mere distributive justice for which the death of Jesus provides a saving, yet legal solution. Justice is here taken up within the saving promises of God as they have been fulfilled in the crucified and *risen* Jesus, in whom (and in whom alone) God's love triumphs over God's entirely justified wrath. God ultimately operates by a righteousness that transcends our understanding, and for that reason had to be *revealed* in the gospel. As Crisler rightly underscores, this righteousness remains a future hope, even though it has been revealed in Jesus' resurrection. We belong to the risen Lord, but we have not yet been raised from the dead. For the apostle Paul there is a place, indeed, a necessary place, for "lament" in our life between the times. This recognition should not only bring comfort to many, but also bring us to reflection as to whether our own Christian faith corresponds to the apostolic message. There is much to be gained from Crisler's detailed consideration of biblical laments and the particular ways in which Paul has taken them up in his letter to Rome. His work makes a fresh contribution to the growing recognition of the place of lament in the theology of the apostle.

Mark A. Seifrid
Professor of Exegetical Theology
Concordia Seminary, St. Louis

1

Introduction

Israel's scriptures are full of prayers. The Law, the Prophets, and the Writings record people addressing God in different situations for different reasons. Suffering, on an individual or national level, is one of the most common situations in which prayers arise. A common form of prayer in these instances is often referred to as lament (*Klage*). Lament is the quintessential language of suffering in ancient Israel, because it both indicates and interprets pain. It is the next best thing to being present at the historical moment of someone's hurt. One could say that lament is like "tears on papyrus." It is most often associated with jarring cries such as "My God, my God, why have your forsaken me?" Yet, such cries are only the tip of the iceberg in terms of lament's literary features and theology. Although it often goes unnoticed, the letter to the Romans contains a large amount of this kind of language. The presence of lament in Romans is significant for a number of reasons as we will see. Above all, it provides a potential window into the suffering of Paul and his recipients, but only if the letter is read in light of the lament it contains. Herein lies the problem.

It is not easy to identify and analyze OT lament in Romans. After all, lament is a form of prayer and Romans is an ancient letter. Even when Paul explicitly mentions prayer, he does not record the full content of that prayer within the letter. Nevertheless, OT prayer, particularly lament, is echoed throughout the letter. These echoes have the potential to impact how we read Romans and thereby how we understand Paul's thoughts about suffering.[1] That is the focus of this work, to read Romans as lament, assess how

---

1. In his recent tome on Paul, Wright notes the importance of prayer language in the Pauline corpus for understanding Paul's thought. He writes, "We have at several points

that affects our interpretation of the letter, and infer what this tells us about Paul's theology of suffering.

DEFINING LAMENT

The term lament (*Klage*) generally evokes thoughts of sadness or crying due to extreme pain. For some, it is a synonym for the verbal reflexes that are enacted in moments of surprise or tragedy. Expressions such as "Oh my God" are indicative of this response.[2] In the field of biblical scholarship, lament is defined in a few different ways.[3] Some define lament strictly in relation to prayers, songs, or sounds heard at an Israelite funeral.[4] Based on the English word alone, some confine the discussion to the book of Lamentations.[5] Still others want to discuss lament only as it relates to specific vocabulary from the Masoretic Text, the LXX, or Greek New Testament. This approach can be seen in discussions about lament in the NT.[6] There is certainly a place for examining so-called lament vocabulary, but the discussion in this study will not be limited to terminology alone. In any case, none of the preceding definitions capture the multi-layered nature of OT lament that Paul employs in Romans.

When I speak of "lament" in Romans, it refers to the literary features, pattern, and theology of lament that are evoked through various OT citations and echoes. We are not merely dealing with loud shrieks or cries. To be sure, Romans contains some jarring cries of distress:

> O wretched man that I am who will deliver me from the body of this death? (Rom 7:24).
>
> On account of you we face death all day long, we were reckoned as sheep for slaughter (Rom 8:36).

---

noticed Paul's prayers, not simply as pious attachments to the outside of his theological or practical teaching but as their very heart. This is the place to end, and perhaps to begin." Wright, *Paul and the Faithfulness of God*, 1516.

2. On lament as a verbal reflex, see Bauer, "Enquiring into the Absence of Lament," 26–27.

3 For a cautionary word on biblical scholarship's use of the word "lament," see Campbell, "NT Scholarship's Use of Old Testament Lament Terminology," 213–25.

4 Westermann helpfully distinguishes between the lament of the dead, a funeral dirge, and the lament of distress. It is the latter that is the focus of this work. See Westermann, *Praise and Lament in the Psalms*, 168.

5 In discussing my research on lament in Romans, this is often the first association that others make. It is the thought that lament is a synonym for funeral dirges or the book of Lamentations.

6 E.g., Öhler, "To Mourn, Weep, Lament and Groan," 150–65.

> For I myself was wishing to be accursed from Christ for my brethren, my fellow kinsmen according to the flesh (Rom 9:3).

However, these cries alone do not define lament in the letter. They are only part of a wider nexus of literary features and theological motifs. Simply put, lament is an event involving the lamenter, God, and enemies. The event often follows a flexible five-fold sequence involving: prior promise, suffering, cry of distress, deliverance, and praise.[7] In this event, tension arises between what God has promised and what the lamenter experiences at the hands of enemies. That tension elicits a cry of distress in which lamenters request that God deliver them from their enemies. God answers that request by saving or somehow reiterating the promise to save. Consequently, the lamenter praises God. This event, or at least portions of it, can be found in various parts of the OT, and, as we shall see, in Romans as well. Furthermore, the theological contours of lament are shaped by the oscillation between hope and suffering, deliverance and defeat, divine presence and divine absence, and between cries of distress and praise. In short, lament is defined by the lamenter's back and forth experience of pain and hope. This same oscillation is evoked in Romans in order to describe the experience of Paul and his recipients who live by faith.

AIM & THESIS

This work aims to explore and articulate the significance of OT lament in Romans. What kind of lament language does Paul use? How does hearing the echoes of lament impact the interpretation of Paul's rhetorical argument? Since lament is the quintessential language of suffering, what does its presence in Romans tell us about Paul's theology of suffering? These are the questions that will occupy our attention in the chapters ahead.

The thesis in what follows is that the experience of OT lamenters is echoed in Romans, and those echoes largely shape the way Paul discusses suffering in the letter. If we read Romans in light of its lament echoes, we discover aspects of Paul's rhetorical argument and theology of suffering that might otherwise go unnoticed. In short, lament amplifies the underlying tension that exists in the letter between what the gospel promises and the suffering that the righteous experience. Although the suffering described

---

[7] This pattern has been adapted based on the work of a few different OT scholars who have dealt at length with biblical lament. E.g., Brueggemann, "The Psalms and the Life of Faith," 3–32; Miller, *They Cried to the Lord*; Westermann, "The Role of Lament," 20–38.

in Romans comes in various forms, the echoes of lament indicate that the all-encompassing cause of pain in the letter is a concern with divine wrath.

The primary echoes of lament are located in Romans 1:16–17; 3:1–20; 7:7—8:1–4; 8:18–39; 9:1–5; and 15:1–6. The echoes in these passages evoke the experiences of those such as Habakkuk, the psalmist, Moses, and Elijah. Their painful experiences are often described through the idiom, pattern, and theology of lament. These lament features are taken up by Paul but also reworked around his particular concerns and historical milieu.

LAMENT IN ROMANS AND THE HISTORY OF RESEARCH

The present analysis of lament in Romans can be located, though not exclusively, in the broader and ongoing discussion about Paul's use of the OT in his letters.[8] Interpreters have long recognized that one cannot understand Paul's argumentation without considering his use and interaction with Israel's scriptures. As Dodd reminds us, "There are two open doors into Paul's world. The one is the Old Testament, which all Christian readers of the epistle should know."[9] Many have heeded Dodd's dictum in their investigation of Romans as any number of commentaries, articles, and monographs indicate.[10] However, far fewer have seen OT lament as a "door" into Paul's thought in Romans.

Of course, it should come as no surprise that interpreters have not given much attention to Paul's use of lament in Romans. NT scholarship as a whole has shown a general lack of interest in exploring lament.[11] The lack of interest can be traced to a few different factors. First, until Hermann Gunkel applied his form-critical analysis to the psalms in the early twentieth century, modern biblical interpreters did not really see lament as a formal category of inquiry. While OT scholarship has been quite productive in analyzing the biblical text in light of the lament form, NT scholarship has

---

8 In the concluding chapter of this work, I will briefly discuss the history of research related to Paul and suffering.

9 The other "door" into Paul's world, according to Dodd, is "Greek thought." Dodd, *The Epistle of Paul to the Romans*, 24.

10 For monographs on Paul's use of the OT in Romans, see e.g., Abasciano, *Paul's Use of the Old Testament in Rom 9:1–9*; Bell, *Provoked to Jealousy*; Berkley, *From a Broken Covenant to Circumcision of the Heart*; Christoffersson, *The Earnest Expectation of the Creature*; Hübner, *Gottes Ich und Israel*; Keesmaat, *Paul and His Story*; Shum, *Paul's Use of Isaiah in Romans*; Wagner, *Heralds of the Good News*.

11 There are a few exceptions. See e.g., Ahearne-Kroll, *The Psalms of Lament in Mark's Passion*; Eklund, *Jesus Weeps*.

tended to lag behind. Second, interpreters have generally seen lament as incongruent with the historical and theological milieu of the early church. Some have dismissed altogether the notion that lament plays any role in the writings of the NT or the experience of Jesus' earliest followers. To many, a cry for deliverance akin to lamenters in the OT is simply misplaced in a first-century religious community that proclaimed the resurrection of its founder. Along these lines, Öhler argues, "The New Testament is characterized by the absence of lament. There are no newly written psalms and songs of lament, indeed that painful turning to God in the face of suffering and death almost seems opposed to the Christian way of life."[12] In light of the vast swath of echoes of lament in Romans, I could not disagree more. Öhler's analysis is an overstatement to say the least. Even more, it betrays a rather thin definition of lament and one that does not accurately reflect the way lament works in the OT or NT.

With all of this said, there are some interpreters who have substantively examined lament in Romans. There have been enough inquiries into the topic to constitute a "history of research." In what follows, I will briefly summarize and critique interpreters who have treated lament in Romans in more than a cursory manner.[13]

The Recontextualization of Lament in Romans

Roy A. Harrisville examines Paul's many citations from the Psalms of Lament in Romans.[14] He attempts to uncover how Paul treats the original context of the psalms, something we will also do in subsequent chapters. Harrisville recognizes that it is difficult to reconcile the original context of these psalms with their usage in Romans. In an effort to solve this dilemma, Harrisville argues that Paul "recontextuazlies" certain Psalms of Lament into the flow of the letter's argument.[15] "Recontextualization," according to Harrisville, means that Paul both added to and subtracted from the form and function of the language as it stood in its original context.

Harrisville's analysis of Psalm 44:23 (43:23 LXX), which Paul cites in Romans 8:36, provides an example of his recontextualization theory.

---

12 Öhler, "To Mourn, Weep, Lament and Groan," 150.

13 I have only included works here that examine lament throughout the entire letter. There are a few interpreters, most notably Gaventa, Seifrid, and Stuhlmacher, who have analyzed Rom 7 in light of OT lament. I will discuss their contributions in chapter 5.

14 See Harrisville, "Paul and the Psalms," 168.

15 Ibid.

Harrisville argues that Paul recontextualizes this lament citation in a number of ways. First, Paul recontextualizes the psalmist's political enemies. The psalmist complains about military and political opponents, but Paul's enemies in the wider context of Romans 8:35–39 include, "tribulation, distress, or persecution, or famine, or nakedness, or peril, or sword, etc." Second, Harrisville argues that Paul does not adopt the psalmist's "mood." Paul could not possibly react to suffering in the same vein as the psalmist who complains vociferously that God has rejected his people, "Surely you have rejected and humiliated us; and you do not go out with our armies" (Ps 44:10; 43:10 LXX). Therefore, even though the portion of the psalm that Paul cites originally functioned as a complaint like this one, Harrisville does not believe Paul shares in the somber mood or tone of the psalmist. In fact, for Harrisville, Paul cites Psalm 43:23 LXX as a foil for what the apostle is really trying to say. By recontextualizing the psalm, Paul transforms the psalmist's complaint into a "descriptive statement of the Christian life" where the believer is "more than a conqueror."[16] In essence, what served as a cry of distress for the psalmist serves as a cry of victory for Paul.

There are a number of things to note about Harrisville's study. First, he is right to recognize that Romans contains a high volume of Psalms of Lament, but his theory of "recontextualization" is problematic for a number of reasons. Next, if one follows Harrisville's definition of recontextualization, Paul's exegesis of the Psalms of Lament becomes nothing more than proof-texting. For example, if the mood and complaint of Psalm 44 is entirely absent from Paul's argument in Romans 8:31–39, as Harrisville argues, then Paul has simply lifted a phrase out of its context irrespective of the emotionally charged tone it carries. Harrisville's presupposition, at least in this instance, seems to be that if Paul did not explicitly cite certain elements from the Psalms of Lament, then they have no bearing on the interpretation of the wider context in Romans. As he notes, "There are no quotations or allusions respecting the complaint aimed directly at God . . . or from complaints which describe the sinner's distress as illness or disease, physical or mental."[17] This is a misguided conclusion. One of Harrisville's main examples, Psalm 43:23, originally functioned as a complaint against God. The "tone," or "mood," of the psalm that Harrisville contends is absent from Romans is actually incorporated into the letter through the citation of Psalm 43:23. Third, Harrisville does not account for the OT lament-like complaints found in Romans 7:24 and 9:3. As I will discuss later, these are jarring cries that are on par with the painful mood and tone of the Psalms of

16 Ibid., 176.
17 Ibid.

Lament, something Harrisville claims is absent from the letter. One should not conclude that Paul has recontextualized the complaints of the Psalms of Lament into shouts of triumph in Romans, because such a conclusion is not supported by the literary evidence of the letter itself. To some degree, Harrisville's treatment of lament in Romans is typical of NT interpreters who feel that the somber context of the Psalms of Lament cannot possibly be present in a letter expounding the gospel of God.[18] Yet, as I will demonstrate in this study, it is within this very kind of somber and painful experience that Paul expounds the gospel in Romans.

To be fair, Harrisville does not set out to provide an exhaustive treatment of the Psalms of Lament in Romans. He does, however, intend to be comprehensive or draw larger conclusions about what the lament language in Romans could mean for the interpretation of the letter and inferences about Paul's theology of suffering. Overall, recontextualization, though helpful to some degree, cannot account for the full impact of OT lament on Paul's thought in the letter.

Lament as Echoing Theodicy in Romans

Richard B. Hays also recognizes that Romans contains a great deal of OT lament. He does not analyze it in either an isolated or systematic way but as part of his larger, and well-known, project that examines OT intertextuality in the Pauline corpus, particularly Romans.[19] Nevertheless, while lament is not his primary concern, Hays treats the issue with more than a few passing comments. His appraisal of lament in Romans is what I would call "echoing theodicy." Not surprisingly, Hays reads Paul's use of lament in Romans in a way that supports his overarching thesis about the letter, namely that Paul attempts to defend God's ways with Israel. Some of Hays's observations about lament in Romans will be helpful for the present study.

First, Hays identifies "clusters" of lament echoes throughout the letter.[20] He argues that these clusters evoke key themes from OT lament that Paul takes up in Romans. For example, Hays posits that the citation of Habakkuk 2:4 in Romans 1:17 evokes a "theodicy theme." As he puts it, "Hab 2:4 speaks directly to the theological problem of God's faithfulness to Israel."[21] This means that Paul is not proof texting Habakkuk. To the contrary, Hays recognizes that Habakkuk 2:4 is an "answer to the prophet's claim (Hab 2:1)

---

18 Cf. Öhler, "To Mourn, Weep, Lament and Groan," 150.
19 See Hays, *Echoes of Scripture*, 38.
20. Ibid.
21 Ibid., 39.

against the apparent injustice of God's ways, complaint intoned through the first chapter of the book."[22] Hays rightly concludes that Paul is evoking themes from Habakkuk through his citation, particularly themes intertwined with lament. However, as I will discuss later, theodicy is not the theme ultimately being evoked. Respectfully, Hays fails to appreciate the original function and theology of lament language taken up by the prophet. Theodicy is not the best description of what is taking place in Habakkuk or Romans. What Paul evokes through his citation is answered lament. It is an answer that comes through the revelation of God's righteousness. This is something slightly different from theodicy. Habakkuk's questions of "how long" and "why" that Hays rightly hears in Romans 1:16–17 are not ultimately about theodicy. They are about relief. That is what Habakkuk wants; therefore, that is what Paul wants as well. I will have much more to say about this in the chapters ahead. In any case, Hays' more general observation about the evocation of larger lament themes through the citation of one lament text is a fundamental tenet of the present study. The alternative to this position is to maintain that, at best, Paul haphazardly attempts to throw the authority of the OT behind his own arguments, or, at worst, that he is pilfering the OT for theologically innocuous nomenclature.[23] Neither alternative is consistent with the function of OT lament in Romans.

A second observation by Hays that will prove helpful for the present study is the importance he places on Psalm 69:9 (Ps 68:10 LXX) for understanding Paul's others uses of the Psalms of Lament in the letter. Hays explains:

> According to Rom 15:4–6, then, the purpose of Scripture—and the lament psalms are particularly in view here—is to provide a christologically grounded model of steadfastness to sustain hope in the midst of adversity, so that members of the community can continue to act for the edification of others even in the midst of opposition and temporary disunity.[24]

For Hays, the Messiah is the speaker in Psalm 69. The Messiah's hope in the midst of suffering, as cited by Paul, becomes paradigmatic for the believing community in Rome. Furthermore, according to Hays, the Messiah's paradigmatic suffering and hope is linked to the issue of theodicy. Hays writes, "Many of the psalms, even where they employ first-person singular discourse, are not strictly individual; they address the crisis of theodicy

---

22 Ibid.
23 For this argument, see e.g., Sanders, *Paul: A Very Short Introduction*, 66–70.
24 Hays, *The Conversion of the Imagination*, 113.

created by God's apparent abandonment of his covenant people."[25] As in his analysis of Paul's Habakkuk citation, Hays filters the use of Psalm 69, and other Psalms of Lament, through the interpretive lens of theodicy. Once again, I respectively object to describing the Psalms of Lament, or Romans, as theodicy. Lament is not ultimately the langue of theodicy but of suffering. Theodicy reduces the function of lament language to philosophical dialogue about the ways of God rather than a complaint about pain that also functions as a hope filled request for deliverance. Furthermore, while Hays rightly highlights the importance of Psalm 69:9 for understanding Paul's other uses of the Psalms of Lament in the letter, its interpretive value lies in soteriology rather than theodicy. As I will discuss in chapter 8, Paul's citation of Psalm 69:9 in Romans 15:3 indicates that the answer to lament, and the concern over divine wrath that accompanies it, is found in the saving effect of Christ's suffering rather than the mere imitation of it.

Lament for a Narrative of Justice in Romans

Sylvia C. Keesmaat is another Pauline interpreter who has examined the high volume of lament in Romans.[26] She argues that Paul employs the Psalms of Lament in order to speak about God's justice, particularly his faithfulness to Israel. In this way, her approach is akin to Hays' work, as she acknowledges. In addition to Hays, Keesmaat also utilizes the works of Walter Brueggemann and Richard A. Horsley.[27] She posits that Paul uses the Psalms of Lament in order to commend faith to the Romans in the face of empirical enemies. Keesmaat explains, "As Israel's faith was always formed and lived in the shadow of empire, so also is the faith that Paul commends to the Christian community in Rome at the heart of the empire."[28] Her thesis combines Horsley's imperialistic reading of Romans with Brueggemann's argument that lament can be defined by "disorientation" and "reorientation."[29] She describes the latter two terms as follows:

> Laments describe an experience of disorientation by complaining that reality is not as it should be. When the wicked prosper and the righteous are oppressed, something is awry in

---

25 Ibid., 118.

26 Keesmaat, "The Psalms in Romans and Galatians," 139–61.

27 See Brueggemann, "The Costly Loss of Lament," 98–111; Horsley, *Paul and Politics*; Elliott, *The Arrogance of the Nations*.

28 Keesmaat, "The Psalms in Romans and Galatians," 139.

29 For an extended discussion of these terms, see Brueggemann, "Psalms and the Life of Faith," 3–32.

covenantal life. Psalms of thanksgiving, sometimes psalms of recital, give to a reorientation that has come through a time of confusion and trouble to a new place of hope and resolution.[30]

Keesmaat applies Brueggemanns' categories of "disorientation" and "reorientation" to Paul's use of Psalms of Lament in Romans 1:16–17, 3:10–20, 8:31–39, 10:18, 11:1–2, 9–10, and 15:3. According to Keesmaat, these psalms evoke a certain context, or world. She explains, "Paul has also evoked the world of lament, where the question of God's faithfulness and justice is up for grabs, where the psalmist insistently petitions God to do something about the injustice and rejection that he has faced."[31] Such a context, or world, is indicative of the one in which the Christians at Rome lived. From Keesmaat's perspective, they could either find righteousness in the "imperial narrative of Caesar or in the story of Israel as reinterpreted in the light of the story of Jesus."[32] She concludes her analysis noting:

> By the end of the epistle to the Romans, Paul—both through his argument and psalmic allusion—has evoked another story, another set of symbols, and another praxis that stand in judgment over the story, symbols and praxis of the empire that surrounded on every side the house churches in Rome.[33]

The "other story," for Keesmaat, is the story of God's faithfulness to Israel, despite living under the shadow of imperial Rome.

The present work has some synergy with Keesmaat's analysis. First, she rightly notes that Christians in Rome faced suffering and questions analogous to those raised in the Psalm of Lament. The use of lament in Romans evokes some of the themes associated with these particular psalms. Moreover, like Hays, Keesmaat argues that lament is a fundamental part of the thesis statement in Romans 1:16–17.[34] Next, I agree with Keesmaat's observation that in his citations Paul does not exchange the painful tone of the Psalms of Lament with a more triumphant one in Romans. For example, unlike Harrisville, and more in line with what I will argue later, Keesmaat does not interpret the citation of Psalm 44:23 in Romans 8:36 in purely triumphant terms. She understands that the citation functioned as a complaint in its original context and that Paul maintains that complaint in his argument. Finally, while I will not employ the terms "disorientation" and

30 Keesmaat, "The Psalms in Romans and Galatians," 141.
31 Ibid., 141.
32 Ibid., 139.
33 Ibid., 157.
34 Ibid., 141.

"reorientation" in this work, Keesmaat is right to observe that Paul's use of lament evokes a "world of lament" which interpreters should recognize in their treatment of the letter.

Despite these agreements with Keesmaat, my fundamental disagreement with her analysis is at the level of identifying the enemies in Romans. She seems to limit the enemies who afflict Paul and his recipients to Imperial Rome. Consequently, Keesmaat does not really acknowledge a cause of suffering beyond Rome. Her analysis gives one the impression that suffering in Romans is not directly related to sin or divine wrath. Yet, in the letter itself, Paul incorporates lament language to describe a far wider range of combatants and problems. Most notably, sin is described as an enemy in the vein of OT lament and its ongoing affliction in the lives of Paul and his recipients raises questions about divine wrath.

Midrash and Lament in Romans

Although he only deals with lament in Romans 9–11, David R. Wallace's monograph length treatment of the issue warrants his inclusion in the present discussion. Wallace argues that lament and midrash shape Paul's argument in Romans 9:1—11:36. With respect to lament's impact on the literary structure of this portion of the letter, he posits that Romans 9:1–5 and 11:33–36 form "an *inclusio*, moving the reader from grief to praise."[35] He explains, "Paul's content and arrangement in these chapters follow an Old Testament lament pattern of an address, body, and a final praise. In the address, the speaker establishes his right to speak, he emphasizes the covenant, and he invokes God's action on Israel's behalf."[36] For Wallace, Paul does not directly invoke God to action for Israel; therefore, he "builds suspense concerning Israel's outcome."[37] After the intercession in Romans 9:1–5, which Wallace argues echoes Moses' intercession from Exodus 32, "Paul uses logical arguments within a lament sequence to defend God's faithfulness."[38] Paul intercedes for Israel and then turns his focus to "God's character in his choosing the 'younger' son."[39] Therefore, from Romans 9:6—11:33, Paul defends God's dealings with Israel. Another way that lament shapes Paul's argument in these chapters, according to Wallace, is the shift to praise in 11:33–36. He observes, "Paul's lament ends with praise to

35. Wallace, *Election of the Lesser Son*, 11.
36 Ibid., 12.
37 Ibid.
38 Ibid.
39 Ibid., 53.

God for his merciful and wise plan for Israel."[40] Finally, it is worth noting that, in addition to Moses, Wallace argues that Paul identifies himself with other OT intercessors such as Isaiah, Jeremiah, and Elijah.[41]

While there are some commendable aspects to Wallace's treatment of lament in Romans 9–11, I find it lacking in a number of ways. First, Wallace does not thoroughly investigate the lament form in light of its OT roots. This is evident in his discussion about the pattern of lament in Romans 9–11 which he identifies as "address, body, and a final praise."[42] As I will discuss in the next chapter, the pattern of lament is far more complex than this. By reducing the pattern to a very general movement, Wallace misses the full impact of lament on Paul's argument in Romans 9–11. Second, he gives almost no consideration to the echoes of Moses' intercessory laments from Exodus 32–34 in Romans 9:1–5. He only observes that "Paul relates to Moses's experience in some degree."[43] This undercuts the full impact of hearing the echoes from Moses' intercessory lament on the interpretation of Romans 9:1–5. Third, Wallace's treatment of lament is really limited to the observation that, like OT lament's shift from cry to praise, Paul begins with a cry in Romans 9:1–5 and ends with praise in Romans 11:33–36. Between those two points Paul uses logical arguments to defend God's faithfulness. However, as we will see, the nature of lament itself and its impact on Romans 9–11 goes far beyond the shift from lament to praise.

Lament as the Language of Suffering in Romans

Mark A. Seifrid's assessment of OT lament in Romans is closest to my own.[44] In fact, as will be evident, much of the present work is built upon Seifrid's observations. Specifically, Seifrid's manner of assessing how Paul incorporates lament themes into his letter is fundamental to my own approach. In a number of places, he consciously engages with the use of lament in Romans and allows that interaction to shape his interpretation of Paul's argument. This is especially evident in Seifrid's interpretation of Romans 7 and 9–11. He does not limit his analysis to specific citations or allusions but includes wider echoes of lament located throughout the letter. For example, in his analysis of Romans 9:1–5, Seifrid observes, "It is the promise of Israel's salvation, not the visible evidence of it, that provokes Paul's lament there

---

40 Ibid., 223.
41 Ibid., 238.
42 Ibid., 12.
43 Ibid., 38.
44 See Seifrid, *Romans*, 607–94.

and that likewise elicits his own hymn of praise in 11:33–36."[45] Like Wallace, but with greater theological insight, Seifrid observes the shift from lament to praise in Romans 9–11. He is aware that everything between the beginning and end of this section is impacted by lament. As Seifrid notes, "Paul's opening lament provides the conceptual framework for the entire discourse, including the hymn of praise, which, according to the pattern of the psalms of lament, reaffirms the hope of the promises, contrary to all outward appearances."[46]

Both at the exegetical and theological level, Seifrid considers how Paul evokes and incorporates the literary and theological features of OT lament. Although his concern is with the broader analysis of how Paul uses the OT in Romans, Seifrids' observations about lament are foundational to my own analysis. Most importantly, his argument that Paul's use of lament incorporates OT lament's theology of suffering in the letter is pivotal to my own thesis and approach.

APPROACH TO THE STUDY

Our approach in what follows consists of specific starting points that in turn shape the interpretive steps taken in the analysis. First, one cannot understand the full impact of OT lament in Romans without recourse to its original context. One piece of lament always works in concert with another. Those other "pieces" are only found in the wider passages from which an OT citation or echo arises.[47] Consequently, whenever we encounter a lament citation or echo in the letter, our first step will be to analyze how that piece of lament functioned in its original context. Specifically, we will consider how the lament "fragment" functioned within its larger lament pattern and what theological themes are present in it.

Next, the version of Israel's scriptures used by Paul most often follows or resembles the LXX. To be sure, there are instances in which Paul's citations do not follow the LXX.[48] Nevertheless, with a number of other Pauline interpreters, I agree that generally speaking Paul's "citations characteristically

---

45 Ibid., 638.

46 Ibid.

47 As Wright notes regarding the use of Israel's scriptures, "Whole passages, whole themes, can be called to mind with a single reference." Wright, *Paul and the Faithfulness of God*, 176–77. Similarly, a single lament reference can evoke whole laments and their accompanying theological themes.

48. Sometimes that divergence is explainable. See e.g., Paul's version of Hab 2:4 in Rom 1:17. However, at other times, the divergence is not easily explained.

follow the Septuagint."[49] Consequently, in this work, all OT references and my translations of them will follow the LXX unless otherwise indicated.

Third, Romans, like the rest of the NT, contains intertextual echoes from the OT.[50] Intertextuality is "the imbedding of fragments of an earlier text within a later one."[51] These fragments occur in the form of citations, allusions, and echoes. In this work, a citation is defined as an explicit reference to an OT text that is often accompanied by some kind of introductory formula.[52] An allusion is defined as an explicit reference to OT passages without explicit citation of an OT text.[53] An echo is defined as phrases, expressions, or words in Romans that evoke a text from Israel's scriptures, but that text is not necessarily cited nor alluded to by Paul. Echoes will often be connected to formal citations or allusions but not necessarily so.[54] Given the frequent occurrence of intertextuality in Romans, we will focus our attention on echoes of OT lament. Lament echoes will be identified and then analyzed for their impact on Paul's rhetorical argument. The method employed for identifying these lament echoes is based in large part on Hays' seven tests for "hearing" echoes. These tests include: (1) *Availability*—Was the proposed source of the lament echo available to Paul when he wrote Romans? (2) *Volume*—How many words or syntactical patterns from the lament source occur in Romans? (3) *Recurrence*—How often does Paul cite the proposed lament text elsewhere? (4) *Thematic Coherence*—How well does the lament echo fit with Paul's argument in the letter? (5) *Historical Plausibility*—Could Paul have intended the lament echo? Could his readers have detected the lament echo? (6) *History of Interpretation*—Have other interpreters heard these echoes of lament? and (7) *Satisfaction*—Do the echoes of lament illuminate the surrounding discourse of the letter?[55] Once the lament echoes have been identified, we will turn our attention to analysis. Specifically, we will consider what "poetic effect" the echoes have

---

49 Hays, *Echoes of Scripture*, x–xi. For a thorough discussion on this issue generally, see Koch, *Die Schrift als Zeuge des Euangeliums*. For a discussion related specifically to Romans, see Stanley, *Paul and the Language of Scripture*, 83–184.

50 This starting point has been well established by a number of interpreters, most notably Hays.

51 Hays, *Echoes of Scripture*, 14.

52 See, e.g. Rom 4:22; 9:7; 10:13; 10:18; 11:34; 15:10, 11. For a discussion on OT introductory formulas in Paul's letters, see Bruno, "Readers, Authors, and the Divine Author," 312; Watson, *Paul and the Hermeneutics of Faith*, 43–47.

53 See e.g., Rom 5:12–21.

54 There are OT lament echoes that occur in Rom 7:7–25 and 9:1–5, but these passages contain no formal OT allusions or citations.

55 Hays, *Echoes of Scripture*, 29–32.

on Paul's argument. In other words, what "larger meanings" are produced in Romans when the interpreter hears Paul's use of lament.

Finally, the exegetical findings that emerge from reading Romans as lament will be brought to bear on the motif of suffering in the letter. We will consider what light is shed on Paul's theology of suffering in light of the fact that he employs so much of the quintessential language of suffering in his letter. This discussion will be set within the larger history of research on Paul and suffering.

It is this final step that we are working towards in each and every chapter. In chapter 2, I will give an overview of OT lament. We will consider OT lament's history of interpretation, literary features, and theology. This will lay the proper ground work for subsequent discussions about lament in Romans. Chapter 3 will examine three echoes of lament in Romans 1:16–17 and their impact on Paul's thesis statement. Next, in chapter 4, we will look at Paul's extensive use of lament in Romans 3:1–20. Here we will see how Paul uses OT lament to describe the justification of God, Jews and Gentiles "under sin," and the cry for mercy in the face of eschatological judgment. Chapter 5 deals with the letter's most explicit use of the lament pattern, Romans 7:7—8:4, as well as Paul's description of sin in the vein of enemies bemoaned in OT lament. In chapter 6, we will consider Paul's two-fold use of OT lament: (1) to explain the interplay between hope and suffering which creation, the children of God, and the Holy Spirit participate in; and (2) to answer complaints/concern with inexplicable suffering at the hands of God. Chapter 7 addresses the widespread use of lament in Romans 9–11. Here we find Paul's intercessory cry of distress for unbelieving Israel that is subsequently answered by God. In chapter 8, we will consider the pedagogical effect of OT lament, integrated with the crucifixion scene, on Paul and his recipients. Finally, in chapter 9, the exegetical findings of reading Romans as lament are brought to bear on the issue of Paul and suffering. Here we will consider how the OT echoes of lament in Romans point to an all-encompassing source of pain, namely the tension between the promise of the gospel and the wrath of God.

2

The Literary Form and Theological Message of Old Testament Lament

On the heels of citing Psalm 68:10, an individual lament, Paul explains, "For as many things that were written beforehand, they were written for our instruction, in order that through endurance and through the encouragement of the scriptures we might have hope" (Rom 15:4). Paul believes that Israel's scriptures have something to offer the Christians in Rome. They are in fact didactic (διδασκαλία) in nature. This obviously includes OT lament which, as I will show in subsequent chapters, permeates the entire letter. Yet, what does OT lament teach Paul's recipients? That is the question that will occupy our attention throughout the entirety of this work. Before seeking an answer in the letter itself, we need to familiarize ourselves with the literary form and theological message of lament as it stands in the OT. As Francis Watson encourages Pauline interpreters, "If Paul's readers are to read his own texts critically and with understanding, they must join him in reading the scriptural texts to which he appeals."[1] This chapter is an effort to do just that. In order to read Romans as lament, we must first establish the form, function, and theology of lament in the OT.

What follows is an attempt to "tune" the reader's "senses" to hear the echoes of lament in Romans.[2] Specifically, with respect to the form of

---

1. Watson, *Paul and the Hermeneutics of Faith*, 78.

2 As Oswald Bayer puts it, "Once the senses have been sharpened by the Old Testament, one can also recognize the 'eschatology of answered lament' in the New Testament." Bayer, "Toward a Theology of Lament," 213.

lament, we need to acquaint ourselves with the participants and pattern of lament. Additionally, we must also consider how lament communicates the pain of its participants. Finally, given the form and function of lament, we need to lay out the basic contours of the theology of lament. We begin with a brief look at the contributions by two of the leading lights of lament interpretation within OT scholarship.

THE CONTRIBUTIONS OF GUNKEL & WESTERMANN TO THE STUDY OF OT LAMENT

A number of monographs on OT lament have appeared over the past several decades.[3] This flurry of works is an indication that many have noticed the "costly loss of lament" in OT interpretation and theological formation.[4] My purpose here is not to review all of those works but rather discuss the contributions of two leading lights in the field whose work has influenced virtually all subsequent discussions. They are Herman Gunkel and Claus Westermann.

The Father of the *Gattungenforschung*

At the turn of the twentieth century, form critics intensified the search for the socio-historical conditions (*Sitz im Leben*) that gave rise to OT literature.[5] Among those involved in this work, Herman Gunkel became known as the "father of the *Gattungenforschung*." His work on the Psalms of Lament is seminal and quite extensive. He made a number of contributions to the study of lament that I want to highlight.

To begin, Gunkel makes a distinction between lament and lamentation. As I mentioned in the previous chapter, these two forms should not be confused with one another. Gunkel was one of the first to recognize this. Many of his efforts are focused on individual and communal psalms to which he applied the label *Klage*.[6] Gunkel posits that the *Sitz im Leben* of a communal lament (*Klage*) was a "lament festival" or "fast" rather than a

---

3 See e.g., Broyles, *The Conflict of Faith and Experience*; Boyce, *The Cry to God in the Old Testament*; De Vos, *Klage als Gotteslob aus der Tiefe*; Basson, *Divine Metaphors*; Floysvik, *When God Becomes My Enemy*; Mandolfo, *God in the Dock*.

4 Brueggemann, "The Costly Loss of Lament," 98–111.

5 See Schultz, "Form Criticism and the OT," 233.

6 Subsequent interpreters have adopted the label, and it continues to serve as a label for the genre today. See Coetzee, "A Survey of Research on the Psalms of Lamentation," 151.

funeral service.⁷ He explains the difference, "The funeral service knows no hope and does not occur in the sanctuary, since according to the ancient belief of Israel, the dead have no relationship to Yahweh."⁸

Second, Gunkel identifies a number of literary features common to the Psalms of Lament. Communal and individual laments share many of these features, but Gunkel argues that the latter are "far more richly" developed than the former.⁹ Gunkel's observations can be grouped according to the following: participants, complaints, theology, and shift in mood.¹⁰ For Gunkel, the participants in a communal lament, that is the lamenter, God, and enemies, are not involved in a conversation. Instead, the speaker is giving a speech. That is why, at least according to Gunkel, the speaker often addresses God as "you." The complaints directed towards the "you" involve various misfortunes and contain supplications for a reversal of those misfortunes. For Gunkel, the complaints are almost exclusively political. Theologically, the people interpret their political misfortune as a revelation of divine wrath. This elicits questions such as "why" and "how long." Moreover, the community petitions a change in God's judgment against them by appealing to "all kinds of rationale for stirring divine intervention." There is frequently an appeal to God's reputation and grace. Lastly, with respect to the shift in mood within lament, Gunkel observes that there is often an expression that indicates the "certainty of being heard."

Third, Gunkel's contributions also include an attempt to explain what he perceives as the eventual disappearance of the Psalms of Lament within Israel's history. He argues that these psalms originated in the Israelite cult but that gradually lament became "separated from its cultic context."¹¹ Consequently, lament prayer "developed into a kind of spiritual poetry whose form gradually became compromised by mixtures with other genres."¹² He goes on to surmise that by the Maccabean era the original genre of lament had come to an end.

There are other contributions that could be mentioned here. Most notably, Gunkel had a large impact on form criticism in general.¹³ However, my focus is not form criticism as it relates to reconstructing the history of

---

7 Gunkel, *Introduction to the Psalms*, 82–83.

8 Ibid., 85.

9 Ibid., 122.

10 For a fuller discussion of the literary characteristics discussed here, see Gunkel, *Introduction to the Psalms*, 85–93.

11 On Gunkel's thesis, see Westermann, *Praise and Lament in the Psalms*, 16.

12 Ibid., 16.

13 Ibid.

Israelite literature.[14] The benefit of Gunkel's analysis for the present study is the contributions outlined above, particularly the literary and theological features that he identifies.

The Exegete and Theologian of the *Klage*

Westermann's investigation builds on Gunkel's work. However, while still probing the historical and literary dimensions of OT lament, Westermann also demonstrates a great concern for exegesis and the theological implications of lament in the OT. He defines lament as "an event between the one who laments, God, and the enemy."[15] In this "event" of lament, Westermann sees a number of defining characteristics but also an eventual disappearance of the prayer form within Israel. There are many contributions that could be highlighted here, but I will limit myself to the ones that are most germane to the present study.[16]

First, regarding the participants of lament, Westermann makes a number of helpful observations about enemies. He analyzes the participants according to their actions and nature. Westermann summarizes the actions of enemies under three headings: (1) they set traps; (2) they are like wild beasts on the lamenter; and (3) they are like attacking soldiers.[17] Additionally, he describes their actions as "preparatory." Enemies plan ahead and utter threats. They also surround and encircle their victims. They approach, draw near, and arm themselves all before attacking. With respect to the nature of enemies, Westermann describes them as "perverse, sacrilegious and godless."[18] The pinnacle of the enemies' perversity is that they no longer acknowledge God at all. The actions and nature of the enemies are so disturbing to lamenters that they actually begin to meditate upon them to the

---

14 In this study, I have chosen to focus on the literary form of lament rather than attempt to reconstruct the historical setting behind lament. The latter endeavor is worthwhile and has a number of contributors. For an overview of such an approach, see e.g., Brueggemann, "The Formfulness of Grief," 84–88; Ferris, *The Genre of Communal Lament*, 1–4.

15 Ibid., 213. He also observes that the "lament of the individual" is by nature "trichotomous." In other words, it always involves the three participants: I—the lamenter; You—God; Them—enemies. See Westermann, *Praise and Lament in the Psalms*, 182.

16 Some readers might feel that I am not highlighting some of Westermann's more significant contributions. I would simply note that my purpose here is not to give an exhaustive critique of Westermann. Rather, I am simply attempting to review those contributions of Westermann that are most helpful for interpreting OT lament.

17. Westermann, *Praise and Lament in the Psalms*, 189.

18 Ibid., 190.

same extent that they meditate on God. The enemies are not only located outside the Israelite community in the form of political opponents but also within the community.

Next, Westermann offers insight into the complaints within a lament, particularly the questions that lamenters ask. For example, he identifies the question "why" as the earliest and simplest form of lament.[19] Westermann argues that the question "why" assumes that the lamenter's suffering is related to alienation from God. It is actually a question about divine absence rather than theodicy in the philosophical sense. He observes, "The question 'Why?' asks why God has rejected, abandoned, or forgotten his people. In the blow he has suffered, the lamenter has experienced God's denial."[20] Westermann also treats the question "how long?" It is not a complaint about a "sudden blow" but "constant duress."[21] Moreover, the question of "how long," like "why," is also a question about God's absence. In addition to analyzing the complaints that lamenters express through questions, Westermann also looks at complaints that come in the form of statements. Such statements are often found in individual laments with "startling bitterness."[22] Yet, they stop short of condemning God.

Third, Westermann distinguishes somewhat between the "lament of the people" and the "lament of the individual." In the former, everything is concentrated in the one motif of an accusation against God, whether by a question or statement.[23] That accusation can arise in times of war where the lamenter, on behalf of the entire community, complains about enemies. Westermann claims that in the "lament of the individual" the motif of accusations against God is toned down. It is not entirely missing, as evidenced by Psalms 12 and 21.[24] Nevertheless, the accusation is made "much less frequently and obviously with less force and vigor." The complaints about God's absence in individual laments are often contained in "negative petitions."[25] Westermann also argues that the enemies in the "lament of the people" are "totally" different from those in the "lament of the individual."[26] In the "lament of the people" the enemies are clearly "political." However, in the

19 Ibid., 197.
20 Ibid., 176–77.
21 Ibid., 177.
22 Ibid., 177.
23 Ibid., 177–78.
24 As I explained in the previous chapter, throughout this work all references to the Psalms will follow the chapter and versification of the Rahlfs' edition of the LXX.
25 Ibid., 185.
26 Ibid., 193.

"lament of the individual," the enemy threatens the lamenter personally. In this instance, "The lamenter alone is under duress. Never is it even implied that the lamenter belongs to a circle of friends who are being assailed."[27]

Fourth, Westermann argues that in the post-exilic period lament as a prayer form almost completely disappears in Israel. Petitions without lament and prayers of repentance become the norm in the literature of the era.[28] The only residue of lament is found not in prayer but in free standing statements not explicitly directed to God.[29] Lament is eventually separated from prayer entirely.

Finally, Westermann's greatest contribution may be the pattern of lament that he detects in various OT genres that he says has a fundamental place in Israel's story. He describes the basic structure, or pattern, of a lament psalm in five parts: address, lament, turning toward, petition, and vow of praise.[30] In his reflection on the lament pattern in Exodus 1–15 and Deuteronomy 26:5–11, two passages that retell a pivotal part of Israel's story, he describes the pattern piece by piece. Regarding these passages, he notes "The events making up the deliverance form a sequence which is always encountered (though it is not always the same) wherever a deliverance is related: distress, a cry of distress, a hearkening (promise of deliverance), deliverance, response of those saved (the praise of God)."[31] Westermann believes the pattern of lament in these passages establishes "the place of the lament in the theology of the Old Testament."[32] Specifically, lament and the saving acts of God are indissolubly linked. Where there is deliverance there is a cry of distress.[33]

As we move forward with our overview of OT lament, the influence of Gunkel and Westermann will be clear. Westermann's influence will be especially noticed because of his exegetical and theological work in lament. That is intentional. His observations more closely coincide with the focus of this work.

---

27 Ibid., 193.

28 Westermann points to examples in Ezra 9, Dan 9, and 3 Macc 6:1–15. See many other passages in Westermann, *Praise and Lament in Psalms*, 201–12.

29 See, e.g. 1 Macc 2:6.

30 Ibid., 170.

31 Ibid., 259–60.

32 Ibid., 260.

33 See Exod 2:23–24; 3:7–9; Deut 26:7.

THE LITERARY FORM OF OLD TESTAMENT LAMENT

If we are to fully appreciate the echoes of lament in Romans, we must first familiarize ourselves with the various literary features of this prayer form. These features include the participants, metaphors, and expressions of lament. The discussion here is not meant to be exhaustive.[34] I am simply laying the necessary groundwork for analyzing the specific uses of lament in Romans. Such analysis requires a working knowledge of the lament form which I am providing here. To reiterate, as I noted in the previous chapter, I am using the term lament as a reference to an entire form of prayer and not merely a cry of distress.

Participants of Lament

Following Gunkel and Westermann, Janowski identifies three participants in OT lament. He describes them as *Gottklage*, *Ichklage*, and *Feindklage*.[35] Lament inherently involves the lamenter, God, and enemies. Each participant has different traits and plays different roles in the event, or experience. Those traits and roles will be discussed throughout this chapter. What I offer here is some basic elements of their identity in OT lament.

At the most basic level, the lamenter is someone who suffers and cries out to God for deliverance. This description can be seen in any number of cries such as "Save me (σῶσόν με), O God, because the waters have entered unto my soul" (Ps 68:2). Lamenters may cry out for what they suffer personally, communally, or even as a figure who intercedes for others. Ferris sees a slight distinction between individual and communal lamenters. He describes the individual lament as something that "was composed to be used by and/or on behalf of an individual to express sorrow and grief over some perceived calamity which had befallen or was about to befall him and to appeal to God for deliverance."[36] Contrastively, the communal lament is something "composed to be used by and/or on behalf of a community."[37] Ferris' description of individual and communal lamenters holds true in the Psalms of Lament and other genres of the OT. As we will see, Romans echoes both individual and communal laments. Some prime examples include the echoes of individual lament in Romans 7:7–25 and the citation of

---

34 For a thorough treatment, see e.g., Westermann, *Praise and Lament in the Psalms*, 16–94.

35 Janowski, "Klage," 4:1390.

36 Ferris, *The Genre of Communal Lament*, 10.

37 Ibid.

a well-known communal lament, Psalm 43, in Romans 8:36. Westermann also describes an intercessory or mediating lamenter. He defines the mediating lament as "A special form inasmuch as it deals with the affliction of the people, but the one who laments is an individual whose position among the people is ordained by God."[38] Such a figure is seen "most vigorously" in Moses, but it is also present "from Elijah through Amos and Hosea, to Jeremiah and the Servant of God in Second Isaiah."[39] The most prominent examples in Romans are the echoes of Moses' intercessory lament for Israel in Romans 9:1–5 and Elijah's lament for/against Israel in Romans 11:2–5.

God is the second participant of lament. The lamenter's complaints, petitions, and praise are always directed towards him.[40] He receives the lamenter's cries, because in OT lament he is the one who can deliver those who are suffering. God's involvement in the event is often marked by the vocative address such as κύριε or ὁ θεός. This is readily seen in many Psalms of Lament, "O Lord (κύριε), do not rebuke me in your anger nor discipline me in your wrath" (Ps 37:2).[41] The divine vocative can appear in both cries of distress and praise. In Romans, the divine vocative appears in both cries of distress and praise that echo this feature of OT lament. For example, we will see this in our discussion of Romans 7:24–25 where Paul's cry of distress quickly shifts to praise, "But thanks be to God (θεῷ) through Jesus Christ our Lord (κυρίου)." It is also present in Paul's intercessory lament for Israel where the cry of distress shifts to praise for Jesus' deliverance, "The one who is God (θεός) over all blessed forever, amen" (Rom 9:5).

The third participant in lament is the enemy, or enemies, who are a never-ending source of distress to the lamenter.[42] Their identity covers a wide range of entities, but they can be broadly classified as "external" and "internal." There is overlap between these two classifications, so that the descriptions of external enemies are often taken up in describing internal ones. There are three images routinely applied to enemies in the Psalms of Lament.[43] Lamenters, both in their praise and complaints, describe enemies as attacking armies:

---

38 Westermann, *Praise and Lament in the Psalms*, 196.

39 Ibid., 196.

40 See e.g., Pss 6:4; 7:3; 12:1; 24:1.

41 See e.g., Pss 25:1; 26:7; 43:27; 68:7.

42. For a helpful discussion on enemies in the Psalms of Lament, see Westermann, *Praise and Lament*, 180–81, 188– 95; Kraus, *Psalms 1–59*, 95–99.

43 I am following Kraus' categories here. See Kraus, *Psalms 1 –59*, 95.

> If an army (παρεμβολή) should marshal itself against me, my heart will not fear; if war (πόλεμος) should rise up against me, in this I hope. (Ps 26:3)
>
> "Who reckon unrighteousness in their heart, all day long they were setting up for wars (πολέμους). (Ps 139:3)[44]

The movements and strategies of an attacking army, such as overpowering and surrounding, are sometimes applied figuratively to the lamenter's enemies.[45] Enemies can also be likened to hunters and fishermen who prey upon the lamenter. Their movements and strategies are also a part of their descriptions:

> You will bring me out from this trap (παγίδος), which they hid for me, because you are my protector. (Ps 30:5)
>
> Because for no reason they hid for me the ruin of their trap (παγίδος), without cause they reviled my soul. (Ps 34:7)

Like hunters, the lamenter's enemies are crafty, deceptive, and opportunistic.[46]

A third image applied to enemies is that of a wild animal seeking something to devour:

> Many young bulls (μόσχοι) surround me, fat bulls (ταῦροι) encompass me; they open their mouth against me like a lion (λέων) who seizes and roars. (Ps 21:13–14)
>
> When those who do evil were coming near to me in order to devour (φαγεῖν) my flesh those who afflict me and my enemies were weakened and they fell. (Ps 26:2)

In addition to these images, enemies in OT lament are known for their deceitfulness and blatant disregard for God.[47] They act with utter impunity as if God will not judge them for the pain they cause, "The fool has said in his heart 'There is no God'" (Ps 12:1). This does not indicate an atheistic worldview but rather the degree to which enemies discount their future judgment. They afflict others as if "there is no God" who will actually see what they do and judge them for it, "For he has said in his heart, 'God has forgotten (ἐπιλέλησται), he has turned his face so as not to see (μὴ βλέπειν) at all'" (Ps 9:32).[48]

---

44 See also Pss 67:31; 75:4.
45 See e.g., Pss 37:5; 39:13; 65:12; 68:5; 139:10.
46 See Pss 63:4–5; 139:5–6.
47 See Ps 9:28.
48 Cf. Ps 93:7.

It should also be noted that external enemies are often political/militaristic in nature while internal enemies usually involve sin and guilt. The former can be seen in one of Israel's earliest cries of distress, "And the Lord said to Moses, 'I have surely seen the affliction of my people who are in Egypt (Αἰγύπτῳ) and I have heard their cry from their taskmasters; for I know their pain'" (Exod 3:7). Israel's enemies who elicit cries of distress are often political forces such as Egypt, Assyria, and Babylon. However, external enemies are not limited to foreign opponents but also include figures from within the Israelite community, even those close to the lamenter, "For if an enemy reviled me, I could endure it, and if the one who hates me boasted against me, I would have been hidden. But you are my peer, my guide and my acquaintance" (Ps 54:13–14). Internal enemies, most often discussed in the Psalms of Lament, are often associated with sin, lawlessness, and guilt:

> For my lawlessness (ἀνομίαι) has gone over my head, like a heavy load they have been made heavy upon me. (Ps 37:5)
>
> Deliver me from all my lawlessness (ἀνομιῶν), you gave me as a reproach to the fool. I was silent and I did not open my mouth, because you are the one who made me. Remove from me your blows; I have fainted from the strength of your hand. (Ps 38:9–11)

The latter example indicates another layer to the internal enemy of sin, namely the divine wrath that the lamenter faces for lawlessness. We will explore this further in a moment. Here I would simply note that divine judgment is often associated with both internal and external enemies. Simply put, lamenters often link enemy activity to God's wrath being leveled against them.[49]

As we will see, Romans echoes the kinds of external and internal enemies described here. In discussing sin, cosmic powers, and divine judgment, Paul takes up some of the same imagery used to describe enemies in OT lament. For example, he portrays sin as a deceitful, opportunistic, overpowering, and deadly enemy in Romans 7:7–25. In Romans 8:31–39, Paul catalogues various afflictions caused by unidentified foes and cosmic powers. His explanation echoes the description of the divine action taken against enemies of OT lament as well as doubts about divine wrath often associated with the affliction they cause. In these instances, and others, the enemies in Romans echo those described in OT lament.

---

49 As Terrien explains, "Disasters and maladies were commonly attributed to divine wrath. This, in turn was supposed to have been caused by human sinfulness." Terrien, *The Psalms*, 326.

I have only provided a thumbnail sketch of the various participants involved in OT lament. Our review of lament's idiom, pattern, and theology will provide further insight into those involved in the event of lament. It is an event that has a distinguishable language, a language we need to have our ears attuned to in order to identify and analyze its presence in Romans.

Questions and the Cry of Distress in OT Lament

The language of lament in the OT consists of various cries, metaphors, and expressions. Our discussion cannot be limited to specific terms that bear the meaning of "cry," "lament," or "shout." There is definitely a place for such lexical investigation, but my focus here is much broader.[50] We need to consider the literary features, or distinct idiom, associated with OT lament. This is especially important given the larger aims of the present study. We cannot really hear the echoes of lament in Romans, let alone analyze their interpretive impact, unless we are familiar with the stock language of this prayer form. Once again, the discussion here is not exhaustive. However, it will provide us with the proper framework for identifying and analyzing OT lament in Paul's letter.

We begin with what is most often associated with lament, namely the cry of distress. At its most basic level the cry of distress is a complaint and petition directed towards God.[51] The lamenter complains to God about what he or she suffers and petitions him for deliverance.[52] The lamenter often expresses this cry in the form of a question such as "how long? (ἕως πότε/ ἕως τίνος)" or "why? (ἵνα τί)." Psalm 12:1–2 provides a textbook example:

> How long (ἕως πότε), O Lord, will you forget me forever? How long (ἕως πότε) will you turn your face from me? How long (ἕως πότε) will I set counsel in my soul, having sorrow in my heart all day? How long (ἕως πότε) will my enemy be exalted over me? (Ps 12:2–3)[53]

---

50. For a discussion of lament vocabulary, see Boyce, *The Cry to God*, 7–24; Öhler, "To Mourn, Weep, Lament and Groan," 150–51.

51 As Miller notes, "All of the language of complaint or lament serves to ground the petition, and, like the more explicit motivation sentences . . . to encourage, justify, from the angle of one praying, the intervention of God as a necessary and appropriate step to overcome the suffering and distress." Miller, *They Cried to the Lord*, 87.

52 "Complaint" is not a synonym for the kind of faithless grumbling (διαγογγύζω) that is criticized at various points in Israel's history. See e.g., Exod 16:2, 7, 8; Num 14:2; Deut 1:27; Josh 9:18.

53 For an analysis of Ps 12 (Ps 13 MT) as an exemplar for understanding individual laments, see Janowski, "Das verborgene Angesicht Gottes," 25–53.

As noted earlier, Westermann interprets the "how long" question as a complaint about the duration of pain rather than a "sudden blow."[54] Embedded in the complaint "how long" is the lamenter's petition that God bring an end to the extended time of pain. Most often, lamenters want to know "how long" their enemies will afflict them, "how long" the Lord will be angry with them, or "how long" enemies will carry on without be judged. These various nuances are demonstrated in the following:

> How long (ἕως πότε), O God, will the enemy reproach? Will the enemy provoke your name forever? (Ps 73:10)[55]
>
> How long (ἕως πότε), O Lord, will you will be angry forever? How long will your zeal be kindled like a fire? (Ps 78:5)[56]
>
> How long (ἕως πότε), O Lord, will sinners? How long (ἕως πότε) will sinners boast? (Ps 93:3)[57]

As we shall see, although Romans does not contain the explicit phrase ἕως πότε or ἕως τίνος, echoes of the complaint "how long?" can be heard in the letter. We will find it in places such as Romans 9:1–5 where Paul's complaint echoes the quatrain of ἕως πότε from Psalm 12. Like an OT lamenter, Romans echoes concerns about the duration ("how long") of enemy activity and divine wrath.

With respect to the question "why" (ἵνα τί), Westermann reminds us that the complaint, or petition, in this instance has to do with God's absence in the midst of the lamenter's suffering.[58] The most well-known example is found in Psalm 21:2, "My God my God, pay attention to me; why (ἵνα τί) have you abandoned me?" Once again, the question functions as both a complaint and petition. More than an explanation in the philosophical vein of theodicy, the lamenter wants a return of God's presence in order to bring an end to the suffering. The question "why" is often coupled with phrases that further explicate the lamenter's frustration with God's absence. They include but are not limited to: "why" do you reject; "why" do you forget; "why" do you hide; "why" do you not forgive; "why" do you make me look at evil; "why" are you angry. I offer only a small sampling here:

---

54 Westermann, *Praise and Lament*, 177.
55 Cf. Ps 81:2.
56 Cf. Ps 79:5; 88:47; Jer 4:21; 12:4.
57 Cf. Job 19:2; Hab 1:2.
58 Westermann, *Praise and Lament*, 176–77.

> For you, O God, are my strength; why (ἵνα τί) have you rejected (ἀπώσω) me? And why (ἵνα τί) do I go about being sullen faced while my enemy afflicts me? (Ps 42:2)[59]
>
> I will say to God my protector, 'Why (ἵνα τί) have you forgotten (ἐπελάθου) me? Why (ἵνα τί) do I go about being sullen faced while my enemy afflicts me? (Ps 41:10)[60]
>
> Why (ἵνα τί), O Lord, have you rejected (ἀπωθεῖς) my soul? Why do you turn your face (ἀποστρέφεις τὸ πρόσωπόν σου) from me? (Ps 87:15)[61]
>
> Have you certainly not rejected Judah, and your soul left from Zion? Why (ἵνα τί) have you mocked us, and there is no healing to us? We waited for peace, and there were not good things; for a time of healing and behold terror. (Jer 14:19)
>
> Why (ἵνα τί) do you show (ἔδειξας) to me toils and pain, so as to look (ἐπιβλέπειν) upon misery and ungodliness? (Hab 1:3)[62]
>
> Why (ἵνα τί) have you rejected (ἀπώσω) forever, God? Why has your anger been kindled (ὠργίσθη ὁ θυμός) against the sheep of your pasture? (Ps 73:1)[63]

Though articulated in various ways, and containing various nuances, all of these phrases containing ἵνα τί, or a grammatical equivalent, express a complaint and petition regarding divine absence. The lamenters need God to be with them in order to deliver them from their enemies, evil, and God's own wrath. Paul's letter to the Romans does not contain the explicit question ἵνα τί. However, the larger concern embedded in the question is echoed at various places in the letter. For example, the echoes of lament in Romans 8:31–39 indicate possible disquietude about God's absence in the midst of pain. The echoes of lament in this section of the letter evoke the "why" type of question.

Cries of distress can be expressed in other ways besides questions. They can also come in the form of assertions about enemies and God. We will discuss this further in a moment. Here I would simply note that the cries of distress expressed through questions encapsulate the kind of deliverance that the lamenter seeks. In short, lamenters seek deliverance from

---

59. Cf. Ps 43:24–25.
60. Cf. Lam 5:20.
61. Cf. Ps 87:15.
62. Cf. Job 3:12; 10:18; Jer 20:18.
63. Cf. Exod 32:11.

enemies and divine wrath. They want the deliverance to come sooner rather than later, and they know it will require God's presence.⁶⁴

Metaphors and Expressions Involving the Lamenter

Lament language contains certain metaphors and expressions that describe the condition, or role, of the lamenter, God, and enemies. This language gives further shape to the participants that we outlined above. In anticipation of reading Romans as lament, it will be helpful to review some of this language as it appears in various genres of the OT.

Lamenters live in the tension that exists between what they suffer and their expectation that God will bring their pain to an end. The language associated with lamenters is defined by a condition of distress and hope that is conveyed in various ways. First, the lamenter's condition is sometimes likened to an animal that is weak, helpless, and vulnerable. One such animal metaphor involves sheep (πρόβατα):

> For on account of you we face death all day long, we have been reckoned as sheep (πρόβατα) for the slaughter. (Ps 43:23)⁶⁵

> Why (ἵνα τί) have you rejected forever, God? Why has your anger been kindled against the sheep (πρόβατα) of your pasture? (Ps 73:1)

In the OT, πρόβατα is often a reference to Israel.⁶⁶ Lamenters are sometimes distressed by the fact that God can both deliver his sheep from enemies and hand them over to their enemies. The sheep are dependent upon God for his protection and yet vulnerable to his judgment as well. This same dynamic is echoed in Romans. It is especially evident in Romans 8:31–39 where Paul's citation of Psalm 43:23 likens his recipients to sheep who are dependent on God for their protection and yet vulnerable to his judgment as well.

Next, OT lament uses spatial metaphors to describe the condition of lamenters. Writers frequently locate lamenters in a pit (λάκκος). The literal sense of λάκκος is often used to describe the location of imprisoned figures

---

64 Miller sums it up nicely, "When one is in distress and trouble, the questions that always come roaring to the forefront of the mind and heart—and here articulated in prayer—are 'Why is this happening?' or, to God, 'Why are you doing this (letting this happen, etc.)?' and the complaining query, 'When is this going to end? or 'How long do I have to endure this suffering?'" Miller, *They Cried to the Lord*, 72.

65 See also Ps 43:12; 94:7.

66 See e.g., Mic 2:12; 5:7; 7:14; Jer 3:21; 50:6; 50:17; Ezek 34:5, 6, 8, 10, 11, 15, 17.

such as Joseph, Jeremiah, and Daniel.⁶⁷ In OT lament, it is often a reference to an enemy's attempt to kill the lamenter, or a reference to the afterlife in Hades (Sheol):

> They killed my life in the pit (λάκκῳ) and they placed a stone over me. (Lam 3:53)⁶⁸
>
> Lord, you brought my life up from Hades (ᾅδου), you saved me from those who go down to the pit (εἰς λάκκον). (Ps 29:4)⁶⁹

It is from this pit that the lamenter will often cry out for deliverance, "I called upon your name, O Lord, from the pit (ἐκ λάκκου) below" (Lam 3:55).⁷⁰ The lamenter's position in the pit conveys the threat of death and separation from God. Similarly, lamenters use the image of "distance," or "withdraw," in their complaints and petitions about separation from God:

> Why, Lord, have you withdrawn (ἀφέστηκας) at a distance (μακρόθεν)? Why do you overlook us in times of need in tribulation? (Ps 9:22)
>
> Do not abandon me, Lord; my God, do not withdraw (ἀποστῇς) from. (Ps 37:22)

Separation from God worries lamenters, because the divine presence is required for their deliverance.⁷¹ Moreover, the implications of God's withdraw from the lamenters is that they are somehow wicked or unrighteous. After all, God's warning to Israel is that he will withdraw from them if they are disobedient to him.⁷² The psalmist acknowledges this noting, "Salvation (σωτηρία) is far (μακράν) from sinners, because they have not sought your righteous requirements" (Ps 118:155). This dynamic only adds to the lamenter's consternation over being separated from God. As we will see, Romans echoes the lamenter's consternation. It is especially heard in Romans 8–9. Paul, like the OT lamenter, cries out to God "from the depths" (ἐκ βαθέων) (Ps 129:1).

Often times, lamenters state their condition plainly or use inarticulate sounds to express their pain. The Psalms of Lament contain a number of such confessions that describe the lamenters' current state of affairs:

---

67 See e.g., Gen 37:20, 22, 24, 28, 29; 40:15; Jer 44:16; 45:6, 7, 10, 11, 13; Dan 6:9, 13, 15, 18, 20, 23.

68 Cf. Ps 7:16; 39:3; 87:7.

69 Cf. Ps 27:1; 142:7.

70 Cf. Ps 39:2–3; Jonah 2:2–9.

71 See e.g., Ps 21:1.

72 See e.g., Deut 31:18.

The Literary Form and Theological Message of Old Testament Lament   31

> I was miserable (ἐταλαιπώρησα) and bent down completely, all day long I was going around sullen faced. (Ps 37:7)
>
> I am poor (πτωχός) and needy; the Lord will take care of me. You are my helper and protector; my God, do not delay. (Ps 39:18)

In the lament language of the LXX, we often find ταλαιπωρέω or its cognates (i.e. ταλαιπωρία; ταλαίπωρος).[73] The lamenter's misery and poverty can emanate from enemy activity or divine wrath. In instances of the former, Psalm 11:6 stands out, "Because of the misery (ταλαιπωρίας) of the poor (πτωχῶν) and because of the groaning (στεναγμοῦ) of the poor, now I will rise, says the Lord, I will set them in salvation, I will deal openly with him." Here we find a cluster of terms associated with the lamenter's condition including ταλαιπωρία, πτωχός, and στεναγμός. They indicate a state of great loss and need. The term στεναγμός, or cognates, often expresses the inarticulate sounds made by lamenters in the midst of their misery and poverty.[74] It is associated with the physical act of crying, "I have grown weary in my groaning (στεναγμῷ), I will wash my couch each night, with my tears (δάκρυσίν) I will drench my bed" (Ps 6:7). Misery and crying are also associated with instances where lamenters express concerns over divine wrath, "For I was silent, my bones became old because I was crying (κράζειν) all day long; because day and night your hand was heavy upon me, I was turned to misery (ταλαιπωρίαν) while a thorn was fixed in me" (Ps 31:4). The misery, poverty, groaning, and tears of lamenters express the outcome of what enemies do, as well as what God does or does not do. The lament language in Romans echoes the same condition. This is especially evident in the miserable condition (ταλαίπωρος) of the "I" who cries out in Romans 7:24 and the tripartite groaning (στεναγμός) of creation, God's children, and the Holy Spirit in Romans 8:19–27. The misery and groaning in the letter, like that in OT lament, is linked to both enemy and divine activity.

The condition of lamenters is also indicated by the way their bodies are described. The eye (ὀφθαλμός) of the lamenter receives a great deal of attention:

> Have mercy on me, O Lord, because I am afflicted; my eye (ὀφθαλμός) has been disturbed, my soul and my belly. (Ps 30:10)
>
> My eyes (ὀφθαλμοί) have been worn out with tears, my heart has been disturbed. (Lam 2:11a)

---

73   For ταλαιπωρέω, see Ps 16:9; Joel 1:10; Jer 4:13, 20; 9:18. For ταλαιπωρία, see Pss 31:4; 39:3; 87:19; Isa 47:11; Jer 5:26; 15:8. For ταλαίπωρος, see Ps 136:8; Isa 33:1.

74   For στεναγμός, see Pss 30:11; 37:10; 78:11; 101:6; 102:20; Job 3:24; 23:2; Mal 2:13; Isa 51:11; Jer 4:31; 51:33; Lam 1:22. For στενάζω, see Job 24:12; 30:25; Isa 24:7; 59:10; Jer 31:19; Lam 1:8; 1:21; Ezek 21:11, 12; 26:15, 16.

The eyes are obviously highlighted because of the tears that flow from them.[75] The description of the eyes is indicative of the sad, disturbed, and desperate condition of the lamenter. Lamenters also speak about their bones and inward parts, "I have been poured out like water, and all my bones (ὀστᾶ) were scattered, my heart (καρδία) became like wax being melted in the midst of my belly (κοιλίας)" (Ps 21:15). The outward and inward condition of the lamenter's body speaks to his or her overall condition before enemies or God. The pain inflicted by their activity, or even inactivity, is manifested in the physical and mental anguish described by lamenters.[76] In Romans 7:7–25, we will find an "I" whose condition echoes this feature of OT lament. Paul accentuates the turmoil taking place within the body of the "I."

Metaphors and Expressions Involving God

We now turn our attention to the expressions and metaphors that are employed to describe the actions of God. In the broadest sense, God's actions are described both positively and negatively. Positively, lamenters often describe God as a refuge, judge, and savior.[77] Negatively, he is described in terms of hiddenness, absence, and rejection.

Positive descriptions of God's actions revolve around the lamenter's need for deliverance that takes on different divine forms. First, in OT lament God saves through protecting his people. This can often be heard in petitions, "Incline to me your ear, make haste to deliver (ἐξελέσθαι) me; be for me a God who protects (ὑπερασπιστήν) and saves (σῶσαί) me in a house of refuge (καταφυγῆς)" (Ps 30:3). The terms ὑπερασπιστής, καταφυγή, and βοηθός are often found in Psalms of Lament where the lamenter is in need of divine protection and shelter.[78] There is a hope and expectation that God will keep lamenters, or the communities they speak for, safe from those who oppress them just as he promised. In these instances, deliverance takes the form of protection. It is what Basson refers to as the "refuge-savior" motif.[79]

---

75 See e.g., Job 17:7.

76 See Job 30:27.

77 Basson argues that the three most important divine metaphors in the PssLm are refuge/savior, judge, and shield. See Basson, *Divine Metaphors*, 76–85.

78 The nouns ὑπερασπιστής and καταφυγή occur frequently in the Psalms of Lament. They express the lamenter's need for protection and shelter from enemies. For ὑπερασπιστής, see Pss 17:3, 31; 26:1; 27:7, 8; 30:5; 32:20; 36:39; 39:18; 58:12; 70:3; 83:10; 113:17, 18, 19; 143:2. For καταφυγή, see Pss 9:10; 17:3; 31:7; 45:2; 58:17; 70:3; 89:1; 90:2, 9; 93:22; 103:18; 143:2. For βοηθός, see Ps 9:10; 17:3; 18:15; 26:9; 27:7; 29:11; 32:20; 39:18; 45:2; 51:9; 58:18; 61:9; 62:8; 69:6; 70:7; 71:12; 77:35; 80:2; 93:22; 113:17, 18, 19.

79 Basson, *Divine Metaphors*, 76–85. See also, Terrien, "The Metaphor of the Rock

The Literary Form and Theological Message of Old Testament Lament

In OT lament, God also saves through judgment. Here God as judge is a positive image. This image is evident in both the petitions and praise of lamenters:

> Judge (κρῖνον) them, O God; let them fall from their plotting; according to the multitude of their ungodliness drive them out, because they have rebelled against you. (Ps 5:11)[80]

> The righteous will rejoice, whenever he should see vengeance (ἐκδίκησιν) against the ungodly; he will wash his hand in the blood of the sinner. (Ps 57:11)

Lamenters desire that God would act as ὁ κρίνων on their behalf, "God is the one who judges (ὁ κρίνων) in the earth" (Ps 57:12).[81] They are confident he will judge with righteousness (δικαιοσύνη).[82] His decisions and actions will result in the defense and deliverance of the weak. Therefore, lamenters plead "Judge (κρίνατε) the orphan and the poor, justify (δικαιώσατε) the downcast and needy (Ps 81:3). In these cases, divine judgment is favor towards the needy but punishment towards the unrighteous enemies.

It should also be noted that in some instances lamenters recognize their need for forgiveness in order to obtain a favorable judgment. Whether lamenters are afflicted from their own sin and guilt or external enemies, there are occasions when they seek mercy in judgment:

> Have mercy (ἐλέησον) on me, O God, according to your great mercy and according to the multitude of your compassions blot out my transgression of the law (ἀνόμημα). (Ps 50:3)

> And do not enter into judgment (κρίσιν) with your servant, because no living thing will be justified before you. (Ps 142:2 LXX)

Nevertheless, even in these situations, God as judge remains a positive image. Lamenters expect God to both judge their enemies and yet have mercy towards them in judgment. Either way, God acts to deliver his people through judgment.

While not entirely separate from the portrait of judge, we can also speak of God as savior. The action taken by God to save lamenters is often signaled through the use of σῴζω or ῥύομαι.[83] We can categorize this

---

in Biblical Theology," 157–71.

80. See also the imperative κρῖνον used in requests against enemies in Pss 53:3; 81:8.

81. The terms most frequently used for a positive portrayal of God's judgment in the Psalms of Lament are κρίνω, κρίσις, ἐκδίκησις, and ἐκδικέω.

82. See Pss 9:5, 9; 34:24; 50:6; 57:2; 71:2; 95:13; 97:9.

83. The verb σῴζω appears over seventy times in the LXX Psalms and ῥύομαι over sixty times. Just within the psalms, there are a number of others terms related to God

action in four ways: (1) the people God saves; (2) what he saves from; (3) the means or manner by which he saves; and (4) why he saves. With respect to the first category, broadly speaking, God saves the righteous, the lowly, and needy. These are not separate parties but ultimately one and the same. There are numerous examples in the Psalms:

> My righteous help is from God who saves (σῴζοντος) the upright (εὐθεῖς) in heart. (Ps 7:11)[84]

> The Lord is near to those who are crushed (συντετριμμένος) in heart and he will save (σώσει) the humble (ταπεινούς) in spirit. (Ps 33:19)[85]

> For he delivered (ἐρρύσατο) the poor (πτωχόν) from the mighty hand and the needy (πένητα), to whom there was not help. (Ps 71:12)

The "righteous" (δίκαιος/εὐθύς) in the Psalms are those who seek God and cry out to him, "Hear, O Lord, my voice, from which I cried out (ἐκέκραξα); have mercy on me and hear me. My heart said to you, 'He sought (ἐζήτησεν) my face;' your face, O Lord, I will seek (ζητήσω)" (Ps 26:7–8).[86] Yet, the righteous are also poor and needy. Their needs stem from external enemies who afflict them as well as their own sin and transgressions.[87] They are crushed (συντετριμμένος) by both political opponents and their own guilt.[88]

With respect to what God saves from, he saves from enemies, threats of death, and death itself. Once again the Psalms provide plenty of examples:

> Deliver (ῥῦσαί) me from (ἐκ) those who do lawlessness and from (ἐξ) men of bloodshed save (σῶσον) me. (Ps 58:3)

> Many are the tribulations of the righteous, and he will deliver (ῥύσεται) them from (ἐκ) all of them. (Ps 33:20)

> To deliver (ῥύσασθαι) their souls from death (ἐκ θανάτου) and to nourish them in famine. (Ps 32:19)

There is an ablative sense (ἐκ/ἀπό) to what God does here. He acts to move the lamenters away from what afflicts and endangers them. The danger is often external enemies, though not always. There are also instances

---

saving his people. They include: ἐξαιρέω, λυτρόω, ῥύστης, σωτηρία, and σωτήρ.

84 See also Pss 5:13; 13:5; 19:7; 33:16; 36:17, 39; 63:11; 93:15; 139:14.
85 See also Pss 17:28; 81:3; 137:6.
86 See also Pss 39:17; 68:7; 69:5; 118:176.
87 See e.g., Pss 36:39–40; 38:9.
88 See e.g., Ps 50:19.

in which God must save lamenters from their own sin and guilt, "Deliver (ῥῦσαί) me from (ἀπό) all my lawlessness (ἀνομιῶν)" (Ps 38:9a).[89] The implication here is that God must act to deliver lamenters from his own wrath for their sin. In any case, whether God saves from enemies or sin, it is ultimately deliverance from death.

When we consider the means or manner of God's deliverance, we find a variety of expressions. God saves "by his right hand," "by his name," "by looking," "by protecting," "by judging," "by forgiving," and the like. The psalmist also indicates the means or manner by which God does not deliver, namely not by human might, "For they did not inherit the land by their sword and their arm did not save (οὐκ ἔσωσεν) them, but your right hand and your arm and the light of your face, because you delighted in them" (Ps 43:4). At the risk of oversimplifying the matter, we could say that in the Psalms God saves "by his mercy, righteousness, and truth." Various images may be employed to describe how God saves, but the Psalms abbreviate those ways as ἔλεος/ἐλεέω, δικαιοσύνη/δικαιόω, and ἀλήθεια. In complaints, petitions, and praise, these terms appear and evoke far more than a divine attribute or quality. They are theological abbreviations for the way God saves whether it is described as "by his hand, strength, name," etc. In many instances, two, or even three, of these terms appear together to communicate how God saves:

> I did not hide your righteousness (δικαιοσύνην) in my heart, I spoke your truth (ἀλήθειαν) and your salvation (σωτήριον), I did not hide your mercy (ἔλεος) and your truth (ἀλήθειαν) from the great assembly. (Ps 39:11)

> Yet his salvation (σωτήριον) is near for those who fear him so that his glory dwells in our land. Mercy (ἔλεος) and truth (ἀλήθεια), righteousness (δικαιοσύνη) and peace have kissed. (Ps 84:10–11)

The point here is that, collectively, these terms are theological abbreviations for the wider soteriology contained in the Psalms of Lament.

It is helpful to offer a brief synopsis of how these terms function as a compressed statement of that wider soteriology. Upon closer investigation of the LXX Psalms, we find that δικαιοσύνη is consistently used in relationship to God's judgment and salvation. God's δικαιοσύνη can signal how he judges (κρίνω) "against" enemies and yet "for" the righteous, something that will result in deliverance for the latter, "And he will judge (κρινεῖ) the world in righteousness (δικαιοσύνη), he will judge the people in equity" (Ps 9:9). Yet, δικαιοσύνη is also explicitly linked to verbs like σώζω or ῥύομαι:

---

89. See also Pss 39:13–14; 50:11–14.

36   Reading Romans as Lament

> In you, O Lord, I have hoped, may I not be ashamed forever; in your righteousness (δικαιοσύνη) rescue (ῥῦσαί) me and deliver (ἐξελοῦ) me. (Ps 30:2)

> In your righteousness (δικαιοσύνη) rescue (ῥῦσαί) me and deliver (ἐξελοῦ) me, incline your to me and save (σῶσόν) me. (Ps 70:2)

In these instances, the forensic element is axiomatic to the term, and the aim is still salvation. Overall then, δικαιοσύνη, as it is often used in the Psalms, is a positive term involving judgment that leads to salvation. That is why lamenters appeal directly to God's righteousness.[90] They are asking that God judge them favorably and their enemies with punishment. The result will be salvation.

With respect to ἔλεος (ἐλέεω), deliverance can involve a number of things:

> Lord, do not rebuke me in your anger (θυμῷ) nor discipline me in your wrath (ὀργῇ). Have mercy (ἐλέησον) on me, Lord, because I am weak; heal me, Lord, because my bones are distressed. (Ps 6:2–3)

> I said, "Lord, have mercy (ἐλέησον) on me; heal my soul, because I have sinned (ἥμαρτον) against you. (Ps 40:5)

> And by your mercy (ἐλέει) you will destroy my enemies. (Ps 142:12a)

As these examples indicate, divine mercy involves God removing his wrath from the lamenter, forgiving the lamenter, and or destroying the lamenter's enemies.[91]

Both δικαιοσύνη and ἔλεος are also intertwined with the psalmist's use of ἀλήθεια. The various occurrences of ἀλήθεια are linked to God's prior promise of deliverance, "But I in my prayer to you, O Lord; at an acceptable time, O God, in the multitude of your mercy (ἐλέους); hear me in the truth of your salvation (ἀληθείᾳ τῆς σωτηρίας)" (Ps 68:14). "Truth" is linked to a word/message of salvation given by God that he proclaims, remembers, and rules by:

---

90 The noun δικαιοσύνη appears over thirty times in the Psalms. In all of those occurrences, δικαιοσύνη is linked positively with judgment and salvation.

91 Ps 142 is an example of God doing all three on behalf of the lamenter in the same event. See Ps 142:1–3, 12.

And do not remove utterly the word of truth (λόγον ἀληείας) from my mouth, because I have hoped in your judgments. (Ps 118:43)[92]

He remembered (ἐμνήσθη) his mercy (ἐλέους) to Jacob and his truth (ἀληθείας) to the house of Israel. (Ps 97:3)[93]

For the psalmist, God's ἀλήθεια defines all of his ways, "All the ways (ὁδοί) of the Lord are mercy (ἔλεος) and truth (ἀλήθεια) to those who seek his covenant and his testimonies" (Ps 24:10). "Truth" is an abbreviation for the prior promise of salvation that the lamenter depends on and that God acts upon. As Bayer reminds us, "Without promise there is no cause for lamentation."[94] In light of the way the Psalms of Lament incorporate ἀλήθεια, we could add "Without a prior promise, God does not act." This brings us to our fourth question related to God's saving actions. Why does he save?

Ultimately, God saves those who cry out to him, because he promised that he would. This is not only encapsulated in the lamenter's constant appeals to God's ἀλήθεια and all that the term signals. It is also stated explicitly by God, "'Because of the misery of the poor and because of the groaning of the needy, now I will rise,' says the Lord, 'I will set them in salvation (ἐν σωτηρίᾳ), I will deal openly with him'" (Ps 11:6). God's prior promise is the basis *par excellence* for his work. When the psalmist asks for God to save for any other reason, it is organically rooted in the promise. For example, lamenters often ask for God to save for his name's sake, "Rise, Lord, help us, and ransom (λύτρωσαι) us on account of your name (ἕνεκεν τοῦ ὀνόματος)" (Ps 43:27).[95] Yet, the referent of ὄνομα is ultimately a God who promised to ransom Israel.

Having considered the positive portrayals of God in lament, we can now turn our attention to the more negative expressions of his actions. What stands out in the Psalms of Lament is the complaint that God is distant, hidden, or has inexplicably rejected his people.[96] As noted earlier, the lamenter will cry out, "Why, O Lord, have you withdrawn at a distance? Why do you overlook us in times of need?" (Ps 9:22). There are times when God, at least in some sense, is not present to deliver those who cry out to him. Otherwise, the complaint would be nonsensical. A similar description of this divine inactivity involves the hiding of God's face, "Do not turn away

---

92 Cf. Pss 88:6, 50; 118:160; 131:11; 145:6.
93 Cf. Ps 105:8.
94 Bayer, *Living by Faith*, 69.
95 See e.g., Ps 22:3; 24:11; 30:4; 73:10; 105:8.
96 On divine rejection, see Melanchthon, *Rejection by God*, 54–75.

(μὴ ἀποστρέψῃς) your face (πρόσωπον) from me, do not move away in anger (ὀργῇ) from your servant; be my help, do not dismiss me and do not abandon (ἐγκαταλίπῃ) me, O God my savior" (Ps 26:9). The turning, or hiding, of God's face is an alternate way of describing divine absence or separation. As Balentine puts it, "When God hides his face, or when he does not see, or answer the suppliant, it is tantamount to cutting off all contact with man."[97] Moreover, it evokes the Deuteronomic warning to Israel, "But I will certainly turn (ἀποστροφῇ ἀποστρέψω) my face (πρόσωπον) away from them in that day on account of all their evils, which they did, because they turned to foreign gods" (Deut 31:18).[98] In this way, God's hiddenness and withdraw are interpreted as wrathful acts. Yet, as the Psalms of Lament indicate, such wrath and rejection is often inexplicable. A prime example is found in Psalm 43, a classic communal lament. The lamenter cries out, "But now you have rejected (ἀπώσω) and disappointed (κατῄσχυνας) us and you will not go out with our armies" (Ps 43:10). God's rejection, at least in this instance, is inexplicable as the lamenter indicates "All these things have come upon us, and we did not forget you and we did not sin against your covenant" (Ps 43:18). God rejects them, but it is not because they have ignored the Deuteronomic warning. The lamenter simply cannot explain God's absence and rejection. Moreover, the inexplicable nature of the rejection only compounds the community's pain.

There is much more to say about the expressions and metaphors used in OT lament to describe God's actions. I have simply provided a framework for identifying and analyzing these particular echoes in Romans. What we will find in Paul's letter is echoes of both the lamenters' positive and negative portrayals of God. OT lament, especially the Psalms of Lament, supply Paul with the language and theological framework he uses to describe God's deliverance and judgment in Jesus Christ. Much of what is outlined here is echoed in some shape or form in Romans. The positive references of refuge, judge, and savior are all present. Paul takes up the soteriological language of lament, particularly δικαιοσύνη, and reworks it around the gospel he preaches. Yet, we will also find negative images related to divine distance, hiddenness, and rejection.

Metaphors and Expressions Involving Enemies

When we turn our attention to the language that lamenters use to describe their enemies, a few things stand out. First, enemies are the antithesis of

---

97 Balentine, *The Hidden God*, 57.
98 The lamenter in Ps 26:9 evokes this Deuteronomic warning.

the righteous lamenters, and it is eschatological judgment that stands at the heart of this antithesis.⁹⁹ The Psalms indicate from the outset how God judges these two groups differently, "On account of this the ungodly (ἀσεβεῖς) will not rise in the judgment (κρίσει) nor sinners (ἁμαρτωλοί) in the counsel of the righteous; for the Lord knows the way of the righteous, but the way of the ungodly (ἀσεβῶν) will be destroyed" (Ps 1:5–6). The use of κρίσις in this instance is ultimately a reference to final judgment, in whatever way the psalmist might have understood it. This can be seen in the way the psalmist speaks of God as the eternal king who judges the nations, "The Lord will reign (βασιλεύσει) forever and ever, you, O nations (ἔθνη), will perish (ἀπολεῖσθε) from his earth" (Ps 9:37). It is also evident in the way lamenters refer to the descent of their enemies to Hades, "Let the sinners be turned to Hades (ᾅδην), all the nations who forget God" (Ps 9:18). Of course, this is not to ignore the present judgment that lamenters wish to see doled out to their enemies. In any case, when lamenters petition God to judge their enemies, there is both a present and eschatological dimension to it.

Next, as noted previously, lamenters often liken the actions of their enemies to the movements of wild animals or flood waters. Their harmful speech is compared to poisonous snakes, "They have sharpened their tongue like that of a snake (ὄφεως), the poison of asps (ἰὸς ἀσπίδων) is under their lips" (Ps 139:4).¹⁰⁰ In describing the sense of being surrounded by enemies, the lamenter evokes the image of ravenous bulls or dogs that encircle their prey, "Many oxen (μόσχοι) have encircled (περιέσχον) me, fat bulls (ταῦροι) have surrounded (περιέσχον) me" (Ps 21:13).¹⁰¹ Their actions are also likened to lions.¹⁰² Flood waters are evoked to describe the sense of being surrounded and engulfed by enemies, "They surrounded (ἐκύκλωσάν) me like water (ὕδωρ) all day long, they encompassed (περιέσχον) me together" (Ps 87:18).¹⁰³

Third, the enemies are violent, even warlike. They wish to inflict harm and death on those whom they oppress. This is sometimes indicated through the weapons they have in their hands, "Sinners have drawn their sword (ῥομφαίαν), they have stretched out their bow (τόξον) in order to throw down the poor and needy, to slaughter the upright in heart" (Ps

---

99 In the Psalms of Lament, the terms used to refer to enemies include: ἀσεβής, ἁμαρτωλός, ἄδικος.

100 Cf. Pss 57:5; 90:13.

101 Cf. Pss 21:17, 21; 58:7, 15;

102 See e.g., Pss 7:3; 9:30;

103 Cf. Pss 68:2, 15, 16; 143:7;

36:14).[104] Even the speech of the enemies is like a weapon, "Who sharpen their tongues like a sword (ῥομφαίαν), they stretch out their bitter deed like a bow (τόξον)" (Ps 63:4).

Fourth, the expression ὅλην τὴν ἡμέραν indicates the persistence of enemies against lamenters. They incessantly harm their victims through their speech and violence. We hear this in complaints such as "For on account of you we face death all day long (ὅλην τὴν ἡμέραν), we were reckoned as sheep for slaughter" (Ps 43:23).[105] While the expression is hyperbolic, it does speak to the unceasing oppression that enemies inflict on their victims.

In summary, the enemies in OT lament are described as those who speak, think, and act in a way that is harmful and deadly to others. As a whole, the various images associated with enemies present them as overpowering, persistent, violent, and deceitful. Their deceit is practiced either through flattery or false testimony against lamenters. Worst of all, as we have already discussed and will discuss further, they act with impunity. They do not believe that God will judge them presently or eschatologically for their actions. Their disposition is "The Lord will not see" (Ps 93:7a).

As we will see, Paul takes up many of these metaphors and expressions to describe enemies in Romans. The two passages that stand out the most are Romans 3:10–18 and 7:7–25. The former is a virtual "catena of lament" in which Paul likens both Jew and Gentile to enemies of OT lament who speak and act as if God will not judge them. In the case of Romans 7:7–25, Paul's description of sin matches the description of enemies in OT lament. Specifically, like those enemies, sin is deceitful, overpowering, and deadly.

THE THEOLOGY OF OLD TESTAMENT LAMENT

The best way to discuss the theology of OT lament is in light of its inherent pattern or sequence. There are at least five parts to OT lament which include: (1) prior promise; (2) suffering; (3) cry of distress; (4) deliverance; and (5) praise. The pattern is flexible and may not always occur in this particular order. The constituent parts can vary in order, be absent entirely, or be assumed, but not explicitly stated. My focus here is not solely the literary phenomenon of this pattern but the theology it expresses. This discussion is critical to the present study, because both the pattern and theology of OT lament are echoed in Romans.

---

104 Cf. Pss 21:21; 58:8; 77:62; 143:10.
105 See Pss 37:7, 13; 55:2; 72:14; 87:18.

The Literary Form and Theological Message of Old Testament Lament 41

Prior Promise in Lament

The complaints and petitions of lamenters would never be uttered without the existence of a prior promise. It is one of the main catalysts for the lamenters' cries of distress. Clearly, the OT contains a number of specific promises that God makes to his people. Some of the most well-known promises are located in texts such as Genesis 12:1–3, 2 Samuel 7:11–13, Ezekiel 11:19– 20, and Jeremiah 31:31–34. In these passages, God promises to "bless" Israel with a great name, land, an eternal king, a new heart, and a new covenant. However, what we find in OT lament, especially in the Psalms of Lament, is that these specific promises are part of a larger and more fundamental word from God. They point to the promise of God's δικαιοσύνη.

The righteousness of God (δικαιοσύνη τοῦ θεοῦ) that lamenters hope for is revealed in divine judgment and salvation.[106] When God judges and saves, he is revealing his righteousness. The expectation of God's judgment and salvation emanate from a prior promise spoken in creation and the history of Israel. When God judges and saves in the world, those actions reveal the larger promise of God's righteousness in creation and Israel.[107] The psalmist praises God for this very thing:

> The Lord made known his salvation (σωτήριον), before the eyes of the nations he revealed his righteousness (δικαιοσύνην). (Ps 97:2)
>
> He remembered his mercy (ἐλέους) to Israel; and his truth (ἀληθείας) to the house of Israel; all the ends of the earth have seen the salvation (σωτήριον) of our God. (Ps 97:3)
>
> He comes to judge (κρῖναι) the earth; he will judge (κρινεῖ) the earth in righteousness (δικαιοσύνῃ) and his people in equity. (Ps 97:9)

As we will see in the following chapter, Romans 1:16–17, Paul's thesis statement, echoes this psalm. What is important for the moment is that the revelation of God's righteousness is not only cause for praise in the Psalms but also a cry of distress. That is because the promise of God's righteousness encapsulates all the promises and hopes of creation and Israel. Everything that God promises to do in the OT involves judgment and salvation. In other words, every promise is rooted in the fundamental promise of God's

---

106 For a discussion of righteousness language in the OT, see Seifrid, "Righteousness Language in the Hebrew Scriptures and Early Judaism," 415–42.
107 Ibid., 441.

righteousness. Where judgment is absent, or seemingly misplaced, and when salvation does not come, there is a cry of distress. That is because such suffering is in tension with the prior promise of God's righteousness.

Suffering and the Cry of Distress in Lament

The tension between God's prior promise and the lamenter's suffering indicates that the pain in question is more complex than oppression at the hands of enemies. To be sure, as we have seen, the actions and speech of enemies cause tremendous suffering. Political and internal enemies cause all kinds of trouble for individuals and the nation. There is an expectation of judgment and deliverance per God's prior promise. When that does not happen, the suffering not only remains but is exacerbated. It is exacerbated by the fact that God is not acting in accordance with his promise. God is not judging his people's enemies as he pledged and thereby delivering them. In other words, the δικαιοσύνη is hidden rather than revealed. In this way, the lamenter's suffering is compounded.

The complexity of the suffering stems from the fact that lamenters can find themselves in the role of both the righteous and the unrighteous. As the righteous, lamenters have hope that God will answer their cries of distress, "The righteous (δίκαιοι) cry out, and the Lord heard them, and he delivered them from all their tribulations" (Ps 33:17). On the other hand, lamenters know they are not righteous before God and are deserving of judgment, "Against you only have I sinned and done what is evil before you, in order that you might be justified in your words and you might overcome when you judge" (Ps 50:6). In these instances, lamenters understand their judgment but still cry out for deliverance on the basis of God's mercy.[108]

There is yet even another scenario that adds to the complexity of the lamenter's suffering. It is when lamenters cannot understand why God is treating them more like his enemies than his people. We considered this already in our discussion of Psalm 43 where the psalmist professes the nation's innocence and complains about God's inexplicable rejection. In all of these instances, the lamenters can only ask that God act in his righteousness.

The complex nature of suffering in OT lament is often indicated by the lamenter's cry of distress. As we have seen, cries consist of a complaint and petition. Complaints and petitions often come in the form of questions such as "why" and "how long." Why is God absent in the midst of suffering? How long until the absence, and thereby the pain, come to an end? The cry can also be a declarative statement, "You have rejected and disappointed us" (Ps

---

108 See e.g., Ps 142.

43:10a). On the whole, cries of distress express the lamenter's concern over God's absence and rejection in the midst of suffering, whether explicable or inexplicable. That absence and rejection contradicts God's prior promise of righteousness. When divine judgment is absent from the lamenter, whether the absence is a justifiable action against the lamenter, or an inexplicable threat to the lamenter, a cry of distress goes up. None of these scenarios results in salvation. Therefore, God's righteousness is not revealed. What we find then is that the complexity of the lamenter's suffering is juxtaposed with the complexity of God's δικαιοσύνη.

Deliverance and Praise in Lament

If the promise, suffering, and cry of distress in OT lament are bound up with God's righteousness, his deliverance obviously is as well. We cannot make too much of the fact that the psalmist links judgment and salvation to righteousness:

> And he will judge the world in righteousness (ἐν δικαιοσύνῃ), and he will judge the people in equity. (Ps 9:9)

> In you, O Lord, I have hoped, may I not be ashamed forever; in your righteousness (ἐν τῇ δικαιοσύνῃ) deliver me and rescue me. (Ps 30:2)

In the theology of OT lament, God both judges and saves ἐν δικαιοσύνῃ. The participants, expressions, metaphors, and pattern of lament helps explain what that means. For God to judge "in righteousness" is to judge the lamenters' enemies. Yet, it also means that his judgment against the lamenter will be merciful. For God to save "in righteousness," is to deliver lamenters from their enemies, whether external or internal ones, through judgment. All such action will mean God has acted in accordance with his promise which is absolutely necessary if the lamenter's pain is to be alleviated.

When the lamenter's pain is alleviated in accordance with God's prior promise, there is a shift towards praise. This is the fifth, though not permanent, movement in the pattern of lament. Villaneuva reminds us that in the Psalms of Lament there is a constant oscillation between the cry of distress and praise.[109] In any case, when there is a shift towards praise, it is defined by an exultation of God's judgment and salvation. In other words, there is praise for Gods' righteousness:

---

109 See Villaneuva, *The Uncertainty of a Hearing.*

> But I have hoped in your mercy (ἐλέει), and my heart will exult (ἀγαλλιάσεται) in your salvation (σωτηρίῳ). (Ps 12:6)
>
> And my tongue will meditate (μελετήσει) on your righteousness (δικαιοσύνην), all day long your praise (ἔπαινον). (Ps 34:28)

The content of the praise reinforces the idea that the theology of OT lament is ultimately defined by the interplay between the promise of righteousness, suffering due to the absence of righteousness, crying out for righteousness, and being delivered by righteousness.

SUMMARY

I have attempted to demonstrate that OT lament involves much more than a loud cry. Pioneering figures such as Gunkel and Westermann have made that abundantly clear. Lament is an event that involves God, the lamenter, and enemies. The interplay between these three is expressed through various expressions and metaphors. Lament also indicates that suffering and God's righteousness are complex theological issues in the OT. Both on an individual and national level the pattern of lament shapes the way divine promises and suffering are experienced. It is an experience defined by the oscillation between hope and disappointment, between judgment and deliverance, between promise and pain. Such oscillation is not only definitive of OT lament but also the experience of the gospel as Paul describes it in Romans. The echoes of OT lament resounding throughout the letter indicate that Paul sees the experience of those justified by faith in Christ commiserate with OT lamenters. Both find themselves grappling with the intersection of God's promised righteousness and the reality of suffering. Of course, as we will see, Paul appropriates OT lament in discussing the gospel. This naturally adds to the complexity of OT lament and how it functions in Paul's thought. Nevertheless, by hearing the echoes of lament in Romans, the lament found in Israel's scriptures, we are better able to take on the exegetical and theological gaps in the letter. The imaginary leap from the pain discussed in Romans to our understanding does not have to be bridged by appeals to salvation history, Stoicism, and the like. Instead, we need to read Romans as lament, because, as I will demonstrate, Paul's thinking is teeming with the participants, expressions, metaphors, and theology of this ancient prayer form.

3

The Gospel as the Answer to the Righteous Lamenter (Romans 1:16–17)

ROMANS 1:16–17 FUNCTIONS AS the letter's densely packed thesis statement.[1] It contains a number of well-known expressions that have occupied the attention of Pauline interpreters for quite some time. The attention is deserved, because the exegetical decisions made here impact the interpretation of the entire letter. The lion's share of interpretive energy usually goes to unpacking the meaning of δικαιοσύνη θεοῦ. Frequent questions also arise about the prepositional phrase ἐκ πίστεως εἰς πίστιν, the identity of ὁ δίκαιος, and what ἐκ πίστεως modifies in the Habakkuk citation. While these issues are of paramount importance to the interpretation of Romans, they are not the direct focus of this chapter. The more immediate aim is to ascertain how reading Romans 1:16–17 in light of its OT lament echoes impacts our interpretation of these key verses and the letter as a whole.

The main argument in what follows is that the intertextual echoes in Romans 1:16–17 evoke the experience of figures depicted in certain OT lament texts. Consequently, the much ballyhooed "righteous one" is best understood as a kind of lamenter whose suffering and cry of distress are answered in the gospel Paul preached. There are three specific OT lament echoes emanating from the Psalms of Lament and Habakkuk. These echoes call to mind parts of the pattern and theology of lament that we reviewed

---

1. Most interpreters agree that Rom 1:16–17 is the thesis statement of the letter. As Käsemann puts it, these two verses are the "theme of the whole epistle." Käsemann, *Romans*, 21.

in the previous chapter. We will examine these specific echoes with an eye towards their original and broader contexts. Most importantly, we will assess their impact on the interpretation of Paul's thesis statement and other parts of the letter.

IDENTIFYING AND TESTING THE ECHOES OF LAMENT IN ROMANS 1:16–17

Before assessing the interpretive impact of the lament echoes on Romans 1:16–17 and beyond, we need to identify the echoes in these two verses, evaluate them in their original OT contexts, and test their presence in Romans. There are three echoes of OT lament present in Romans 1:16–17. They originate from three places: a certain kind of Psalm of Lament related to "disappointment," Habakkuk, and Psalm 97.

Psalms of Lament and Disappointment with a Prior Promise

Paul asserts at the beginning of Romans 1:16 "I am not ashamed of the gospel." Interpreters usually treat the verb ἐπαισχύνομαι in one of two ways. Some see a reference to Jesus tradition such as that found in Mark 8:38, "For whoever should be ashamed of (ἐπαισχυνθῇ) me and my words in this adulterous and sinful generation, also the son of man shall be ashamed of (ἐπαισχυνθήσεται) him, whenever he should come in the glory of his father with the holy angels." If this is the background for Paul's use of ἐπαισχύνομαι in Romans 1:16, the point would be that the apostle is publicly testifying about Jesus in accordance with his eschatological warning. Alternatively, some interpreters associate ἐπαισχύνομαι with Paul's discussion about the foolishness of the gospel in 1 Corinthians 1:18–31. While there is no semantic link with ἐπαισχύνομαι, conceptually there might be a connection between Romans 1:16 and Paul's assertion that "we preach Christ crucified, to Jews a stumbling block, to Gentiles foolishness" (1 Cor. 1:23). The implication would be that Paul is not "ashamed" to preach what is a stumbling block to Jews and foolishness to Gentiles. Both of these interpretations assume that Paul is concerned with public "shame" before others, whether it is the kind of shame Jesus warned about or shame associated with an offensive and foolish message. However, without dismissing either of these interpretations out of hand, we must also consider ἐπαισχύνομαι in light of the Psalms of Lament that contain the αἰσχύν—root. Few interpreters of

Romans have examined this background.² This opens us to the possibility that Paul's concern in Romans 1:16 is not merely with "shame" in preaching but "disappointment" with what the gospel promises. The latter concern is found in a number of Psalms of Lament.

As I noted in the previous chapter, *prior promise* is one of the key elements in the pattern of lament. A lamenter often oscillates between hope and disappointment in the promise God gives. Disappointment with a promise in the Psalms of Lament of the LXX is often expressed through words of the αἰσχύν—root. Terms such as αἰσχύνω, ἐπαισχύνομαι, and καταισχύνω appear frequently in instances where the lamenter's concern is not simply public shame.³ Lamenters often make assertions or requests related to potential or real disappointment. The disappointment stems from the tension between hope in what God promised and the actual experience of the lamenter. While the absence of a fulfilled promise might result in public shame, the shame alone is not the cause of the lamenter's pain. The shame is only a result of the more fundamental cause of disappointment, namely hope in a prior promise that is either threatened or not yet realized. A few examples will suffice at this point:

> Our fathers hoped (ἤλπισαν) in you, they hoped (ἤλπισαν), and you delivered them; they cried to you and they were saved, they hoped (ἤλπισαν) in you and they were not disappointed (κατησχύνθησαν). (Ps 21:5–6)

> In you, O Lord, I have hoped (ἤλπισα), may I not be disappointed (καταισχυνθείην) forever; in your righteousness save me and deliver me. (Ps 30:2)

> O God, I have hoped (ἤλπισα) in you, may I not be disappointed (μὴ καταισχυνθείην) forever. In your righteousness save me and deliver me, incline your ear to me and save me. (Ps 70:1–2)

The contrast between ἐλπίζω and καταισχύνω is clear. What is also clear from these examples is that the language of the αισχύν—root, frequently used in the Psalms of Lament, is associated with disappointment. To put it another way, there is an emphasis on the lamenter's hope left unrealized. The specific object of hope is the promise of salvation. That is why the lamenter mentions past saving acts and then requests deliverance in the

---

2 Gerhart Herold is an exception to this interpretive trend. Herold examined the word group in the LXX and assessed its relevance for the interpretation of Rom 1:16–18. See Herold, *Zorn und Gerechtigkeit Gottes bei Paulus*, 28–69.

3 See e.g., ἐπαισχύνομαι in Ps 118:6; καταισχύνω in Pss 6:11; 13:6; 21:6; 24:2, 3; 30:2, 18; 34:4; 43:8, 10; 52:6; 69:3; 70:1; 73:21; 118:31, 116; αἰσχύνω in Pss 6:11; 24:3; 30:18; 34:4, 26; 68:7; 69:3, 4; 70:13, 24; 82:18; 85:17; 108:28; 118:46, 78, 80; 128:5.

present (σῶσόν με).⁴ It is also worth noting that in Psalms 30:2 and 70:2 the lamenter asks to be saved specifically by means of God's "righteousness" (ἐν τῇ δικαιοσύνῃ). As the wider contexts of these two psalms indicate, divine δικαιοσύνη involves God's protection and deliverance from enemies who plot against and afflict the lamenter.⁵ Additionally, a number of other psalms link divine δικαιοσύνη with God's salvation, a salvation that comes through the judgment of enemies.⁶

Testing Echoes of Disappointment

Whether or not these specific kinds of Psalms of Lament are echoed in Romans 1:16–17 can be assessed by briefly applying Hays' seven tests for hearing intertextual echoes in Paul.⁷ First, in terms of "availability," Psalms of Lament that wrestle with disappointment over a prior promise are indeed available to Paul. He clearly cites a number of Psalms throughout Romans and other letters, so that it is reasonable to conclude Paul had access to the kinds of Psalms mentioned above.⁸ Next, the "volume" of the echoes is substantial as evidenced by the repetition of words occurring in Romans 1:16–17 and the Psalms of Lament in question. The specific semantic congruence includes ἐπαισχύνομαι, δικαιοσύνη (especially as it relates to θεός), and σωτηρία. Third, the echoes here also pass the test of "thematic coherence." Paul revisits the theme of disappointment with faith in the gospel in Romans 5, 9, and 11, items that will be addressed in subsequent chapters.⁹ Fourth, it is "historically plausible" that Paul would be influenced by and even appropriate this group of Psalms of Lament to articulate the experience of the Jew and Gentile who believe in the gospel. That historical plausibility is grounded in Paul's well-established use of the Psalms and immersion in a Jewish milieu that often appropriated Israel's Psalms.¹⁰ Fifth, although the echoes I am suggesting here are seldom adopted by interpreters, they

---

4. The parallel request for deliverance in Ps 70:2 is ῥῦσαί με.
5. See e.g., the complaints about the ἐχθρός in Pss 30:9, 12, 16, 20; 70:10.
6. See e.g., Pss 9:9, 35:7, 65:4
7. Hays, *Echoes of Scripture*, 29–32.
8. See Rom 3:4, 3:10, 13, 14, 18, 4:7, 8, 8:36, 10:18, 11:9, 15:3.
9. See Rom 5:5, 9:33, 10:11.
10. Hengel notes, "Like a strict orthodox Muslim today, numerous orthodox Jews and quite a few Swabian pietists, Paul knew large parts of his Holy Scripture off by heart. This would be true above all of the Greek psalter, the prayer book of Judaism. In many respects his language is shaped by that of the psalms." Hengel, *The Pre-Christian Paul*, 36.

are not without precedent in the "history of interpretation." For example, Hays himself observes "*Aischynein* and its near relatives *kataischynein* and *epaischynesthai* appear repeatedly in the very prophecies and lament psalms from which Paul's righteousness terminology is also drawn."[11] Finally, the proposed echoes do in fact pass Hays' test of "satisfaction." They "illuminate the surrounding discourse" in a way that offers more explanatory power than the more common readings of ἐπαισχύνομαι which find the interpretive key either in Jesus tradition or Pauline statements about kerygma in the Corinthian correspondence. We will return to the issue of "illumination" shortly. I would simply note at this point that the proposed echoes related to Paul's use of ἐπαισχύνομαι pass most of Hays's tests for hearing intertextual echoes.[12]

The Divine Answer to Habakkuk's Cries

Paul ends his thematic statement by citing a portion of Habakkuk 2:4, "But the righteous one will live by faith." It is a citation that has received a great deal of attention from interpreters. Most of their focus revolves around whether the prepositional phrase ἐκ πίστεως modifies ὁ δίκαιος or ζήσεται. However, my focus is on the original and wider context of Habakkuk that Paul evokes by citing one small portion of it. The specific portion in question is neither "small" in Habakkuk nor a mere "proof text" for Paul.[13] Instead, Habakkuk 2:4 is the divine answer to the prophet's laments, and the citation of that answer in Romans 1:17 echoes the entire experience of the prophet. It is an experience defined by a certain pattern and theology described in the previous chapter. As is common in OT lament, the divine answer originally given to a suffering Habakkuk, that the "righteous one will live by faith," can only be understood in light of the book's lament pattern and theology. Moreover, Habakkuk's pattern and theology of lament is the hermeneutical key to understanding Paul's citation. Therefore, it is necessary to lay out the basic pattern and theology of lament that originally surrounded Habakkuk 2:4.

---

11 Hays, *Echoes of Scripture*, 38.

12 The only "test" I did not mention in my analysis is what Hays calls "recurrence." There is no specific recurrence of echoes from the Psalms of Lament related to disappointment within the letter. Nevertheless, the test of "thematic coherence" is closely linked to "recurrence," and, as I mentioned already, the letter does contain a theme or motif of disappointment with faith in the gospel. On "recurrence," see Hays, *Echoes of Scripture*, 30.

13 Sanders, *Paul: A Very Short Introduction*, 66–70.

To begin, it is important to remember that questions are part of the stock language of OT lament. As I discussed in the previous chapter, a lamenter will ask a question in order to complain and make a request to God. Habakkuk commences with two classic questions of lament:

> How long (ἕως τίνος), O Lord, will I cry out and you certainly shall not hear? I will cry to you while being mistreated and you will not save? Why (ἵνα τί) do you show me troubles and pains, so as to look upon misery and ungodliness? Justice has been opposite of me, and the judge takes. On account of this the law has been scattered, justice is finally not accomplished, because the ungodly oppresses the righteous one (τὸν δίκαιον); on account of this justice will go out twisted. (Hab 1:1–4)

The complaint embedded in Habakkuk's questions is that God has not answered his request to be delivered from ungodly enemies within Judah. Consequently, in the absence of a divine response, Habakkuk can also complain that there is no justice in the nation and the righteous are oppressed. From the perspective of the pattern of lament, Habakkuk trusted in the *prior promise* that God would deliver the righteous. However, instead of deliverance from the ungodly, Habakkuk *suffered* at their hands; therefore, there is a *cry of distress*. If we are following the pattern, the next element we expect to find is *deliverance*. That deliverance comes via two divine responses to the prophet's cries.

The initial response to Habakkuk's cry for deliverance is enigmatic and actually elicits another cry from the prophet rather than the relief he desperately seeks. God promises to do something quite unbelievable, "Behold, despisers, and look and marvel greatly and be terrified, because I am doing a work in your days, which you certainly shall not believe (οὐ μὴ πιστεύσητε) even if someone should tell it to you" (Hab 1:5). Specifically, he promises that he will bring the Chaldeans to pour out judgment upon Judah (Hab 1:6–11). Habakkuk responds to God's answer with another cry of distress which entails yet more questions:

> Are you not from the beginning, Lord, my Holy God? And we certainly shall not die. Lord you have appointed them for judgment; and he formed me so as to convict me with correction. Your eye is pure so as not to see evil, and you are not able to look upon afflictions; why do you look upon despisers? Will you be silent while the ungodly devours the righteous (τὸν δίκαιον)? (Hab 1:12–13)

The Gospel as the Answer to the Righteous Lamenter 51

Once again, the questions function as both complaint and request. Habakkuk complains that God would respond to his cry for help by sending ungodly Chaldeans against Judah and requests that God would act in accordance with his righteous nature. The appeal to God's righteousness is implied in Habakkuk's assertion that "Your eye is pure so as not to see evil, and you are not able to look upon afflictions" (Hab 1:13). The "evil" in question is the prospect of ungodly Chaldeans devouring the righteous while God remains silent (Hab 1:13–17). That silence is broken in God's second answer to Habakkuk who has cried out and now anxiously awaits a response (Hab 2:1).

God commands Habakkuk to write down his response to the prophet's cries of distress (Hab 2:2). The response comes in the form of a vision (ὅρασις) that God reveals to him. The prophet describes that vision in Habakkuk 2:5—3:19. In short, it is a vision of God pouring out his judgment through the unrighteous Chaldeans against the unrighteous Judeans. Yet, the divine wrath is also doled out to the Chaldeans. God appears as a warrior whose actions strike fear in the heart of Habakkuk. In fact, the prophet makes yet one more request as God's wrath is revealed to him. He cries out "When my soul is disturbed by your wrath (ὀργῇ) remember mercy (ἐλέους)" (Hab 3:2). Despite his trepidation, Habakkuk sees that the divine wrath and judgment against the unrighteous will ultimately result in salvation for the righteous. This is clear from Habakkuk's closing *praise*, the fifth movement in the pattern of lament, when he exclaims, "But I will be glad in the Lord, I will rejoice in God my savior (σωτῆρί μου). The Lord God is my power (δύναμίς) and he will order my steps until the end; he causes me to mount on the high places so as to overcome in his song" (Hab 3:18–19). This exclamation signals a fundamental shift from Habakkuk's cries of distress in the beginning of the book to praise at its close. The cause of the shift is the salvific vision laid out in Habakkuk 2:5—3:19. This brings us back to Habakkuk 2:2-4.

The divine answer in Habakkuk 2:2-4 is best understood in light of the prophet's preceding cries, subsequent vision of deliverance, and eventual praise. In other words, one must interpret Habakkuk 2:2-4 in light of the book's pattern and theology of lament. The overarching divine answer to Habakkuk's cries is:

> And the Lord answered me and said, "Write the vision clearly upon the tablet, in order that the one who reads them might pursue it. Because the vision is still for its time and it will rise in the end and will not be in vain; if it should be late in arriving, wait for it, because the one who is coming will come and he certainly shall not delay. If he should shrink back, my soul will

not delight in him; but the righteous one will live by faith in me." (Hab 2:2–4)

While in Romans 1:17 Paul only cites the final line of Habakkuk 2:4, in context, that line is part of a larger answer to the prophet's cries of distress. Several features in Habakkuk 2:2–4 are deserving of attention.

First, as in common in OT lament, God exhorts Habakkuk to "wait" (ὑπόμεινον) for deliverance.[14] Habakkuk sees the vision of deliverance outlined above, but he will not immediately experience it. He will have to wait for it. God assures Habakkuk that his waiting will not be in vain (οὐκ εἰς κενόν). To put it another way, the prophet will not ultimately be disappointed, or have his hope of deliverance dashed. The hope resides ultimately in the one who is to come (ἐρχόμενος ἥξει) (Hab 2:2). Although later Christian interpreters identified ἐρχόμενος as a Messianic figure, the larger context of Habakkuk identifies the ἐρχόμενος as θεός himself.[15] This is clear in Habakkuk 3:3 "God (θεός) will come (ἥξει) from Teman, and the holy one from the thick shadowy mountain." It can also be seen in a number of other references related to the arrival of θεός in the prophet's vision.[16] Second, the antithesis of waiting on the deliverance is to "draw back" (ὑποστείληται) from it, something that is quite displeasing to God.[17] Contextually, the verb ὑποστέλλω signals unbelief, even fear, in the vision of deliverance.[18] One might grow weary of waiting on deliverance or, fear the judgment associated with that deliverance.[19] In either instance, God does not delight (εὐδοκεῖ) in the one who "draws back" from the vision of deliverance.[20] The verb εὐδοκέω with θεός as the subject is common in OT lament where God's delight in someone will result in their deliverance.[21] Divine "delight" in this case rests upon whether or not the lamenter waits for, or believes in the vision of God's arrival to save and to judge. Finally, based on the wider context of the book, the identity of ὁ δίκαιος in Habakkuk 2:4 is the prophet and those who lament like him. The substantival adjective ὁ δίκαιος occurs in Habakkuk 1:4, 13 and 2:4. The latter two uses are contrasted with the ἀσεβής person. There

---

14. See e.g., Pss 26:14; 36:34.

15. See Heb 10:37–38.

16. The rest of the vision in Hab 3 also exemplifies this identification. See Hab 3:4–6, 10, 13.

17. LEH, 637.

18. This is not a common verb in the LXX. See e.g., Exod 23:21; Deut 1:17; Job 13:8; Wis 6:7; Hag 1:10.

19. E.g., Hab 3:2.

20. Cf. MT version of Hab 2:4.

21. See e.g., Pss 39:14; 43:4.

is no explicit reference to ἀσεβής in Habakkuk 2:4, but in 2:5 we do find mention of the "one who is drunk and the despiser who boasts." Such an individual obviously does not live by faith in the vision of God's judgment and deliverance. Consequently, God does not delight in that ungodly one. In short, Habakkuk, the righteous one, lives by faith that God has answered his cry, albeit unbelievably, in the vision of his arrival to judge and save.

Testing Echoes of Habakkuk's Lament

In this reading of Habakkuk, there are plenty of implications for how we interpret Paul's citation. We will return to that interpretation shortly. For the moment, I simply want to test the presence of echoes from Habakkuk 2:4 and its wider context of lament in Romans 1:16–17. Does Paul's thematic statement echo Habakkuk's cries of distress and the divine answer to those cries including the vision of God's arrival to judge and to save? In answering this question, we will consider the following echoes of Habakkuk in Romans 1:16–17: (1) the cries of distress in Habakkuk 1:2–4, 12–17; (2) the divine answers in Habakkuk 1:5–11, 2:2–4; and (3) the visions in 2:5—3:19. All of these echoes of lament pass Hays's tests for hearing intertextual echoes.

To begin, these echoes of lament are obviously "available" to Paul given the fact that he cites Habakkuk 2:4. They also pass Hays's test of "volume." Paul's citation signals obvious semantic links between Habakkuk and Romans 1:17. Yet, the "volume" of the echoes from Habakkuk can also be heard on a conceptual level. While the verb ἀποκαλύπτω, a key term in Romans 1:17, does not appear anywhere Habakkuk, the idea of revelation is a key motif in the book. We noted earlier that just prior to Habakkuk 2:4 God commands Habakkuk to write down the ὅρασις that he sees (Hab 2:2–3). The term obviously carries a revelatory sense. Both Habakkuk and Paul equate deliverance with revelation or a vision. Next, the echoes of lament in Romans 1:16–17 also pass the tests of "recurrence" and "thematic coherence." There is a recurrence of Habakkuk 2:4 in Galatians 3:11, and, as I will discuss further in a moment, Habakkuk's lament-laden themes of cries for judgment and deliverance are key in Romans as well. With respect to the "history of interpretation," many interpreters have suggested that one must understand the citation of Habakkuk 2:4 in light of its larger context.[22] Fewer have emphasized the echoes of Habakkuk's lament form and theology in Paul's citation.[23] Nevertheless, such a reading is not entirely without exegetical precedent. Finally, the echoes of lament in Romans 1:16–17 do in

---

22 See Watts, "For I Am Not Ashamed of the Gospel," 3–25.
23 For one exception, see Hays, *Echoes of Scripture*, 36–41.

fact "illuminate surrounding discourse." I will discuss this at length below. I would simply note at this point that the echoes of lament from Habakkuk shed light on some of the key expressions in Paul's thematic statement, namely ἐπαισχύνομαι, δικαιοσύνη θεοῦ, ἀποκαλύπω, and ὁ δίκαιος.

From Lament to Praise for the Revelation of Righteousness

In Psalm 97:2, the psalmist exclaims "The Lord made known his salvation, before the nations he revealed his righteousness." Interpreters have observed for some time that Romans 1:17 echoes this psalm.[24] What receives less consideration is how the echo of a thanksgiving psalm is connected to the echoes of OT lament in the rest of the thesis statement. Before assessing that connection, it is necessary to treat Psalm 97:2 in light of its original context and briefly consider how its passes the tests for intertextual echoes.

Salvation and judgment are the focal points of the praise in Psalm 97. In fact, these two divine actions are highlighted through the literary *inculsio* in verses 1 and 9:

> Sing to the Lord a new song, because the Lord has done amazing things; his right hand saved (ἔσωσεν) for him and his holy right arm. (Ps 97:1)

> For he is coming (ἥκει) to judge (κρῖναι) the earth; he will judge (κρινεῖ) the world in righteousness (δικαιοσύνη) and the people in uprightness. (Ps 97:9)

Both the believing community and creation itself praises God for his judgment and salvation (Ps 97:4–8). They praise God for "revealing" judgment and salvation as well as "remembering" his mercy and truth towards Israel:

> The Lord made known (ἐγνώρισεν) his salvation (σωτήριον αὐτοῦ), before the nations he revealed (ἀπεκάλυψεν) his righteousness (δικαιοσύνην αὐτοῦ). He remembered (ἐμνήσθη) his mercy (ἐλέους αὐτοῦ) towards Jacob and his truth (ἀληθείας αὐτοῦ) to the house of Israel; all the ends of the earth have seen the salvation (τὸ σωτήριον τοῦ θεοῦ ἡμῶν) of our God. (Ps 97:2–3)

The parallelisms in these lines, a literary feature so common to the psalms, are informative here.[25] For example, further explanation of σωτήριον

---

24 See e.g., Schreiner, *Romans*, 66.
25 On parallelisms in the Psalms, see Futato, *Interpreting the Psalms*, 33–40.

αὐτοῦ is provided by the parallel phrase δικαιοσύνην αὐτοῦ. The latter phrase indicates the manner by which God saved those who now praise him, namely through the judgment of their enemies. A number of psalms indicate that God delivers his people through the judgment of their enemies, and the theological shorthand for this manner of salvation is δικαιοσύνη.[26] Additionally, the verb μιμνήσκω in 97:3 parallels γνωρίζω and ἀποκαλύπτω in 97:2. Therefore, the revelation of God's righteousness before the nations is also a remembrance of the mercy he promised to Israel. The parallel to the noun ἔλεος is ἀλήθεια. The promise of mercy, or righteousness, to Israel is "truthful" as indicated by the universal wide salvation God revealed.

It should also be noted that Psalm 97, while technically not a lament, does assume certain lament features. Specifically, it assumes the activity of enemies, a cry of distress, and deliverance. For example, references to God's "right hand" in 97:1 evoke cries elicited by enemies in the Psalms of Lament:

> Now I know the Lord saves (ἔσωσεν) his anointed; he will hear him from his holy heaven; in mighty deeds is the salvation of your right hand (ἡ σωτηρία τῆς δεξιᾶς αὐτοῦ). (Ps 19:7)
>
> In order that your beloved might be delivered, save with your right hand and hear me. (Ps 59:7)[27]

Within the larger collection of the psalms, any praise for salvation makes little sense without the interpreter's assumption that the speaker had previously been in distress and requested deliverance. Therefore, praise in the psalms is either implicitly or explicitly contrasted with cries of distress. In this way, it is safe to assume that the speaker in Psalm 97 has moved from a cry that God would save from enemies to praise that he has revealed his righteousness.

Testing Echoes of Psalm 97

If there are echoes of Psalm 97 in Romans 1:16–17, it would obviously have implications for how we interpret Paul's thought and the echoes of lament we have been discussing up to this point. There is no question that the echoes of Psalm 97 pass a number of Hays's tests. Psalm 97 is "available" to Paul, and the "volume" of the echo is substantial. The shared vocabulary of Psalm 97 and Romans 1:16–17 includes ἀποκαλύπτω, σῴζω/σωτηρία, and δικαιοσύνη. There is also "thematic coherence" between the two texts. They both highlight that God has revealed his righteousness/salvation. It is

26 I discussed two of these psalms earlier. See Pss 30:2; 70:2.
27 See also Pss 20:9; 43:4; 44:5; 62:9; 73:23; 73:11; 76:11; 108:6; 137:7; 138:10.

"historically plausible" that Psalm 97 influenced Paul's thinking in Romans 1:16–17 given the simple fact that the psalms often shape various facets of his thought. Within the "history of interpretation," many interpreters have posited Psalm 97 as part of the background to Paul's thematic statement.[28] Finally, the echoes of Psalm 97 as I have described them here "illuminate the surrounding discourse." Specifically, as I will demonstrate later, the echoes of Psalm 97 fit nicely with the echoes from various Psalms of Lament and Habakkuk. It signals a shift from lament to praise, a shift which hinges on the revelation of God's righteousness that had been promised and requested. In this way, Psalm 97 is a key component of lament echoes in Romans 1:16–17.

READING ROMANS 1:16–17 IN LIGHT OF OT LAMENT ECHOES

We have evaluated lament echoes in their original contexts and tested their presence in Romans 1:16–17. It is now time to assess their interpretive impact on Paul's thematic statement, and, at least to a certain extent, the wider contents of his letter. There are some simple but important interpretive questions to ask. What difference does it really make if we "hear" the echoes of lament in Romans 1:16–17? How does it impact our understanding of what Paul says? These are the kinds of questions to which we now turn our attention.

Echoes of Disappointment and the Gospel

One of the echoes of lament we identified in Romans 1:16–17 are the Psalms of Lament that speak of "disappointment" ($αἰσχύν$—root). In these instances, the lamenter is specifically distressed by disappointment, or at least the potential for disappointment, in God's prior promise to deliver those who cry out to him. A lamenter's faith, or hope, in what God promised either has been or ultimately could be for naught. If this is the kind of experience evoked in Paul's thematic statement, as I am suggesting here, and it is the scenario that stands behind his assertions about the gospel, it raises two questions. First, what pain are Paul and his recipients experiencing that could potentially result in disappointment with the gospel? Second, what is Paul's response to such circumstances?

---

28 See Seifrid, *Christ Our Righteousness*, 45. However, Watson raises questions about the impact of this psalm on Rom 1:16–17. See Watson, *Paul and the Hermeneutics of Faith*, 49–50.

With respect to the first question, any answer must consider the clues provided by the letter itself. Subsequent chapters will provide a full treatment of these clues. Here I would simply note that suffering in Romans, the kind of suffering that could result in disappointment with the gospel, emanates from five interrelated sources: (1) divine wrath; (2) the personified enemy of sin; (3) inexplicable rejection by God; (4) Israel's unbelief; and (5) ecclesiastical judgmentalism. There are indications in the letter of a concern with the relationship between divine judgment, both present and future, and ongoing struggles with sin.[29] There are also suggestions in the letter that some in Rome felt God had inexplicably rejected them, or that Paul saw the potential for that conclusion in the face of their pain.[30] Either way, it could lead to disappointment in the gospel. Similarly, Paul voices concern about Israel's unbelief and its implications for the gospel he preaches. He articulates that concern, not coincidentally, through the use of OT lament language.[31] Finally, Paul addresses the controversy embroiling Jewish and Gentile Christians in Rome. He criticizes an eschatologically damaging form of judgmentalism.[32] In short, all of the sources of suffering that Paul addresses have the potential to "disappoint" his faith in the gospel and that of his Roman recipients. Just as the suffering experienced by lamenters in the Psalms of Lament could result in disappointment (either presently or eschatologically) in what they hoped for, the pain of Paul and the Romans could have a similar result.

I recognize that my reading of ἐπαισχύνομαι and the rest of Romans 1:16–17 diverges from the tendency to associate Paul's "shame" language solely with Jesus tradition or the wisdom tradition from the Corinthian correspondence, as mentioned previously. Both of those readings are related to the kerygma of the gospel. Nevertheless, a reading based on OT lament echoes related to "disappointment" does not preclude Jesus or wisdom tradition readings altogether. Paul is clearly eager to preach the gospel (εὐαγγελίσασθαι) to those in Rome (Rom 1:15). One could even say that he is "not ashamed" to preach it there. But we should not limit the meaning to public embarrassment or kerygmatic concerns. The lament echoes, along with the emphasis on suffering in the rest of the letter, indicate a potential for eschatological disappointment with the gospel Paul unashamedly preached.

29. Not coincidentally, those portions of the letter contain a high volume of lament language, most notably Rom 3:9–20 and 7:7–25.

30 Rom 8:18–39 is especially important here. Once again, not surprisingly, there is a high volume of lament echoes in this portion of the letter.

31 See Rom 9:1–5.

32 See Rom 14:10–23 and 15:1–6.

When Paul asserts that he is not "ashamed/disappointed" in the gospel, he has in mind the sources of suffering that I briefly outlined above. His statement is not entirely detached from the "shame" of preaching the gospel, but it is not entirely defined by that concern either. Moreover, Paul has an immediate response to the suffering that could potentially "disappoint" one's faith in the gospel. Romans 1:16–17 is the response *in nuce* while the rest of the letter offers a more extensive explanation.

The shorthand response is marked by the two γάρ conjunctions in Romans 1:16 and 17. Paul is not disappointed/ashamed in what the gospel promises, despite what he suffers, because (γάρ) he sees the gospel as the δύναμις θεοῦ εἰς σωτηρίαν. The genitive θεοῦ has a number of syntactic possibilities, but the simple idea of source best fits the context and comports with Paul's use of similar phrases elsewhere.[33] The phrases τὸ εὐαγγέλιον and δύναμις θεοῦ mark a convertible proposition, so that God's power which results in (εἰς) salvation and the gospel are one and the same.[34] The second γάρ in 1:17 signals Paul's explanation as to why the gospel is God's power to save. It is because in the gospel the δικαιοσύνη θεοῦ is revealed (ἀποκαλύπτεται). Here we are faced with one of the thornier exegetical issues in the letter. Therefore, it is necessary to pause and briefly review the more salient points of the discussion before analyzing the phrase in light of the OT lament echoes which are our primary concern.

Even before the New Perspective led to a fresh appraisal of the expression, the meaning of δικαιοσύνη θεοῦ has occupied the attention of interpreters for quite some time.[35] From the patristic era until the Reformation, various proposals were put forward that attempted to explain what Paul meant when he asserted that the "righteousness of God" is revealed in the gospel. Longenecker has helpfully classified those various approaches as either attributive/subjective or communicative/objective.[36] While each approach possess its own unique nuances, generally speaking, either Paul is speaking about God's just nature and action or about God's gift of a right standing to the sinner. Longenecker identifies Tertullian and Ambrosiaster as the first proponents of the attributive/subjective reading. Both were

---

33. The exact same phrase δύναμις θεοῦ as a description of the gospel appears in 1 Cor 1:18. In that context, source seems to be the best syntactical option. See also 1 Cor 1:24, 2:4.

34 On convertible propositions, see Wallace, *Greek Grammar*, 40–46.

35 For one of the most recent discussion on the phrase from a New Perspective interpreter who still sees some value in the "old" perspective, see Dunn, "What's Right about the Old Perspective on Paul?" 214–19.

36 Longenecker, *Introducing Romans*, 294.

influenced by the Latin rendering of δικαιοσύνη θεοῦ as *iustitia Dei*. Ambrosiaster observes:

> It is the justice of God (*iustitia Dei*), because he has given what he has promised; hence the one who believes that he has acquired that which God had promised through his prophets shows that God is just and becomes a witness to his justice.[37]

The shift from Ambrosiaster's attributive/subjective interpretation takes place with Augustine's communicative/objective reading which interprets δικαιοσύνη θεοῦ as a reference to God's unmerited grace. Augustine argued that righteousness is something God gave to the repentant sinner. According to Longenecker, the respective readings of Ambrosiaster and Augustine are melded together in the Middle Ages. Thomas Aquinas exemplifies this move in his assertion that δικαιοσύνη θεοῦ is that "by which God is just and by which he justifies human beings."[38] The Reformation saw the emergence of Luther's interpretation, which, like Augustine's, emphasized the unmerited grace of God. From Longenecker's perspective, Luther interpreted δικαιοσύνη θεοῦ as a:

> Divine gift (i.e. in the objective or communicative sense) that puts the person who receives that gift "by faith" in an entirely new relationship with the one true, righteous Divine Being (i.e. in a state of "forensic justness or rightness") and causes that person to live in an entirely new way both personally and in society (i.e. in an experience of "ethical justice or rightgeousness").[39]

So, from the patristic era until the Reformation, we find primarily three different interpretations of δικαιοσύνη θεοῦ: (1) attributive/subjective; (2) communicative/objective; and (3) a kind of combination of both (e.g., Aquinas).

Post-reformation readings from the past several centuries have not really moved that far away from the approaches outlined above. What does change is an emphasis on interpreting δικαιοσύνη θεοῦ in lights of its Jewish background. For example, Hereman Cremer insists on understanding Pauline righteousness "vis-à-vis the OT Hebrew masculine noun צֶדֶק and its feminine counterpart צְדָקָה."[40] Based on this Hebraic background, Cremer concluded that δικαιοσύνη θεοῦ conveyed two things: (1) "an attribute of God and the quality of his actions"; and (2) "what God accomplishes

---

37 Ibid.
38 Ibid., 296
39 Ibid., 298.
40 Ibid., 299.

redemptively on behalf of his people, often conjunction with the concept of 'salvation.'"[41] More recently, N. T. Wright has placed a premium on the Jewish background of Paul's use of δικαιοσύνη θεοῦ. He interprets the phrase as a compressed statement best understood as God's "covenant faithfulness." Wright explains:

> The best argument for taking *dikaiosyne theou* in Romans 1:17, 3:21, and 10:3 as "God's faithfulness to the covenant with Abraham, to the single-plan-through-Israel-for-the-world," is the massive sense it makes of passage after passage, the way in which bits of Romans often omitted from discussion, or even explicitly left on one side as being irrelevant to the main drift of the discourse, suddenly come back into focus with a bang.[42]

The narrative sequence, represented in the compressed phrase "single-plan-through-Israel-for-the-world" is Wright's exegetical key to the letter, including his interpretation of δικαιοσύνη θεοῦ. Therefore, for Wright the "righteousness of God" is God's covenant faithfulness that ultimately serves as "the original divine answer to the problem of Adam."[43]

Given this reception history of δικαιοσύνη θεοῦ, how is the interpretation of the phrase impacted by the OT lament echoes that accompany it, particularly echoes related to disappointment/shame? The primary impact is that the echoes evoke a particular "backdrop" or narrative substructure for understanding the phrase.[44] Specifically, it is a "backdrop," or "story," of a righteous lamenter who suffers, cries out for God to save "in his righteousness" as he promised, and believes that hope in the divine promise will not ultimately disappointment, neither presently or eschatologically.[45] In the Psalms of Lament where lamenters mention disappointment/shame over God's prior promise, they often ask God to save by his "righteousness." The implication is that they expect deliverance to come in a particular manner. The specific manner is God's judgment of the lamenter's enemies which results in deliverance. In Romans 1:16–17, Paul is the lamenter who, although suffering and crying out for God to save by his righteousness, does not believe his faith in the gospel will end in disappointment. That is because Paul believes the δικαιοσύνη θεοῦ has been revealed in the gospel. In the

---

41 Ibid.

42 Wright, *Justification: God's Plan and Paul's Vision*, 179. For a similar explanation, see also Wright, *Romans*, 396–406.

43 Wright, "Romans and the Theology of Paul," 32.

44 On narrative substructure in a Pauline letter, see Hays, *The Faith of Jesus Christ*, 73–205.

45 Cf. Ps 30:2; 70:2.

death and resurrection of Jesus, God judged his enemies so as to save the righteous. The presence of this backdrop does not rest solely upon the OT echoes related to disappointment/shame. As we will see, the lament echoes from Habakkuk also contribute to this reading.

Echoes of the Divine Answer to Lament

Habakkuk 2:4 provides more for Paul than the justification nomenclature that is found throughout Romans. Habakkuk as a whole actually offers the larger pattern and theology of that provides an interpretive background, framework, or narrative for understanding Romans 1:16–17. In short, as I outlined it above, Habakkuk suffers from sin, lawlessness, and impending judgment in Judah. He cries out about these sources of suffering asking classic questions such as "why" and "how long." The two-pronged answer to Habakkuk's cries is that God is doing something unbelievable through the invading Chaldeans and that the "righteous one" must believe in the vision of divine judgment and deliverance that is to come. What I want to consider here is how the lament sequence in Habakkuk, evoked in Romans 1:16–17 through the citation of Habakkuk 2:4, impacts the way we interpret some of the key phrases in Paul's thematic statement.

We begin with the identity of ὁ δίκαιος. We have already established that the "righteous one" in Habakkuk is someone like the prophet himself who cries out to God in the face of suffering and believes the divine response that follows. The divine response is that the "righteous one" is someone who believes in the vision of impending judgment and salvation. It is my contention that ὁ δίκαιος in Romans, both in 1:17 and beyond, should be identified as a similar kind of figure. There are a number of figures in Romans who, like Habakkuk, suffer, cry out, and receive an answer grounded in judgment and salvation. We will examine these figures throughout the course of the present work. For the moment, it is sufficient to note that figures such as Abraham, David, Elijah, and Moses—all of whom make an appearance in Romans—are sometimes described through the use of lament.[46] A common thread between them is that, like Habakkuk, they suffer, cry out, and receive a promise of judgment and salvation. Yet, given the fact that the Habakkuk citation is in the letter's thesis statement, the lamenting figure of the prophet seems to shape Paul's understanding of ὁ δίκαιος the most. This means that divine answer to Habakkuk, the one cited in Romans 1:17, is especially important for understanding not only ὁ δίκαιος but other phrases in the thesis statement as well.

46. See Rom 4; 9:1–3; 11:1–6.

The verb ἀποκαλύπτεται in Romans 1:17 is a second phrase that needs to be considered in light of the echoes of lament from Habakkuk. Paul explains that the gospel is the power of God that results in salvation to the one who believes, because in the gospel the δικαιοσύνη θεοῦ ἀποκαλύπτεται. The latter conception plays an important role in the way God responds to Habakkuk's cries of distress. He reveals a vision (ὅρασις) of future judgment and salvation that Habakkuk must believe.[47] Similarly, God's response to the righteous lamenters in Romans is the revelation of judgment and salvation in the εὐαγγέλιον. Of course, one of the primary differences between Habakkuk's ὅρασις and Paul's εὐαγγέλιον is that the former is portrayed as not having occurred yet. Contrastively, the judgment and salvation promised in the gospel has already taken place through the death and resurrection of Jesus.[48] The answer to Habakkuk's distress is the vision of the judgment and salvation to come, but the answer to Paul's distress is the revelation of the judgment and salvation that has already taken place in Christ. Nevertheless, it does not follow that Paul confines judgment entirely to the past. He closely links the revelation of God's righteousness in the gospel and the revelation of divine wrath presently and eschatologically in Romans 1:18. He explains "For the wrath of God is being revealed (ἀποκαλύπτεται)" (Rom 1:18). Moreover, even beyond Romans 1:18–32, Paul shows concern with wrath and judgment throughout the letter.[49] Yet, even with the prospect of present and future judgment, and the distress it causes, Paul points the Romans to the gospel.

Finally, the phrase δικαιοσύνη θεοῦ is illuminated by hearing the echoes of Habakkuk's lament language as well. While Habakkuk does not contain the actual phrase, it still provides, especially via the prophet's lament language, insight into what Paul means by it. The connection between Paul's statement in Romans 1:17 and Habakkuk 2:4 is not solely defined by πίστις. The noun does act as a hook word in Paul's explanation that God's righteousness is revealed "from faith (πίστεως) to faith (εἰς πίστιν)" and the citation from Habakkuk "But the righteous one will live by faith (πίστεως)." Nevertheless, Habakkuk and Romans are also linked by their shared object of faith, namely the righteousness of God revealed in the divine vision and or message. As I have noted numerous times already, by citing Habakkuk 2:4, Paul evokes the entire scenario in which the prophet was told "But the righteous one will live by faith." It is a scenario in which God responds to the suffering and cries of Habakkuk by revealing a vision of future judgment

---

47 See the use of ὅρασις in Hab 2:2–3.
48. See Rom 3:21–26; 4:25.
49 See e.g., Rom 2:1–16; 5:6–10; 14:1–18.

and salvation. Historically, God would judge Judah through the Chaldeans and yet judge the Chaldeans as well. Only those who believed the vision, even if they had to wait for it, would actually live beyond the judgment and experience deliverance. The combination of judgment and deliverance, even deliverance through judgment, as the answer to Habakkuk's cries is not missed by Paul. He simply refers to it as δικαιοσύνη θεοῦ.

An Echo of Lament to Praise

Earlier, we identified Psalm 97 as a third OT echo in Romans 1:16–17. Psalm 97 works in concert with the lament language from certain Psalms of Lament and Habakkuk. Based on the latter two sources of echoes, Paul's righteous lamenter wrestles with disappointment in what God promised and yet finds an answer in the revelation of God's righteousness. As is common in the form and theology of OT lament, this should result in praise for the revelation of God's righteousness. We find that expected praise through the echo of Psalm 97.

The point here is that the echo of Psalm 97 in Romans 1:16–17 must ultimately be read in light of its original context and alongside the specific pattern and theology of lament evoked through the lament echoes we have been discussing. As we saw previously, the psalmist praises God for making known (ἐγνώρισεν) his salvation (σωτήριον) (Ps 97:2a). The parallelism in 97:2b clarifies that such knowledge is revelation (ἀπεκάλυψεν) and the salvation is righteousness (δικαιοσύνην) (Ps 97:2). Just as in Habakkuk, δικαιοσύνη in Psalm 97 combines God's judgment and salvation. This is indicated in Psalm 97:9 where the closing praise is "For he will come to judge (κρῖναι) the earth; he will judge (κρινεῖ) the world in righteousness (δικαιοσύνῃ) and the peoples in uprightness." Furthermore, the phrase "before the nations" in 97:2b indicates that the revelation of God's righteousness is universal in scope. Consequently, the revelation of God's righteousness results in universal wide praise "Shout to God, all the earth (πᾶσα ἡ γῆ), sing and be glad and sing with accompaniment" (Ps 97:4). This universal praise for the revelation of God's righteousness, that is salvation through judgment, corresponds to a similar motif in Romans 1:16–17. Although Paul does not explicitly praise God as the psalmist does, the echoes of Psalm 97 evoke such praise. Even more, when the echo from Psalm 97 is combined with the other lament echoes, a figure emerges who has shifted from a cry of distress to praise. The revelation of God's righteousness in the gospel is the catalyst here, and throughout the letter, for the shift. Regardless of where the pain comes from, or the cry such pain elicits, the gospel is the divine answer which turns lament to praise.

READING THE REST OF ROMANS IN LIGHT OF THE ECHOES IN 1:16-17

When we read Romans 1:16–17 in light of its OT lament echoes, four salient points related to the interpretation of the letter emerge. First, since OT lament plays such a significant role in the thematic statement, it stands to reason that it will have a prominent role in the rest of Romans as well. Interpreters often point out that Romans 1:16–17 is a compressed statement which receives fuller treatment in the letter. Therefore, the presence of lament in the compressed statement means it is probable to occur elsewhere. Subsequent chapters will confirm this probability and deal extensively with those occurrences.

Second, the catch phrase of the entire letter, δικαιοσύνη θεοῦ, must now be interpreted against the backdrop, or narrative, of lament that is echoed in Romans 1:17. The explicit phrase occurs again in Romans 3:8, 3:20–21, and 10:3. As I will demonstrate in the chapters ahead, these three uses of the phrase, like the one in Romans 1:17, are linked literarily and conceptually to OT lament. The phrase assumes, and in fact has explicit connections to, a pattern and theology of lament. Nevertheless, the OT echoes surrounding δικαιοσύνη θεοῦ in Romans 1:17 are determinative for interpreting subsequent uses. Specifically, the righteousness of God is what the "righteous one" cries out for in the face of suffering and eventually praises God for when it is revealed.

Third, the lament echoes in Romans 1:16–17 shed light on the identity of ὁ δίκαιος throughout the letter. The "righteous one" from the larger context of Habakkuk informs us about the identity of that figure in the thematic statement and beyond. The lament echoes evoke a framework, or narrative, for understanding ὁ δίκαιος that is defined by the figure's suffering, cry of distress, and divine answer. For Paul, ὁ δίκαιος suffers from a variety of sources, cries out for deliverance, and always "hears" the divine answer to those cries in the gospel. What we will find later is that while the sources of suffering vary in Romans, as do the cries of distress, the divine answer to the prospect of final "disappointment" with the gospel is the same. The gospel reveals God's righteousness, which is what ὁ δίκαιος needs and was promised. Consequently, the "righteous one" praises God as the psalmist does in Psalm 97.

Finally, the echoes of lament in Paul's thematic statement imply that suffering is at the heart of the letter's purpose. OT lament is the language of suffering. It is used in moments of profound pain and distress. Therefore, its presence in Romans 1:16–17 is quite telling. It tells us that both Paul and his recipients are suffering. The specific causes of their suffering are not spelled out in these two verses, but they do emerge in the course of Paul's argument. To reiterate, Paul's citation of Habakkuk 2:4, originally the divine response to the prophet's cries of distress, indicates that faith in the gospel is the divine answer to all that ails the "righteous one." Paul will drive this point home throughout his letter with further use of OT lament language. Nevertheless, the divine answer cited from Habakkuk 2:4 becomes determinative for Paul's subsequent reflection on how the gospel answers the suffering and cries of distress experienced by the righteous.

4

The Gospel as the Answer to the Unrighteous Lamenter (Romans 3:1–26)

PAUL'S MOST EXTENSIVE USE of OT lament occurs in Romans 3:1–20. Some interpreters assume that in this section of the letter Paul is simply concluding what he has already laid out in 1:18—2:29.[1] But the high volume of lament echoes in these verses indicates something more is going on. Here we need to keep in mind one of the primary diagnostic questions behind this entire work. Why does Paul use OT lament language? In this instance, why is there so much lament language in Romans 3:1–20?

In answering that question, the overarching thesis of this chapter is that the lament language in Romans 3:1–20 casts Jew and Gentile as two participants common to OT lament. They act as both unrighteous enemies of God who do not fear him and guilty petitioners who plead for his mercy. By taking up both roles, the δικαιοσύνη θεοῦ is revealed in that God judges his enemy and delivers the one who seeks his mercy. As in the case of Romans 1:17, echoes of OT lament have implications for how we understand δικαιοσύνη θεοῦ in 3:5 and 3:21–26.

The process here is similar to the one we followed in the previous chapter. We will identify the OT lament usage and evaluate it in its original context. We will then consider how reading Romans 3:1–20 in light of its

---

1. E.g., Achtemeier opens his remarks on Rom 3:9–20 noting, "The time has come to cast a balance, to reach a conclusion, and that is what Paul is about in these verses." Yet, he does note that Paul's conclusion, like so often in argumentation, points beyond itself. Achtemeier, *Romans*, 58.

OT lament echoes impacts our interpretation of this section of the letter and others.

IDENTIFYING AND TESTING THE ECHOES OF LAMENT IN ROMANS 3:1-20

The cluster of OT lament in Romans 3:1-20 consists of passages from the Psalms of Lament, Isaiah, and Ecclesiastes. Interpreters do not always appreciate the common thread of lament that runs throughout these passages.[2] There is an assumption, especially with the catena in 3:10-18, that Paul has simply strung together verses that speak to humanity's universal sinfulness.[3] They fail to see that each citation contains lament language that in many instances originally functioned as part of a larger lament pattern. Consequently, there is a failure to fully appreciate the language's interpretive impact on Paul's argument.[4]

Penitential Lament and God's Righteousness (Psalm 50)

In describing how possessing the oracles of God is an advantage to the Jew and defending God's faithfulness in the face of unbelief, Paul cites Psalm 50:6, "In order that you might be justified in your words and you will overcome when you judge." These lines are part of what some have rightly called a "penitential lament."[5] We need to briefly consider the wider context of this penitential lament psalm in order to test and analyze its echoes in Romans 3:1-8.

Psalm 50 contains all the key elements common to the pattern or sequence of lament. The sequence begins with a series of requests in verses 3-4 that are subsequently grounded in the suffering that the psalmist describes in verses 5-8.[6] Verses 9-14 contain another series of requests followed by

---

2. The catena as a whole is sometimes briefly summarized and not much more. See e.g., Dodd, *Romans*, 72.

3 E.g.. Achtemeier explains that Rom 3:10-18 is "a display from Scripture of the universal shortcomings of a humanity in rebellion against its Creator." Achtemeier, *Romans*, 59.

4 E.g., Moo, commenting on Rom 3:10-18, wrongly concludes that these are not "directly related to Paul's purpose." Moo, *Romans*, 203.

5 Although Ps 50 is not always referred to as a lament psalm, it clearly contains the primary features of lament. For OT scholars who classify this psalm as lament, see e.g., Anderson, *Out of the Depths,* 240; Miller, *Interpreting the Psalms,* 53-54.

6 Note the causal ὅτι at the beginning of Ps 50:5.

praise in verses 15–21. Therefore, the suffering, cry of distress, and praise, elements common to the lament pattern, are all present in the psalm.

The psalmist's suffering stems from the awareness that he is guilty of sin and therefore deserving of divine judgment.[7] This awareness is on display from the outset. The psalm commences with a request for mercy and forgiveness, "Have mercy on me (ἐλέησόν με), O God, according to your great mercy and according to the multitude of your compassions wipe out my lawlessness" (Ps 50:3).[8] This initial request is grounded in the duel acknowledgment of guilt and God's "victory" in judgment against him:

> I know my lawlessness and my sin is before me continually. Against you only have I sinned and done what is evil before you, in order that (ὅπως) you are justified (δικαιωθῇς) in your words and you overcome (νικήσῃς) when you judge (ἐν τῷ κρίνεσθαί σε). (Ps 50:5–6)

The lamenter's acknowledgment of guilt serves interlocking purposes. It serves as an acknowledgment that God is righteous and victorious in his judgment against him. Even more, the lamenter acknowledges that God is righteous and victorious in judgment, in order that God might grant him the mercy he requested. Subsequent requests for mercy in 50:7–15, though articulated in various ways, are grounded in the duel acknowledgment of guilt and God's righteous judgment found in 50:5–6.

The victory and righteousness of God described in 50:5–6, as well as the initial request for mercy in 50:3, are further illuminated by the lamenter's final request "Deliver (ῥῦσαι) me from blood guiltiness (ἐξ αἱμάτων) O God, God of my salvation (σωτηρίας); my tongue will exult your righteousness (δικαιοσύνην)" (Ps 50:16). The noun αἷμα refers to the liability for sins that God can punish by death.[9] These are the sins for which the lamenter acknowledged his guilt and God's victory in judgment against him in 50:5–6. Yet, he requests to be delivered from the guilt for this sin and the judgment it incurs. Deliverance (σωτηρία) from guilt and judgment will result in the lamenter's praise for God's δικαιοσύνη (Ps 50:16). When the reference to δικαιοσύνη in 50:16 is read in light of δικαιόω in 50:6, and the psalm as a whole, we see that praise for God's righteousness includes both praise for his righteous judgment (50:6) and deliverance (50:16) from the punishment that judgment demands.

---

7 See the repeated use of ἁμαρτία and ἀνομία in Ps 50:4, 5, 7, 11. See also LEH, 31, 51.

8 See also Ps 50:4.

9 Goldingay, "Psalm 51:6a," 388.

To summarize up to this point, the lamenter in Psalm 50 suffers from his own sin and the wrath that his guilt incurs. His suffering elicits a cry of distress that includes the duel acknowledgment of sin and God's righteous judgment against him as well as the request for mercy and deliverance. We have then a lamenter who plays the role of both enemy and petitioner.

Testing Echoes of Psalm 50

When we turn our attention to testing the echoes of Psalm 50 in Romans 3:1–8, we are looking for both semantic and conceptual links between the two texts. Obviously, the citation of Psalm 50:6 provides an explicit semantic link, but there are other echoes from the larger context of this lament psalm in Paul's argument. With respect to the "recurrence" of Psalm 50 in Romans or Paul's other writings, Romans 7:14 may be the only other echo of this particular psalm. Specifically, in the enigmatic self-description of the "I" in Romans 7, there may be an echo of Psalm 50:7, "For behold I was conceived in lawlessness, I was desired in sin."

The four other tests are more important for our purposes here. First, the "thematic coherence" between the two passages is that both Psalm 50 and Romans 3:1–8 focus on the duel acknowledgment of guilt thereby acknowledging God's justification, or victory, in judgment against the guilty party. Next, it is "historically plausible" that Paul means to evoke the entire context of the psalm given the fact that he explicitly cites a portion of it and given his reflection on the figure of David elsewhere.[10] I have already established that Paul does not extract OT verses, phrases, or words without recourse to their fuller context. Third, within the history of interpretation, it is not unheard of for interpreters to recognize that Paul evokes the entire context of Psalm 50 and not simply one phrase.[11] Finally, reading Romans 3:1–8 in light of the entirety of Psalm 50 does "illuminate the surrounding discourse." I will discuss later the interpretive impact of reading Romans 3:1–8 in light of the entire form and theology of lament from Psalm 50. For the moment, I would simply note that the larger lament features evoked through the citation of Psalm 50:6, particularly the lamenters' duel acknowledgment that serves as the basis for requesting mercy, fit nicely with the way Paul uses OT lament for his argument in Romans 3:1–20 as a whole.

---

10 See e.g., Rom 1:3; 4:6; 11:9.

11 See Hays, *Echoes of Scripture*, 48. Contrastively, Dodd thinks all of Rom 3:1–8, thus including the citation of Ps 50:4, is "obscure and feeble." Dodd, *Romans*, 70.

Unrighteous and Irreverent Before the Cosmic Judge (Ecclesiastes 7 and Psalm 35)

Romans 3:10–18 is often referred to as a *catena* of OT citations. It is more accurately a "catena of lament." Paul employs multiple Psalms of Lament as well as passages that contain features of OT lament. This catena contains an *inclusio* that begins with a citation from Ecclesiastes 7 and ends with a citation from Psalm 35. The lament language borrowed from these two psalms serve as Paul's summative description of Jews and Gentiles under sin (Rom 3:9). Therefore, we need to briefly consider this language in its larger context.

In Romans 3:10, Paul begins his catena of lament by citing Ecclesiastes 7:20 "There is no one righteous (δίκαιος), not even one." There is one textual issue here that needs to be addressed. The phrase "not even one" (οὐδὲ εἷς) is most likely an addition from Psalm 13:1. This redaction by Paul is not really too far afield from the LXX version of Ecclesiastes 7:20 "For there is no righteous man in the earth (ἐν τῇ γῇ), who will do good and not sin." The phrase ἐν τῇ γῇ is replaced with οὐδὲ εἷς, but they both convey the universal unrighteousness of the human being.[12] Even more, on the whole, both Ecclesiastes 7 and Psalm 13 share a rather "jaundiced" view of people.[13] Therefore, despite the conflation of Ecclesiastes 7 and Psalms 13, the former deserves to be treated in its entirety. I will assess the full context of Psalm 13 shortly.

Ecclesiastes is wisdom literature, but it shares some theological traits with lament. This is especially evident in the wider context of Ecclesiastes 7:1–22 where the writer's pessimistic anthropology is expressed through three contrastive pairs: the wise and the foolish; the righteous and the ungodly; the righteous and the wise. The first pair is contrasted in 7:1–12. The "wise" (σοφός) are those who mourn, restrain themselves from anger, and do not romanticize the past.[14] The foolish (ἄφρων) are those who laugh, are quick to anger, and look back with fondness on days gone by.[15] In Ecclesiastes 7:15–18, we find our second contrast between the righteous (δίκαιος) and the ungodly (ἀσεβής). However, the contrast between this pair is somewhat surprising. The writer does not contrast the obedience and blessings of the righteous person to the disobedience and destruction of the unrighteous

---

12. On Paul's redaction in Rom 3:10, see Jewett, *Romans*, 123.

13 Dunn specifically notes, "The somewhat jaundiced view of Qoheleth confirms Paul's own argument that Jewish national understanding of themselves as the 'righteous' is a misunderstanding of covenant privilege and responsibility." Dunn, *Romans*, 150.

14 See Eccl 7:2–4, 9–10.

15 See Eccl 7:1–12.

person as one might expect to find in Jewish wisdom literature.[16] Instead, we find the book's leitmotif of futility (ματαιότης) applied to the contrast between the righteous and unrighteous, "I have seen all things in the days of my futility (ματαιότητός); the righteous one (δίκαιος) being destroyed in his righteousness, and the ungodly one (ἀσεβὴς) remaining in his wickedness" (Eccl 7:15). The writer follows this observation with imperatives to be neither too righteous nor too ungodly (Eccl 7:16–17) and the conclusion that the wisest course of action is to fear God.[17] Finally, in 7:19–22, the writer contrasts the wise and righteous person. The wise person has an advantage over the righteous person, because the former understands that "[t]here is no righteous person in the earth, who will do good and not sin" (Eccl 7:20). In other words, the wise know that neither they, nor anyone else, are ultimately righteous.[18] This realization is driven home by the warning in 7:21–22 that the wise person should not eavesdrop on what his servant says about him, because he will hear his servant cursing him. The servant's cursing is not excused. Rather, the wise person is reminded that he or she does the exact same thing. Therefore, they are also unrighteous. In the theology of Ecclesiastes, it is the realization of this unrighteousness, and the divine judgment it incurs, which makes one wise and ultimately righteous before God.

At this point, we might ask what features of lament are found in Ecclesiastes 7:1–22. The primary feature is its description of the foolish and unrighteous. In OT lament, the foolish and unrighteous are enemies of God while the wise and righteous are delivered by him. Ecclesiastes 7:1–22 provides the unique insight that the foolish and unrighteous do not recognize their unrighteousness while the wise and truly righteous one does. Paul sets the former pair alongside the enemies described in the Psalms of Lament, including Psalm 35 where enemies foolishly and irreverently ignore the prospect of God's judgment.

The end of Paul's *inclusio* is a citation of Psalm 35:2, "There is no fear of God before their eyes." In the larger setting of the psalm, this observation is part of the lamenter's complaint to God.[19] Paul only cites part of the opening line of the psalm. In its entirety it reads, "The lawless one, in order to sin, speaks in himself, there is no fear of God before his eyes" (Ps 35:2).[20]

16 See e.g., Sir 4:11–19.
17 See Eccl 7:18; 12:13.
18 See also Eccl 7:27–29.
19 Ps 35 is mixed in its form, but it is still primarily lament. It contains wisdom and hymnic elements as well. Nevertheless, it is still regarded as an individual lament. See, e.g. Westermann, *The Psalms*, 55.
20 There are a few noteworthy things about the translation of Ps 35:2. First, the

The implication is that the lawless person tells him or herself that they will not face judgment for their lawlessness. In this way, there is no fear of judgment before God. The absence of fear emboldens the opponent's deceit and devious plans which the lamenter describes in 35:3–5. The lamenter's complaint against the opponent shifts to praise and requests for deliverance in 35:6–12. The lamenter extols God's ἀλήθεια, ἔλεος, and δικαιοσύνη. All of these terms are related to the lamenter's need for deliverance from his enemies expressed in his word of praise "you will save (σώσεις) men and animals, O Lord" (Ps 35:7). He conveys the specific means of deliverance in the request of 35:11–12:

> Extend your mercy (ἔλεος) to those who know you and your righteousness (δικαιοσύνην) to those who are upright in heart. Let not the foot of the arrogant come to me, and may the hand of sinners not shake me.

God's mercy and righteousness are seen here as protection from enemies. The lamenter's protection by means of God's mercy and righteousness includes the fall of his enemies. This is indicated in the closing praise "There those who do lawlessness fell, they were driven out and they certainly were not able to stand." Presumably, the enemies are unable to stand before God in judgment. This is the antithesis of the opponents' self-delusional and foolish position lamented in the beginning of the psalm (Ps 35:2). Although there is no fear of divine judgment before the eyes of the opponents, they will "fall" in judgment at the request of the lamenter.

What we find then is that, in their original contexts, the two parts of Paul's *inclusio* of lament functioned as descriptions of wicked enemies who foolishly denied divine judgment. Miller notes that in "lamenting prayers" the fool is also the wicked.[21] That certainly applies here. Although Ecclesiastes 7 does not contain a "lamenting prayer," it does describe the type of enemy we find in explicit lament texts. From Ecclesiastes 7, we see that the wise person is one who knows that no one, including him or herself is righteous. Contrastively, the "righteous" person, the one who fails to realize that "no one is righteous," is a fool. Such a person is also unaware of impending judgment. Similarly, the enemies in Psalm 35 are lawless fools who tell themselves that they will not face God's wrath for their deceit, lawlessness, and devious plans. The lamenter cries out against such enemies, but he also

---

subject of the verb in the MT is פֶּשַׁע. In this reading, it is transgression personified that speaks to the lawless or evil person. Second, the NETS translator renders Ps 35:2a as "Says the transgressor of the law in himself; in order to sin."

21 Miller, *They Cried to the Lord*, 85.

trusts that God will deliver him by judging enemies who are arrogant and foolish enough to have no fear of such judgment.

Testing the Echoes of Ecclesiastes 7 and Psalm 35

With respect to testing the echoes of lament in Romans 3:10 and 18, I will stipulate that Ecclesiastes 7 and Psalm 35 pass the tests of availability, volume, and recurrence. They also pass the test of thematic coherence quite well. In Romans 3:10–18, Paul portrays both Jew and Gentile as the kinds of enemies bemoaned in OT lament. This theme coheres with the foolish and "righteous" figure in Ecclesiastes 7 as well as the deceitful and irreverent opponent in Psalm 35. In terms of historical plausibility, it is reasonable to conclude that Paul intended for these figures to be noticed in Romans 3:10–18. The dichotomy between the righteous and unrighteous was ingrained within Second Temple Judaism and the OT.[22] Yet, in many ways, Paul is turning that dichotomy on its head and using Israel's scriptures to do so. Finally, in terms of satisfaction, I will demonstrate below how echoes from Ecclesiastes 7 and Psalm 35, combined with other lament echoes in Romans 3:10–18, bring Paul's argument to a significant climax in 3:19–20.

Turning Away Without A Cry to God (Psalm 13)

Within the *inclusio* marked by citations in Romans 3:10 and 3:18, the enemies in Paul's catena can be grouped into three categories, the first of which is found in 3:11–12. Here we have a partially reworked citation from Psalm 13 "There is no one who understands, there is no one who seeks God. All have turned away together they have become worthless; there is no one who does good, not even one" (Rom 3:11–12).[23] In the original context of Psalm 13, these lines are part of a complaint about the enemies who afflict God's people (Ps 13:4).

---

22 As a reminder, for testing historical plausibility, Hays notes "One implication of this criterion is to give serious preference to interpretive proposals that allow Paul to remain a Jew." Hays, *Echoes of Scripture*, 31.

23 The largest difference between Ps 13:2 and Paul's citation in Rom 3:11 is that in the former we do not find οὐκ ἔστιν ὁ συνίων, οὐκ ἔστιν ὁ ἐκζητῶν τὸν θεόν. Instead, Ps 13:2b reads τοῦ ἰδεῖν εἰ ἔστιν συνίων ἢ ἐκζητῶν τὸν θεόν. Paul's version adds the negative adverb οὐκ and drops the infinitive of purpose ἰδεῖν which modifies the main verb (διέκυψεν) in 13:2a. One explanation for this difference is that Paul, or the author of this preformed material, wanted it to match the nominative δίκαιος in Rom 3:10. In any case, the sense of the text is not greatly impacted by it.

The lamenter in Psalm 13 describes the nation's enemies in a variety of ways. We need to keep in mind that the psalmist portrays the description of the enemies as originating from above (ἐκ τοῦ οὐρανοῦ) (Ps 13:2). God ultimately describes these enemies. To begin, the enemies are described as foolish, because they do not believe they will face judgment for their deeds. The lamenter complains, "The fool (ἄφρων) has said in his heart there is no God" (Ps 13:1a). As Grogan notes, this atheism is not literal but "practical."[24] Foolish enemies live with a great sense of impunity. They conduct themselves *as if* God is absent to judge them. Fools do not believe they will suffer judgment even though they fail to seek God and harm God's people (Ps 13:1, 4). There is such a lack of concern about divine wrath that the fool lives as if "there is no God" who will actually judge him. Second, this foolish impunity pervades humanity. The psalmist uses a number of phrases to indicate how far this foolishness reaches including: οὐκ ἔστιν ἕως ἑνός, τοὺς υἱοὺς τῶν ἀνθρώπων, and πάντες.[25] Third, their foolish impunity has made the enemies morally worthless from God's perspective. When God looks (διέκυψεν) upon the sons of men, he sees they are corrupted and repulsive in their behavior (Ps 13:1–2). The divine assessment in verse 3 is that "All have turned away (ἐξέκλιναν), together they have become worthless (ἠχρεώθησαν), there is no one who does good, not even one." The sons of men should "turn away" (ἐκκλίνω) from evil, but they turn away from God instead.[26] Consequently, they become worthless (ἠχρεώθησαν). The verb ἀχρειόω, although not occurring frequently in the LXX, is sometimes used in metaphorical references to God's people becoming like a fruitless tree.[27]

The descriptive complaint of the enemies closes in verses 4–5. The psalmist likens them to lawless animals that consume God's people and do not cry out to God for deliverance from the wrath he will surely bring upon them:

> Do all those who do lawlessness not know? Those who consume my people like eating bread do not call upon (ἐπεκαλέσαντο) the Lord. There they act cowardly in fear, where there was not fear, because God is with the righteous generation.

The enemies' lack of a cry (ἐπικαλέω) for deliverance in the face of judgment is the most damning complaint against them. They do not cry out, because they have told themselves God will not judge them—"there

---

24 Grogan, *Psalms*, 59. See also Miller, *Interpreting the Psalms*, 95.

25 Of course, in the context of Ps 13, "all" has to be qualified in light the more positive references to God's people and Israel. See Ps 13:4, 7.

26 For the psalmist's command to turn away from evil, see e.g., Pss 33:15; 36:27.

27 See Jer 11:16; Dan 4:14.

is no God" (Ps 13:1). Nevertheless, although they mistreated God's people without fear of repercussion, they will eventually cower in the face of God's judgment (Ps 13:5).

While the enemy does not cry out for deliverance, the lamenter closes with a plea for help and praise for Israel's salvation. The specific request is "Do not put to shame the counsel of the poor, because the Lord is his hope" (Ps 13:6). The lamenter does not want God's people, the poor, to be disappointed (καταισχύνω) in their hope to be delivered from the enemies just described.[28] Despite the threat of being disappointed in the prior promise, there is praise for Israel's salvation (τὸ σωτήριον τοῦ Ἰσραηλ) (Ps 13:7).

Testing the Echoes of Psalm 13

Given the fact that the echoes of Psalm 13 occur in a portion of the letter filled with OT citations, the most pertinent "tests" are thematic coherence, historical plausibility, and the illumination of the surrounding discourse. In terms of thematic coherence, I would note once again that Romans 3:1–20 is shaping a particular kind of lamenter through intertextual echoes of OT lament. The enemies described in Psalm 13 correspond to that lamenter. Like the enemies in Psalm 13 who conduct themselves with impunity and do not cry out to God for deliverance from his judgment, the Jew and Gentile in Romans 3:1–20 do the same. Additionally, at least based on Paul's statements elsewhere in the letter, it is historically plausible that he intended to identify Jews and Gentiles under sin as the kind of enemies described in Psalm 13. For example, he notes Gentile impunity, the kind lamented in Psalm 13:1–5, in Romans 1:32 describing the Gentiles as those "who although having the righteous requirement of God, that those who do such things are worthy of death, not only do them but also give consent to those who do them." Similarly, his statement in Romans 2:3 most likely questions an impunity among certain Gentiles and Jews "But do you reckon this, O man the one who judges those who do such things and does them, that you will escape the judgment of God?" Finally, the echoes from Psalm 13 illuminate the surrounding discourse of Romans 3:1–20 by connecting the Jew and Gentile under sin to enemies who foolishly act with impunity in their treatment of God's people and refuse to call out for deliverance in the face of the judgment they deny. It is the refusal to cry out that will prove especially important in our analysis below.

---

28. On the use of καταισχύνω and its cognates in Psalms of Lament, see chapter 3.

The Deceitful and Deadly Speech of Enemies

The catena of lament identifies another kind of enemy from OT lament, one bemoaned for deceitful and deadly speech. Romans 3:13–14 cites three Psalms of Lament that collectively echo this kind of opponent, "Their throat is an opened grave with their tongues they deceive, the poison of asps is under their lips; whose mouth is full of cursing and bitterness." The wider contexts reveal that these verses originally functioned as part of a lamenter's wider complaints about enemies. Though the complaints are expressed in various ways, they all cry out against the deceitful and deadly speech of enemies. We will look at each of them in turn.

The lamenter in Psalm 5 requests to be heard by God from the outset of the prayer (Ps 5:2–4). The suffering that elicits this initial request is the activity of enemies. They are lawless and thereby unable to withstand God's judgment "The lawless (παράνομοι) will not remain before your eyes" (Ps 5:6). This is a description of enemies we have already seen in Psalms 13 and 35.[29] However, one unique element in this lamenter's compliant is the assertion of God's disdain for such enemies:

> You have hated (ἐμίσησας) all those who do lawlessness (ἀνομίαν). (Ps 5:6b)

> You will destroy all those who speak the lie; the Lord abhors (βδελύσσεται) the man of bloodshed and deceit. (Ps 5:7)

The verbs μισέω and βδελύσσομαι, with θεός or κύριος as the subject, indicate the intensity of God's wrath against the enemies.[30] The term βδελύσσομαι is sometimes used in contexts where it conveys the sense of being repulsed or even sickened by something.[31] It is to this extent that God abhors the "man of bloodshed and deceit" (Ps 5:7). Subsequent requests in Psalm 5:9–11, also grounded in complaints about enemies, provide further description of them:

> Lord, guide me in your righteousness on account of my enemies, make straight your way before me. For there is no truth in their mouth, their heart is empty; their throat is an open

---

29. See Pss 13:4–5; 35:2.

30. The only other use of βδελύσσομαι in the LXX Psalms with a divine subject is found in Ps 105:40 "And the Lord (κύριος) was exceedingly angry with his people and he abhorred (ἐβδελύξατο) his inheritance." There are a few more instances of μισέω with a divine subject in the LXX Psalms. See Pss 10:5; 30:7; 44:8.

31. In Ps 106:18, as the psalmist recalls God's past dealings with Israel, he describes how rebellious Israelites drew near to death and even "abhorred" (ἐβδελύξατο) the idea of eating any food.

grave, with their tongues they deceive. Judge them, O God; let them fall from their schemes according to the multitude of their ungodliness drive them out, because they have rebelled against you, Lord.

The lamenter requests that God "judge" and "let them (i.e., enemies) fall" based on the fact that the enemies used deceit in their plot against him. Most importantly, scheming to harm others qualifies as rebellion against God. The psalmist conveys their deadly intent by complaining that their "throat is an opened grave" (τάφος ἀνεῳγμένος ὁ λάρυγξ αὐτῶν) and that "with their tongues they deceive" (ταῖς γλώσσαις αὐτῶν ἐδολιοῦσαν). The λάρυγξ, a metonymy for speaking, is likened to a τάφος ἀνεῳγμένος.[32] The metaphorical "open grave" evokes the image of the lamenter slipping into the "tomb," or throat, opened by the enemy. As Broyles explains it, "Here is painted the graphic picture of someone being enticed by their flattering speech and slipping on their smooth tongue into their grave-like throat. They are likened to a slippery chasm to Sheol."[33] The enemies' means of luring their victims to the grave is their deceptive speech (ταῖς γλώσσαις αὐτῶν ἐδολιοῦσαν).

While this deceptive speech harms the lamenter, the ultimate grounds of the request is that the enemies have rebelled (ὅτι παρεπίκρανάν σε) against the Lord (Ps 5:11). Their harm of the lamenter, via caustic speech, is tantamount to rebelling against God. This is the most egregious action of all to which the lamenter appeals in the hope of having the request (κρῖνον) granted.[34] If God judges the enemies, those who hope in the Lord will rejoice (Ps 5:11–12). The shift from cry to praise hinges upon divine judgment against enemies defined by deceitful, deadly, and rebellious speech. The lamenter is confident that God will do just that closing the psalm with the assertion "you will bless the righteous" (Ps 5:13a). Therefore, we gather from the entirety of Psalm 5 that those who use deceitful and deadly speech against the righteous have rebelled against God and face certain judgment. This is the kind of enemy evoked in Romans 3:10–18 and descriptive of Jews and Gentiles under sin, as we will discuss further below.

---

32. Waltke et al., *The Psalms as Christian Lament*, 38–39.

33 Broyles, "Psalms Concerning the Liturgy of Temple Entry," 254. Contrastively, Kraus believes that the language in Ps 5:10 is better understood as a complaint about the enemy's slander. See Kraus, *Psalms*, 156.

34 The imperative κρῖνον is the translator's rendering of הַאֲשִׁימֵם. The latter phrase, a hiphil imperative meaning "declare guilty," is more detailed with respect to what is involved in the judgment. Specifically, God declares the enemy guilty and then carries out punishment in light of that sentence.

Another psalm cited by Paul in Romans 3:13 also originally functioned as part of a complaint against enemies, "The poison of asps is under their lips" (Ps 139:4). The broader description of the enemies in Psalm 139, like Psalm 5, focuses on their deceitful and deadly speech. The first three stanzas of the psalm (2–4; 5–6; 7–9) contain requests for protection and deliverance from enemies who plot (λογίζομαι) harm in their hearts and conceal such plans through their deceitful words.[35] Therefore, the lamenter labels them as evil (πονηρός), unrighteous (ἄδικος), sinful (ἁμαρτωλός), and arrogant (ὑπερήφανος) (Ps 139:2, 5). The complaint also includes colorful metaphors describing the enemies as those:

> Who plot (ἐλογίσαντο) unrighteousness in their heart, all day long they array themselves for war; they sharpen their tongue like that of a serpent, the poison of asps is under their lips. (Ps 139:3–4)
>
> Who plot (ἐλογίσαντο) to trip up my steps; the arrogant hide a trap for me and they stretch out cords, traps for my feet, they have set a stumbling block for me near the path. (Ps 139:5–6)

The metaphors stem from war, wildlife, and hunting.[36] The common thread in each is the constant ("all day long") use of subterfuge and deceit. The primary means of the deceit is through language, either flattery or slander.[37] Nevertheless, the goal of the language is the same, namely harm and death. This is clear in the way the lamenter compares the enemies' speech to the "poisons of asps" (ἰὸς ἀσπίδων) being under their lips, a metonymy for speech that aims to kill. Their deceptive and deadly speech goes hand in hand with their plans, so that the lamenter can use the parallel description "babbling man" (ἀνὴρ γλωσσώδης) and "unrighteous man" (ἀνὴρ ἄδικος) (Ps 139:12). In light of the suffering caused by such plans and speech, the lamenter requests and expects God to save the righteous by judging their enemies, "Charcoals will fall upon them, you will throw them down in fire, in troubles they certainly shall not withstand" (Ps 139:11).[38] Once again, just as we saw in Psalm 5, the lamenter's enemies are violent offenders whose deceitful speech and plans elicit a cry for help and warrant divine judgment against them.

---

35 For λογίζομαι rendered as "to harm," see LEH, 375.

36 See e.g., παρατάσσω, πόλεμος, ἰός, and παγίς. For a brief discussion of how these metaphors are applied to the enemies in OT lament, see chapter 2.

37 Seybold argues that the metaphor indicates speech full of "Verleumdungen." See Seybold, "Zur Geschichte des Vierten David Psalters," 385.

38 See also Ps 139:10, 13.

Finally, Paul cites one more psalm that bemoans the speech of enemies describing them in part as those "whose mouth is full of cursing and bitterness" (Rom 3:14). The terse description is part of Psalm 9:22–39.³⁹ Specifically, it is part of the lamenter's larger complaint to God about the pain inflicted on the "poor" (πτωχός). The shorthand description of the enemy includes ἁμαρτωλός, ἀσεβής, and πονηρός.⁴⁰ Overall, these enemies provoke the Lord to judgment, because they lie in wait (ἐνεδρεύω), even like lions, to harm the poor with impunity (Ps 9:29–32). Just as the enemy described in Psalm 35:2, which ends the catena of lament in Romans, the enemy here does not believe he will be judged for his actions "For he has said in his heart 'I certainly shall not be shaken, from generation to generation without harm'" (Ps 9:27).

The psalmist continues describing the enemy as one "whose mouth is full of cursing (ἀρᾶς), bitterness (πικρίας), and deceit (δόλου), underneath his tongue are pain (κόπος) and grief (πόνος)" (Ps 9:28).⁴¹ Kraus calls the "mouth" of the enemies, or at least the Hebraic terms standing behind ἀρά (אָלָה) and πικρία (מִרְמָה), "an arsenal full of deadly weapons."⁴² The ἀρά (אָלָה) of the enemy could be related to the opponents' vows or invocations during battle. Mowinckel explains "All such words were considered to be powerful and fatal 'curses,' and were even used by the ancients in war, or before a battle, in order to strike the enemy in a way just as effective as the use of a sword or spear."⁴³ In the context of Psalm 9, the cursing and bitterness most likely refers to the enemies' slander against the lamenter. Miller connects such slander to the violation of the ninth commandment noting, "The dangers against which the Ninth Commandment stands as a shield are well illustrated in the Old Testament. The lament or complaint psalms are often petitions to God for help against persons who have endangered the petitioner by false accusations."⁴⁴

What we have then in Psalm 9:22–39 is a lamenter whose enemies slander him with impunity, because divine judgment is apparently distant

---

39 Here is where the MT and LXX diverge in the number of the chapters. The LXX combines Pss 9 and 10 from the MT to form one psalm. Ps 9:22–39 LXX is Ps 10 in the MT. Despite the combination of both psalms in the LXX, I am only treating Ps 9:22–39 LXX.

40 See Ps 9:23, 25, 34, 36.

41 Paul's citation in Rom 3:14 does not contain the additional καὶ δόλου.

42 Kraus, *Psalms 1–59*, 197. For a setting of war and siege where an opponent's ἀρά (אָלָה) is mentioned, see Ps 58:13 (57:13).

43 Mowinckel, *The Psalms in Israel's Worship*, 199.

44 Miller points specifically in the MT to Pss 4:2; 5:6, 9–10; 7:12–16; 10:7–9; 27:12. See Miller, *The Way of the Lord*, 14.

at the moment. That is why the lamenter commences with a classic cry of distress "Why, Lord, have you withdrawn at a distance?" (Ps 9:22a). It also explains the request for God to "Crush the arm of the sinner and evil one, his sin will be sought, and he certainly shall not be found on account of it" (Ps 9:35). The enemy operates with impunity before God in his slander of the lamenter, as indicated in the complaint "For he has said in his heart 'God has forgotten, he has turned his face so as not to see forever'" (Ps 9:32). Yet, as the lamenter's praise indicates, there is an expectation that God has not forgotten altogether. He hears both the lamenter's cry and the enemy's slander (Ps 9:37–39).

We have covered a lot of ground in looking at the fuller contexts of Psalms 5, 10, and 139. To summarize up to this point, the enemies in these psalms plot against the righteous/poor lamenter and use deceptive speech to cover up their intentions. As we saw, the deceitful words could be either flattery or slander, and the various metaphors from war, hunting and wildlife speak to the severity of their actions. The enemies in these psalms also operate with impunity dismissing the threat of God's judgment. The absence of judgment only emboldens them in their deceit and violence. Consequently, the lamenters in these psalms request and fully expect God's deliverance from these enemies by means of divine judgment against them.

Testing the Echoes of Psalms 5, 10, and 139

The tests most pertinent for our purposes here are thematic coherence and illumination of the surrounding discourse. With respect to the former, the coherence between the wider contexts of these psalms and Romans 3:1–20 can be found in the theme of an "enemy" whom God is right to judge. For Paul, God is justified in placing Jew and Gentile under sin just as he is justified in the Psalms of Lament to pour out his wrath on enemies who afflict the righteous. Those who view Romans 3:9–20 as Paul's closing argument about the universal sinfulness of humanity miss this thematic coherence. In fact, the OT citations become a prime example of Paul ignoring the original contexts of these passages. However, the actual "theme" or point of Paul's argument in Romans 3:9–20 is that God is righteous in his judgment against Jew and Gentile, just as he is just to judge the enemies in these Psalms of Lament. Additionally, as we will discuss in greater detail below, the echoes from these Psalms of Lament illuminate the surrounding discourse in a few different ways. When the Jew and Gentile in Romans is read in light of these enemies from the Psalms of Lament, we see that the former operate with impunity like the latter. They are guilty of deceitful and deadly speech.

The Violent and Unpeaceful Path of the Enemies

The citation from Isaiah 59:7–8a is the final piece of Paul's catena that we need to consider. It reads, "Their feet are swift to shed blood, destruction and misery are in their paths, and they have not known the way of peace" (Rom 3:15–17). Isaiah 59:7–8 in its entirety reads:

> Their feet run to evil they are swift to shed blood; and their thoughts are the thoughts of fools, destruction and misery are in their paths. They have not known the way of peace, and there is no justice in their ways; for their paths are twisted, which they travel through, and they do not know peace.

Isaiah's description is part of a larger lament that permeates the entire chapter. As Oswalt describes it, Isaiah 59 is a lament over the "inability to do righteousness."[45] We will briefly evaluate the form and theology of this lament in order to better understand Isaiah 59:7–8 and its echoes in Paul's catena. We are especially interested in Isaiah's description of enemies.

The prophet begins with a question "Is the hand of the Lord not able to save? Or is his ear too heavy so as not to hear?" (Isa 59:1). This question probably reflects a complaint by the people about God's aloofness in the midst of their distress. Isaiah's response indicates that the people's suffering is by no means inexplicable, "But your sins (ἁμαρτήματα) separate (διιστῶσιν) you from God, and on account of your sins (ἁμαρτίας) he has turned his face from you so as not to have mercy" (Isa 59:2). The anthropomorphic reference to God "turning his face" indicates divine rejection and wrath through his absence.[46] God's aloofness, or the people's sense of separation from him, can be explained by the people's sin. Their specific ἁμάρτημα/ἁμαρτία is detailed in 59:3–8. From the perspective of lament, the description functions like a complaint against enemies. The complaint corresponds with the Psalms of Lament that we have been discussing thus far. Like those enemies, God's people in Isaiah 59 use deceitful and deadly speech "Your lips speak lawlessness, and your tongue meditates on unrighteousness" (Isa 59:3).[47] However, the Isaiah 59 complaint also reflects on the violent deeds of the people, "For your hands have been defiled with blood

---

45 Oswalt, *The Book of Isaiah*, 512.
46 On the idiom of God hiding his face, see Balentine, *The Hidden God*.
47 See also Isa 59:4.

and your fingers are in sin" (Isa 59:3).[48] The violence of their lips and hands are compared to a spider's eggs that hatch serpents rather than a useful substance (Isa 59:5–6). One of the implications of the metaphor is that the people were to produce useful, or righteous, works. Instead, their works are lawless (ἀνομία) (Isa 59:6).[49]

In 59:7–8, the writer employs the common OT/Isaianic metaphor of "walking" in order to further describe the people's ἀνομία. They run quickly in their ὁδοῖς to shed blood, and their thoughts are foolish. In their ways, one finds σύντριμμα and ταλαιπωρία (Isa 59:7).[50] The former term can refer to the destruction left after a battle or the breaking of a vessel.[51] As we discussed in the previous chapter, the term ταλαιπωρία is often associated with the misery that ensues from Israel's lawless opponents and enemy forces.[52] It is also a term heard in the complaints of the afflicted.[53] However, in this context, Isaiah charges Israel with causing complaints of misery. They are not in misery, but they are the perpetrators of it. They are guilty of conducting themselves in a less than peaceful and just manner, "They have not known the way of peace (εἰρήνης), and there is not justice (κρίσις) in their ways (Isa 59:8)."

The consequence of the people's unpeaceful and unjust ways, as well as the ultimate cause of their suffering, is described in Isaiah 59:9–15. Their ways result in the absence of justice and righteousness. They are like the blind who grope along the wall waiting for light in the midst of darkness (Isa 59:9–10). The people are likened to those who groan in the face of death.[54] They wait for justice (κρίσις), but it is not present. Salvation (σωτηρία) is far away from them. The γάρ in 59:12 marks the explanation of why they suffer in this way. In short, it is because their lawlessness is before God and their sin resists them, "For our lawlessness (ἀνομία) is great and our sins (αἱ ἁμαρτίαι) resist us" (Isa 59:12). They are afflicted by duel and intertwining opponents, their God who judges them for their guilt before him and their sin. In the case of the latter opponent, Israel's enemy is not merely a

---

48 Cf. Lam 4:14.

49 Cf. Isa 5:1–7.

50 The noun ὁδός occurs three times and τρίβος once in these two verses thereby emphasizing the conduct or "way" of the people. Oswalt notes that words for "way" and "highway" are prominent throughout Isaiah. See Oswalt, *Isaiah*, 516.

51 See Isa 15:5, 30:14, 51:19.

52 See Amos 5:9; Jer 4:20; 6:26.

53 See e.g., Pss 11:6; 68:21; 87:19; Hab 1:3.

54 The use of στενάξουσιν in Isa 59:10 indicates a cry of distress common to the lament pattern.

political entity but sin itself.⁵⁵ Isaiah goes on to confess on behalf of the community that they are guilty of ungodliness, falsehood, and disobedience (Isa 59:13-14). Included in the confession is their unrighteous speech (ἐλαλήσαμεν ἄδικα) and scheming (ἐμελετήσαμεν ἀπὸ καρδίας ἡμῶν λόγους ἀδίκους) (Isa 59:13), something we have seen emphasized in the Psalms of Lament.

Finally, it is worth noting that God's ultimate response to Israel's situation is to arrive as a divine warrior.⁵⁶ He surveys the situation and sees there is no one to help "He looked and there was not a man" (Isa 59:16). Therefore, he comes himself clad in the armor of righteousness, salvation, and vengeance (Isa 59:17). He comes for both wrath and deliverance "For wrath (ὀργή) will come from the Lord like a violent river, he will come with anger (θυμοῦ). The deliverer (ὁ ῥυόμενος) will come on account of Zion and he will turn away ungodliness from Jacob" (Isa 59:19b-20). Just as he would judge a political opponent of Israel in order to free her, he comes to judge the enemy of sin in order to deliver her.

Testing the Echoes of Isaiah 59

The echoes of Isaiah 59 pass a number of tests. To begin, there is a recurrence of this text in Romans 11:26 where Paul cites Isaiah 59:20, "The deliverer will come from Zion, he will turn away ungodliness from Jacob." Therefore, Paul's thought is clearly affected by the contents of the entire chapter and not just the portion he cites in Romans 3:15-17. The citation of Isaiah 59:7-8 also passes the test of thematic coherence. The enemies described in the wider context of Isaiah 59, like the enemies of the Psalms of Lament cited in the catena, are unrighteous in their speech, thoughts, and deeds. Consequently, they face divine judgment. Lastly, with respect to illuminating the surrounding discourse, the full complement of lament language in Isaiah 59 provides a unique echo in Paul's argument. Specifically, both Isaiah and Paul identify the Jew as being under sin and thereby deserving of divine wrath but at the same time in need of divine mercy. Isaiah 59 and Romans 3:9-20 both liken Jews and Gentiles to an unrighteous enemy, but the ending of the former passage evokes hope beyond that judgment. It

---

55 Oswalt observes, "Here is the true enemy against which God has come to make war. It is not the Canaanites who are the enemies of God's people, and thus of God; rather, it is the sin that the Canaanites represent. This is the ultimate development of the Divine Warrior motif in the Bible: God comes to destroy the final enemy of what he has created: not the monster Chaos, but the monster Sin." Oswalt, *The Book of Isaiah*, 527.

56 Cf. God as a warrior in Isa 59:16-21 and Hab 3.

is the hope that though God is right to come as a warrior and dole out wrath he will also come to save.[57]

Request for Mercy in the Face of Judgment (Psalm 142)

In Romans 3:20, Paul writes "Because from the works of the law no flesh will be justified before you, for through the law is the knowledge of sin." Paul's statement echoes Psalm 142:2b "Because no living thing will be justified before you." I will test this echo below. For the moment, I want to evaluate the echo in light of its original context.

Psalm 142 is an individual lament that contains two stanzas, 142:1–6 and 142:7–12. In the first stanza, the lamenter's two requests are grounded in two interrelated sources of suffering:

> Lord, hear my prayer, give ear to my petition in your truth, hear in your righteousness; and do not enter into judgment with your servant, because (ὅτι) no living thing will be justified before you. Because (ὅτι) the enemy pursued my soul, he lowered by life to the ground, he sat me in dark places like the eternal dead; and he exhausted my spirit in me, my heart was disturbed in me. (Ps 142:1–4)

The lamenter suffers and cries out for help, because he is not justified before God and his enemy pursues him. The implicit link between the two sources of suffering is that God hands the lamenter over to the enemy's pursuit, because the lamenter is not righteous before him. As the wider theology in the psalms demonstrates, God delivers the righteous but judges the unrighteous.[58] The enemy afflicts the lamenter externally (physically) and spiritually (internally) (Ps 142:4). The lamenter's only recourse is to remember what God has done in the past in such circumstances and pray, "I stretched out my hands to you, my soul is like waterless ground to you" (Ps 142:6).

The second stanza contains numerous requests grounded in the same two concerns of the first stanza, divine wrath and enemy activity, but also the hope that God would answer:

> Hear me quickly, O Lord, my spirit fails; do not turn your face away from me, and I will be like those who go down to the pit. Make me hear your mercy (ἔλεος) early in the morning, because I have hoped in you; make known to me, Lord, the way in which

---

57 Cf. the request in Hab 3:2.
58 See e.g., Ps 1:5–6.

I should go, because I have lifted my soul to you; deliver me
from my enemies, Lord, because I have fled to you. (Ps 142:7–9)

The request "do not turn your face away from me" is a metonymy that
God not be angry with him and consequently turn him over to enemies.[59]
This request is ultimately grounded in the hope that in such circumstances
God would answer as he promised he would.[60] There are also multiple requests for knowledge and instruction about how the lamenter should walk
before God, or do his will (Ps 142:10). Ultimately, the lamenter believes God
will give him life (ζήσεις με) beyond judgment on account of his name (Ps
142:11a). He also believes that God will lead him out of tribulation by means
of his righteousness (ἐν τῇ δικαιοσύνῃ σου) (Ps 142:11b). The lamenter ends
by praising God for his mercy in the face of divine wrath and enemies, "And
in your mercy (ἐν τῷ ἐλέει σου) you will utterly destroy my enemies and you
will destroy all those who afflict my soul; because I am your servant."

What we find then in Psalm 142 is a scenario in which the lamenter is
pressed on both sides. Like every other living creature, he is not righteous
before God. Consequently, like every other creature, he is afflicted by enemies. Yet, the lamenter is not without hope. The hope remained that God
would answer him in mercy and righteousness (Ps 142:2, 11). The evidence
of that answer would be the destruction of enemies, so that he would no
longer be afflicted externally or internally (Ps 142:12).

Testing the Echoes of Psalm 142

Obviously, the echo of Psalm 142:2 in Romans 3:20 is not an explicit citation. Consequently, it is necessary to apply more tests to this echo than those
applied in the catena. To begin, the psalm is available to Paul as evidenced in
his repeated use of the psalms throughout Romans. The volume of the echo
includes the repetition of δικαιωθήσεται in Psalm 142:2 and Romans 3:20.
The two texts also share the expression πᾶς ζῶν modified by Paul as πᾶσα
σάρξ.[61] There is a recurrence of this echo through a "brief string of words"
from Psalm 142:2 in Galatians 2:16.[62] The thematic coherence between
Psalm 142 and Romans 3:1–20 resides in the lamenter's recognition that he
is unrighteous before God. This is tantamount to confessing that one is an
enemy of God like those described in the Psalms of Lament we discussed

---

59   See Deut 31:17–18; 32:20.
60   See the three ὅτι and what follows them in Ps 142:8–9.
61. On Paul's modification, see Jewett, *Romans*, 265–66.
62   DeSilva, *Galatians*, 44.

above. Yet, the inclusion of the Psalm 142 echo, much like the inclusion of Isaiah 59 in Romans 3:15–17, sheds new light on the kind of "enemy" Paul has in view through his heavy use of OT lament. Specifically, it is an enemy who laments and asks that God act in his mercy and righteousness. It is historically plausible that Paul intentionally echoes Psalm 142 in Romans 3:20. Hays argues that the "psalm's opening and closing verses disclose the spiritual context in which Paul learned the words that he echoes in Rom. 3:20."[63] Within the history of interpretation, a number of interpreters have recognized some kind of connection between Psalm 142 and Romans 3:20, though not necessarily the exact one I am arguing for here.[64] Finally, given what I have laid out thus far with respect to OT lament in Romans 3:1–18, the echo of Psalm 142 contributes to Paul's portrait of the Jew and Gentile who is under sin. As I mentioned already, they are not only enemies in the vein of the opponents decried in the Psalms of Lament. They are also, at least potentially, those who cry out for mercy as the lamenter in Psalm 142 does.

READING ROMANS 3:1–20 IN LIGHT OF ITS OLD TESTAMENT LAMENT ECHOES

We have spent a considerable amount of time identifying and testing OT lament echoes in Romans 3:1–20. I have tried to situate the echoes in their original contexts, so that we might full understand how this full range of echoes impacts our reading of Romans 3:1–20.

Lament as the Advantage of the Jew

In Romans 3:1–2, Paul asks and then answers his own question. Given the end of his argument in Romans 2:28, namely that the "Jew is one inwardly" and "circumcision is of the heart," Paul anticipates the question "What then is the advantage of the Jew?" (Rom 3:1). His answer is "much according to every way," but the only specific example he gives is that they "were entrusted with the oracles of God" (Rom 3:2). The referent of λόγια τοῦ θεοῦ has been identified in various ways.[65] Yet, it is possible that the expression

---

63 Hays, *Echoes of Scripture*, 51.

64 See Sumney, *Reading Paul's Letter*, 72–73.

65 Jewett covers many of the interpretive options noting that the phrase refer to "the messianic promises, the promises to Abraham and the patriarchs, the commandments of the Torah, or even the whole of Scripture." Jewett, *Romans*, 243. Moo suggests the phrase could be "shorthand for those privileges of Israel that Paul enumerates in 9:4

is linked, at least in part, to OT lament, given its heavy influence on this portion of the letter and elsewhere. The reason Paul argues that the Jew's advantage is their possession of the "oracles of God" is because those oracles attest to the fact that God answers the cries of his rebellious people, people like the lamenter in Psalm 50.

One of the only other uses of the exact phrase τὰ λόγια τοῦ θεοῦ in the LXX and New Testament comes from Psalm 106:11, "For they rebelled against the oracles of God (λόγια τοῦ θεοῦ) and they provoked the counsel of the most high."[66] In the wider context of Psalm 106, the psalmist recounts Israel's wilderness warnings. A pattern is described in which Israel rebelled against God, God humbled them, they cried out for help, and God delivered them (Ps 106:10–16). The verb κράζω marks the repetition of this pattern throughout the psalm.[67] When Israel rebelled against God and faced divine judgment, they would cry out (κράζω) for help. Once again, as it is described in Psalm 106:11, their rebellion was against τὰ λόγια τοῦ θεοῦ. Israel disobeyed the Mosaic Law which had come with a warning of judgment. Yet, as the psalmist indicates, Israel also learned that when they rebelled against the oracles they could cry out to God for mercy. In this way, there is a connection between τὰ λόγια τοῦ θεοῦ and lament. It is a connection echoed in Romans 3:1–8.

The lamenter in Psalm 50, cited by Paul in Romans 3:4, vocalizes the kind of cry that Israel needed to utter in their disobedience. Their cry needed to acknowledge that God was right to judge, or was in fact victorious in his judgment against them. This is the cry of distress that Paul wants the Jew to utter in Romans 3:1–20. It is a cry that justifies God in his judgment against them. However, the Jew, like the Gentile, does not cry out in this way. Both are "under sin," and, like the enemies from the Psalms of Lament that Paul cites in his catena, they do not cry out so as to acknowledge that God is righteous in his judgment against them.

Enemies Who Do Not Lament in the Face Divine Judgment

Paul's "catena of lament" helps to further explain the theological abbreviation "all Jews and Greeks are under sin (ὑφ' ἁμαρτίαν)" (Rom 3:9).[68] The explanation of this abbreviation is not located solely in the individual verses

---

–5a." Moo, *Romans*, 183, fn. 27.

66 See 1 Pet 4:11.

67 See Ps 106:6, 13, 19, 28.

68. On "theological abbreviation" in Paul's letters, see Betz, *Galatians*, 27; Crisler, "Locative Language in Romans," 6–21; Wilson, "Under Law in Galatians," 362–92.

as they are stitched together in Romans 3:10–18 but in the echoes of their larger contexts. If we limited ourselves to the catena as it stands, we could conclude that to be ὑφ' ἁμαρτίαν is to be unwise and without a concern to seek God. We could also conclude that those "under sin" are deceitful in their speech and violent in their ways. Simply put, Jews and Greeks are all unrighteous, without knowledge of peace, and without fear of God. This description of Jews and Greeks "under sin" could be gathered without recourse to the wider contexts of the OT lament Paul cites.

However, if we read the catena while hearing the echoes of the wider lament contexts and their interaction with Romans 3:1–20, a certain figure emerges. It is a figure whose caustic speech and violent deeds against others is done with complete impunity (Ps 9; 13; 35). Paul's catena describes a person who, like the enemies in the Psalms of Lament, denies that their actions will incur the wrath of God. Both Jew and Gentile essentially operate as if "there is no God" who will finally judge them (Ps 13:1). There is no fear (φόβος) of eschatological judgment "before their eyes" (Ps 35:1). They do not believe they will be "shaken" on that day (Ps 9:27). They conduct themselves as if God has hidden his face, or "forgotten" to judge them (Ps 9:32). Moreover, a figure emerges who is foolish enough to think he is righteous, rather than wise enough to know that "no one is righteous" (Eccl 7:20). This is a figure that does lawlessness (ἀνομία) and is godless (ἀσεβής), so that he is hated by God (Ps 5:6–7). They scheme against others for their harm constantly, or "all day long" (Ps 139:3). Through the lament echoes, Paul likens the Jew and Gentile to a hunter whose prey is the poor, one who lies in wait for the innocent, or a wild animal that viciously attacks its enemy. Moreover, despite their behavior and guilt, neither Jew nor Gentile "calls upon (ἐπεκαλέσαντο) the Lord" for deliverance from divine judgment (Ps 13:4). They do not lament as they should.

There is one slight exception here. The echoes from the wider context of Isaiah 59, although corresponding to the catena's emphasis on devious speech and violent deeds, present a figure who does in fact cry out to God. Yet, God does not hear the cry, because it is not a request to be delivered from judgment. It is a cry for blessing, and that is why it is not heard. As Oswalt notes, "God cannot pay attention to the people's cries for blessing."[69] His refusal to hear their cry is related to their sin and guilt. As I noted above, Isaiah 59 commences with a complaint about God's aloofness, "But your sins separate you and God, and on account of your sins he has hidden his face from you" (Isa 59:2).[70]

---

69. Oswalt, *Isaiah*, 513.

70 Cf. the warning about the hiding of God's face in Deut 31:17–18; 32:20.

What we have then in Romans 3:10–18 is a description of the Jew and Gentile "under sin" that is dramatically shaped by OT lament.[71] Specifically, they are enemies who afflict others by their speech and deeds, and they do so with complete impunity. They do not fear divine judgment; therefore, they do not cry out for deliverance from it. Without this cry, God is not acknowledged as righteous in his judgment (Rom 3:4) and there is obviously no deliverance from it.

The "Law" Elicits the Lament for Mercy and Righteousness

Clearly, the figure echoed in Romans 3:10–18 does not cry out in the face of divine judgment. The absence of such a cry implicitly denies that God is righteous to judge. That is the most egregious offence of all. Yet, in Romans 3:19–20, another figure who does cry out in the face of judgment is also echoed. Specifically, as I discussed already, there is an echo of Psalm 142. We now turn our attention to the interpretive impact of reading Romans 3:1–20 in light of this echo.

We must begin by identifying the referent of νόμος, used four times in Romans 3:19– 20.[72] Some have suggested that νόμος is a reference to the scriptural citations in 3:10–18.[73] Others see it as a reference to the Mosaic law. On some level, it refers to both, although the Mosaic sense is more pronounced. Paul has shown an explicit concern for the Mosaic law since 2:17. He has argued that God is righteous in his judgment against Jew and Gentile, because they behave like enemies, namely like the lawlessness enemies of OT lament (Rom 3:10–18). Therefore, the enemies of lament echoed in Romans 3:10–18 illustrate that the Jew and Gentile are guilty of breaking the law. Although it is the Jew who is specifically "in the law" (τοῖς ἐν τῷ νόμῳ), as Paul puts it in 3:19, their lawlessness means the Gentiles are culpable as well. If the elect and covenantal Jews could not keep the law, neither can the Gentiles.[74]

Paul and the Romans know (οἴδαμεν) that the law speaks to those "in the law" (i.e., Jews) for a distinct purpose. The purpose of the law "speaking"

---

71 I am borrowing this language from Beverly Gaventa who argues that the Psalms of Lament "shape" Paul's "I" in Rom 7:7–25. See Gaventa, "The Shape of the 'I,'" 77–92. My point here is that Paul's perception of the Jew and Gentile are shaped by the enemies in the Psalms of Lament and elsewhere.

72 BDAG 677–78.

73 E.g., Jewett argues "It is clear from the context that 'law' is being used here in the inclusive sense of all Scripture and that it refers back to the previously cited catena drawn from the Psalms and Isaiah." Jewett, *Romans*, 264. See also Wright, *Romans*, 458.

74 Schreiner, *Romans*, 168.

is in order that every mouth of every enemy, Jew and Gentile, might be shut (φραγῇ) and all the world would be guilty (ὑπόδικος) before God" (Rom 3:19). That is what OT lament says will happen to unrighteous and guilty enemies, "For the mouth (στόμα) of those who speak unrighteousness has been shut up (ἐνεφράγη)" (Ps 62:12).[75] For Paul, every "mouth" in the world has been shut up as an enemy guilty (ὑπόδικος) before God.[76] All that remains is for God to answer the cries against such enemies, cries echoed in the catena of lament, and condemn them. That is because (διότι) there is no one who will be justified "by works of the law" (ἐξ ἔργων νόμου). The law brings knowledge of sin (Rom 3:21).

With all of this in mind, how does the echo of Psalm 142 directly impact the interpretation of Romans 3:19-20? Simply put, it evokes the alternative to the guilty enemy who does not cry out for mercy in the face of judgment. The alternative is to cry out like the lamenter in Psalm 142:2, "And do not enter into judgment (εἰς κρίσιν) with your servant, because no living thing will be justified before you." For Paul, such a cry is elicited by the "law" which, in its polyvalence, reveals to the lamenter that he is a lawless enemy of God who faces certain judgment. The cry also acknowledges that God is righteous in judgment against his enemy, as the law makes clear. Given the echoes from the rest of the psalm, which we reviewed above, it is also a request for God to deliver the lamenter in his mercy (ἐν τῷ ἐλέει) and righteousness (ἐν τῇ δικαιοσύνῃ) (Ps 142:11-12). As the wider context of Psalm 142 indicates, God's mercy and righteousness would entail forgiveness of the lamenter and judgment of his enemy which in this case is sin.[77] This is the cry echoed in Romans 3:19-20. It is a cry for God to act in mercy and in righteousness at the moment of judgment. It is a cry that Paul believes is answered in the gospel that he describes in Romans 3:21-26.

THE GOSPEL AS THE ANSWER TO THE CRIES OF ROMANS 3:1-20

We have already seen in Romans 1:16-17 that the righteous, those such as Habakkuk, cry out and find their answer in the gospel. In Romans 3:1-20, the OT lament echoes indicate that the gospel also answers the lament of

---

75 See also Ps 106:42.

76 For ὑπόδικος as "guilty," see Philo *Spec. Laws* 2.249; Josephus *Vita* 74. See also Seifrid, *Christ Our Righteousness*, 61.

77 As we will see in chapter 5, Paul's most colorful depiction of sin as an enemy is located in Rom 7. Not surprisingly, Rom 7:7-25 depicts sin as an enemy in the vein of the opponents described in the Psalms of Lament.

the unrighteous. On both sides of the catena of lament, there are echoes of a lamenter who acknowledges God is righteous in his judgment against him (Ps 50; Rom 3:4) and one who requests mercy in the face of that judgment (Ps 142:2; Rom 3:19–20). In both instances, it is an unrighteous lamenter who cries out to God. Sandwiched between those echoes is Romans 3:10–18 replete with lament echoes of its own which evoke enemies who refuse to cry out to God as well as those who cry out for judgment against them. As we saw in our analysis of Romans 3:19–20, it is only when the law "speaks" to the unrighteous that a cry for mercy and righteousness might be elicited. When the law elicits that lament, the divine answer comes in the gospel. Therefore, when we hear the OT echoes in Romans 3:1–20, the argument in 3:21–26 becomes an answer to the various cries of distress that have been evoked: (1) the cry that God is righteous in his judgment (Rom 3:4); (2) the cry for God to judge lawless enemies (Rom 3:10–18); and (3) the cry for God to act in mercy and righteousness (Rom 3:20).

The response to all these cries is captured in the theological abbreviation δικαιοσύνη θεοῦ. Not coincidentally, a common thread in the OT lament echoes of Romans 3:1–20 is their shared request for God's δικαιοσύνη:

> Deliver me from blood guilt, O God, God of my salvation; my tongue will exult in your righteousness (δικαιοσύνην). (Ps 50:16)

> Lord, guide me in your righteousness (δικαιοσύνη) on account of my enemies, make straight your way before me. (Ps 5:9)[78]

> Lord, hear my prayer, give ear to my supplication in your truth, hear me in your righteousness. (Ps 142:1)[79]

Whether the lamenter has been defeated in judgment, overcome by enemies, or both, there is a request for God's δικαιοσύνη. From Paul's perspective, the answer to that request is found in the gospel of the crucified and risen Christ, "But now apart from the law the righteousness of God (δικαιοσύνη θεοῦ) has been revealed, being testified to by the law and the prophets, but the righteousness of God (δικαιοσύνη θεοῦ) through faith in Jesus Christ for all who believe" (Rom 3:21–22).

But how does the gospel specifically answer the cries of distress and requests for righteousness echoed in OT lament? On the one hand, Paul answers that question throughout the letter.[80] However, in these verses, he offers an answer *in nuce*. Given the nature of the requests, God needed to

---

78. See also Ps 35:7.
79 See also Ps 142:11.
80 We will explore much of that answer in subsequent chapters.

both condemn his enemies and have mercy upon then. Paul recognizes that in Christ Jesus God did both. He describes Jesus as the one:

> whom God put forth as a propitiation (ἱλαστήριον) through faith in his blood for a demonstration of his righteousness (δικαιοσύνης) on account of the passing over (πάρεσιν) of sins committed beforehand in the forbearance (ἀνοχῇ) of God, for a demonstration of his righteousness (δικαιοσύνης) in the present time, in order for him to be both righteous (δίκαιον) and the one who justifies (δικαιοῦντα) the one from faith in Christ. (Rom 3:25–26)

Paul's references to ἱλαστήριον, πάρεσις, and ἀνοχή all color the meaning of δικαιοσύνη as an answer to lament. In order for God to grant mercy to the Jew and Gentile who requests it (Pss 50; 142), his wrath for their sin must be satisfied. Therefore, God put forth Jesus as the ἱλαστήριον, or mercy seat, where divine wrath is propitiated, thereby answering the lamenter's request.[81] He put forth Jesus as the ἱλαστήριον to demonstrate his righteousness (εἰς ἔνδειξιν τῆς δικαιοσύνης αὐτοῦ) as the lamenter requested. Yet, putting Jesus forth as the ἱλαστήριον also answers the cry of distress against enemies, the kinds of requests echoed in the catena of lament. God had not yet given a complete answer to that request. As Paul puts it, there was a "passing over (πάρεσιν) of sins committed beforehand." While the noun πάρεσις is a *hapax legomenon* in the LXX and NT, the cognate παρίημι occurs more frequently in the LXX and in certain contexts can bear the sense of "leave undone."[82] That is the sense in Romans 3:25. God had not yet brought the fullness of his wrath on the enemies described in Romans 3:10–18. Consequently, he had not yet answered the requests for judgment against them that can be heard in the wider contexts of the OT lament echoed in the catena.

There is no further explanation for God "leaving undone" (πάρεσις) his judgment before the crucifixion, but that should not keep us from noticing the anthropological complexities presented here. There are honest pleas for judgment against enemies in OT lament, which are then echoed in Paul's catena and answered in the gospel. At the same time, he identifies the entire world (πᾶς ὁ κόσμος Rom 3:19) as the very enemies who elicit those kinds of cries for justice. This is where the echo from Psalm 142 enters the picture. Those who cry out against enemies are enemies themselves. Therefore, the only option is to cry out for mercy as the lamenter does in Psalm 142. This cacophony of requests requires a response from God that simultaneously

---

81 For ἱλαστήριον as "mercy seat," see Morris, *The Apostolic Preaching of the Cross*, 159; Seifrid, *Romans*, 620–22.

82 E.g., Ps 137:8.

answers the cry for judgment and mercy towards his enemies. Paul sees this truly unique response in the gospel where God demonstrates that he is both "righteous" (i.e., answers the request to condemn the enemy) and "justifies" (i.e., answers the enemy's request for mercy). The request for condemnation and mercy is at the same time a request for God to reveal his δικαιοσύνη. For Paul, all who lament, whether they are afflicted or causing the affliction, are unrighteous. And the gospel becomes the answer to the unrighteous lamenter who believes, or, more specifically, cries out.

5

The Gospel as the Answer to the Lamenting "I" (Romans 7:7—8:4)

QUESTIONS WILL PROBABLY ALWAYS swirl around the interpretation of Romans 7:7–25. Among their various exegetical disagreements, interpreters seldom agree on the identity of the ἐγώ. Suggestions range from Adam to some kind of rhetorical figure and seemingly everything in between.[1] Yet, one thing is clear. The ἐγώ in this passage is a troubled soul.[2] Paul describes a quite hellish experience. It is the kind of experience that is pertinent to the focus of this work, because it contains the idiom, pattern, and theology of OT lament. There are a number of echoes, particularly from the Psalms of Lament, that collectively portray sin as an enemy who deceives, captures, and kills the "I" in the same vein as enemies of OT lament. Paul uses lament language to describe sin's persistent and overpowering use of the law against the "I." There is also a five-fold pattern of lament: promise, suffering, cry of distress, deliverance, and praise. As noted in previous chapters, this pattern is a fundamental feature of OT lament. Thus, the idiom and pattern of lament contained in Romans 7:7–25 provides another look at how this OT prayer form affects Paul's letter and our reading of it. This in turn will inform an even larger concern with Paul's theology of suffering in Romans.

---

1. For the interpretive history of Rom 7:7–25, see Lichtenberger, *Das Ich Adams und das Ich der Menschheit*, 13–105.

2 The pronoun ἐγώ occurs twenty-six times in Rom 7:7–25. It is obviously a key rhetorical feature of the passage. See Stauffer, "ἐγώ," in *TWNT* 2:356–62.

The main argument in this chapter is that when one reads Romans 7:7–25 in light of its OT lament echoes, the otherwise enigmatic "I" emerges as a figure whose lament is representative of all those who are afflicted by sin's use of the Mosaic Law and who finds an answer in the gospel. Like OT lamenters, the "I" is hard pressed by both an enemy (sin) and divine wrath. The experience of the "I" not only echoes OT lamenters; it also represents struggles of a whole cast of figures, including Adam, Israel, Paul, the Romans, and anyone else plagued by sin's use of the law.

The following analysis takes an approach similar to the two preceding chapters. I will first identify and test the echoes of OT lament in Romans 7:7–25. We will then read the passage in light of these echoes in order to see how they impact the interpretation of the text. Along the way, we will consider how the interpretive approach put forth here fits with other major suggestions from the text's reception history.

IDENTIFYING THE ECHOES OF LAMENT IN ROMANS 7:7–25

In the previous two chapters, the identification and testing of echoes focused on particular OT passages. Here the process is somewhat different, because we are dealing with broader characteristics of the lament genre rather than a handful of specific passages. There is a distinct idiom and pattern that is not necessarily tied to one particular OT text. Furthermore, with respect to testing the echoes, it has been well established in previous chapters that the echoes of lament in Romans pass Hays' seven proposed tests. Therefore, I will stipulate that Romans 7:7–25 passes these tests as well and forego a separate section for testing the echoes both in this chapter and in much of the subsequent chapters.[3] I will briefly touch on the tests in a few instances. The primary focus here is to identify the echoes of the lament idiom and pattern and analyze them in their original settings.

Echoes of ἐγώ

Beverly Gaventa has recently observed that Paul's depiction of the ἐγώ in Romans 7 is "shaped" to some degree by the depiction of the "I" in the

---

3 Hays actually foregoes the explicit tests throughout his work. He notes from the outset, "I do not use these criteria explicitly in my readings of the texts, but they implicitly undergird the exegetical judgments that I have made." Hays, *Echoes of Scripture*, 29.

Psalms of Lament.[4] Paul employs the pronoun twenty-six times, so that it is clearly emphatic.[5] The Psalms of Lament also employ ἐγώ quite often, and the uses normally have two basic functions that are echoed in Paul's use of the pronoun.

First, ἐγώ is often used to emphatically express confidence in God's prior promise despite the suffering presently experienced. In Psalm 12, a classic individual lament, the speaker complains that in God's absence enemies afflict him without hindrance.[6] Nevertheless, the lament closes with the emphatic "But I (ἐγὼ δέ) have hoped in your mercy" (Ps 12:6). The ἐγώ with the postpositive δέ is a frequent occurrence in the Psalms of Lament.[7] Similarly, in Psalm 54, after complaining against enemies and requesting deliverance, there is an emphatic statement of trust in God's prior promise to hear those who cry to him "But I (ἐγὼ δέ) cried to the Lord, and the Lord heard me" (Ps 54:17). The same construction occurs three times in Romans 7.[8]

Second, the ἐγώ frequently appears in the midst of the speaker's complaint and request before God. In Psalm 24:16, the pronoun emphatically marks the lamenter's complaint about enemies and a request for deliverance "Look upon me and have mercy on me, because I (ἐγώ) am alone and poor." Similarly, Psalm 37 contains three emphatic uses of ἐγώ in which the lamenter complains about enemies and his own sin:

> But I (ἐγὼ δέ) like a deaf man was not hearing and like a mute man not opening my mouth. (Ps 37:14)
>
> For I (ἐγώ) am ready for a beating, and my pain is before me continually. For I (ἐγώ) will proclaim my lawlessness and I will worry about my sin. (Ps 37:18–19)

The psalmist places the pronoun at these points in order to accentuate the lamenter's complaint and request. As we will see, these kinds of emphatic uses of ἐγώ are echoed in Romans 7:7–25. Paul's ἐγώ also complains about an enemy but ultimately expresses confidence in God's prior promise of deliverance.

---

4. Gaventa, "The Shape of the 'I,'" 78.

5 See Rom 7:8, 9, 10, 11, 13, 14, 17, 18, 20, 21, 23, 24, 25.

6 We have here the four fold use of the classic lament idiom "how long" (ἕως πότε). See Ps 12:12–13.

7 See e.g., Pss 5:8; 21:7; 25:11; 37:14; 39:18; 59:17. On this point, see Gaventa, "The Shape of the 'I,'" 82.

8 See Rom 7:9, 10, 14.

Echoes of a Deceptive Enemy

In Romans 7:11, the "I" complains "For sin having seized an opportunity through the commandment, deceived (ἐξηπάτησέν) me and through it killed (ἀπέκτεινεν) me." Dunn suggests that ἐξαπατάω and the surrounding context echoes Genesis 3.[9] I will have more to say about this possible echo later. For the moment, I would note that only one layer of the narrative substructure in Romans 7:7–25 is Adamic. Adam's story is only one element of a larger nexus of narratives that are held together by lament. When Paul describes sin as deceptive, it echoes more than the exchange between Adam and the serpent. It echoes a multitude of complaints leveled against enemies in OT lament.

Enemies in OT lament deceive their victims by ambuscade and falsehoods in order to kill them. This is often reflected in the image of a stealthy predator or army:

> You will me out of this trap, which they hid (ἔκρυψάν) for me, because you are my protector. (Ps 30:5)

> For without cause they hid (ἔκρυψάν) for me the ruin of their trap, for nothing they reviled my soul. (Ps 34:7)

> They will dwell near and they will hide (κατακρύψουσιν); they will watch my step, just as they waited for my life. (Ps 55:7)

The metaphors employed here indicate that an enemy's deception is entirely concealed like an army waiting to ambush its opponent or a hunter who has set a trap for its prey.[10] The enemy often conceals the trap through deceptive speech:

> The words of his mouth are lawlessness and deceit (δόλος), he has ceased to be wise and to be good. He plans iniquity on his bed; he stations himself on a road that is not good, he does not despise evil. (Ps 35:4–5)

> They were divided from the anger of his face, and his heart came near; his words were softer than oil and they are darts. (Ps 54:22)

> And they deceived (ἠπάτησαν) him with their mouth and with their tongue they lied (ἐψεύσαντο) to him. (Ps 77:36)

Just as in Paul's catena of lament, and as these examples illustrate, the enemies' words have a harmful and deadly aim. Their words mask that aim

---

9 Dunn, *Theology of Paul the Apostle*, 98–99; 476.

10 As discussed in chapter 2, enemies in the Psalms of Lament are often described as armies, hunters, or wild animals. See Kraus, *Psalms 1–59*, 95–99.

either through false accusations or flattery. As we will see, sin operates against the "I" in a similar manner, because it has the same aim, namely to kill.

The volume of the echo in Romans 7 is marked by a number of things including the use of ἐξαπατάω and a cluster of terms related to death, particularly ἀποθνῄσκω, ἀποκτείνω, and θάνατος. We find the combination of deceit and death in Paul's complaint that "sin having seized (λαβοῦσα) an opportunity through (ἀφορμήν) the commandment deceived (ἐξηπάτησέν) me and through it killed me" (Rom 7:11).

Echoes of an Overpowering Enemy

The portrayal of sin in Romans 7 as an overpowering enemy that makes the "I" fatally miserable echoes the description of the overpowering in OT lament. Lamenters often complain that they cannot match the brute force of their oppressors who take them captive and enslave them through various tactics. The overpowering enemies are both political enemies and personified internal foes. Complaints against such overbearing enemies are scattered throughout Israel's scriptures in both communal and individual settings and subsequently echoed in Romans 7.

It makes sense that Paul's portrayal of sin would echo OT lament in which God's people cried out against enemies far too powerful for them. Israel's history is marked by such cries. When the nation cries out for God to deliver them from Egyptian oppression, it marks one of the earliest complaints we find against overpowering enemies who enslave and afflict. It is a complaint encapsulated a few different times in the book of Exodus:

> After those many days the king of Egypt died. And the sons of Israel groaned (κατεστέναξαν) from their work and they cried out (ἀνεβόησαν) and their cry (βοή) from their works ascended to God. And God heard their cry (στεναγμὸν αὐτῶν), and God remembered his covenant with Abraham and Isaac and Jacob. (Exod 2:23–24)

> And now behold the cry (κραυγή) of the sons of Israel has come to me, and I have seen their affliction, with which the Egyptians afflicted them. (Exod 3:9)

Egypt's strength and brutality, juxtaposed alongside God's prior promise, elicited a cry of distress. Following the Exodus narrative, Egyptian bondage becomes the benchmark for Israel's overpowering enemies whom God must overcome on behalf of his people. Subsequent overpowering enemies elicit the same kind of prayers from lamenters. This is evident in the prayers offered during the conquest and period of the Judges.[11] Both pre- and post-exilic prayers complain about the overpowering nature of Israel's enemies.[12] It should also be noted that often times the pain which leads to these cries of distress is self-inflicted. This is clear in Ezra's post-exilic confession:

> From the day of our fathers we are in great error until this day and on account of iniquities we have been handed over, and our kings, and ours sons in the hand of the kings of the nations in sword, and in captivity, and in plunder and in our open shame, as it is this day. (Ezra 9:7)

Ezra cries out on behalf of the post-exilic community whose affliction at the hands of overpowering enemies is in step with all those who preceded them. This scenario is also reflected in Israel's liturgy.[13] We see the entire scenario summarized in Psalm 105:

> And the Lord was angry with his people and he abhorred his inheritance; and he handed them over into the hands of their enemies, and those who hated them lorded over them; and their enemies afflicted them, and they were lowered underneath their hands. Many times he delivered them, and they rebelled against him in their counsel and they were lowered in their lawlessness. And he saw when they were being afflicted when he heard their supplication; and he remembered his covenant and regretted according to the multitude of his mercy. (Ps 105:40–45)

These verses reflect a common scenario in Israel's history. God is angered by Israel's rebellion; therefore, he hands them over to enemies who overpower them. Consequently, Israel cries out to God for deliverance, and he responds out of mercy and faithfulness to his covenant. Moreover, we can see from Psalm 105 and elsewhere that Romans 7 is not entirely novel in describing sin as an overpowering enemy in the vein of political opponents such as Egypt or Babylon. Israel's scriptures already personified sin in this way. It can be seen in Isaiah 59, a passage Paul cites in his catena of lament.[14] Just as Israel groaned (καταστενάζω) before the might of Egypt, Isaiah groans before the power of sin on behalf of the nation "And they will

---

11. See e.g., Josh 7:6–9; Judg 3:7–11.

12 See e.g., Neh 9:6–38. Although, following Westermann's thesis about the absence of lament in the post-exilic period, Nehemiah's prayer lacks some of the more salient features of lament. See Westermann, *Praise and Lament*, 165–213.

13 See e.g., Ps 77:61; 105:42.

14 See also Gen 4:7 MT.

fall in midday as in the middle of the night, they will groan (στενάξουσιν) as if dying" (Isa 59:10).

Romans 7:7–25 also echoes individual cries against overpowering enemies who are strong, deceptive, and persistent. Either in complaints or expressions of confidence the lamenter often acknowledges the superior strength of an opponent. The latter is exemplified in statements such as "He will deliver me from my powerful enemies (ἐχθρῶν μου δυνατῶν) and from those who hate me, because they were mightier (ἐστερεώθησαν) than me" (Ps 17:18). Such enemies overpower their victims through various strategies such as surrounding, outnumbering, and surprising them. Once again, we find the imagery of predatory hunters and animals in complaints such as "They seize (ὑπέλαβόν) me like a lion ready for prey and like a cub dwelling in hiding places" (Ps 16:12).[15] Additionally, these overpowering enemies are unrelenting in the affliction they cause as evident in the oft heard expression "all day. The lamenter routinely complains with statements such as "My enemies trampled me all day long (ὅλην τὴν ἡμέραν), many are those who battle against me from one high" (Ps 55:3).[16] There is seemingly no reprieve from these overpowering enemies.

There are a few different indications that Romans 7:7–25 echoes the overpowering enemies complained about in OT lament. The volume of the echoes is indicated by the language that OT lamenters and Paul use to describe their enemies. For example, Paul twice states that sin "seized" an "opportunity" to deceive and kill him:

> But sin having seized (λαβοῦσα) an opportunity (ἀφορμήν) through the commandment produced in me all desire. (Rom 7:8)

> For sin having seized (λαβοῦσα) an opportunity through (ἀφορμήν) the commandment deceived me and through it killed me. (Rom 7:11)

Sin is able to "seize" the "I," because it is simply more powerful. Other expressions echo the complaint against an overpowering enemy who captures and defeats the weak in war:

> For the law is spiritual, but I am fleshly having been sold under sin (πεπραμένος ὑπὸ τὴν ἁμαρτίαν). (Rom 7:14)

> But I see another law in my members warring (ἀντιστρατευόμενον) in the law of my mind and taking me captive (αἰχμαλωτίζοντά) in the law of sin which is in my members. (Rom 7:23)

---

15 See also Pss 7:3; 55:6–7; 58:3–4.
16. See also Pss 31:3; 37:7; 73:22; 87:18; 101:9; 139:3.

The expression πεπραμένος ὑπὸ τὴν ἁμαρτίαν is unique in Greek literature, but, along with the participles ἀντιστρατευόμενον and αἰχμαλωτίζοντά, it is language that echoes OT lament's complaint against overpowering enemies.[17] As noted above, OT lament often complains about political enemies who overpower their victims. Romans 7:7–25 echoes that kind of complaint to describe sin. Sin overpowers the "I" in the way the Egyptians, Babylonians, or other opponents afflicted ancient Israel. As we will see, this echo passes the test of both thematic coherence and illumination of the surrounding discourse.

Echoes of Psychological and Bodily Affliction

Romans 7:7–25 also contains a cluster of phrases that complain about how sin afflicts the "I" internally, that is within the σάρξ or σῶμα. This complaint echoes complaints against enemies in OT lament and the trouble they cause inside of those who cry out for help. A number of the echoes come from Psalm 37, an individual lament.[18]

The lamenter in Psalm 37 complains a number of times about the location wherein sin, divine wrath, and enemy activity afflict him:

> There is no healing in my flesh (ἐν τῇ σαρκί μου) from before your anger, there is no peace in my bones (τοῖς ὀστέοις μου) from before my sins. (Ps 37:4)
>
> For my loins (ψύαι) have been filled with scorn, and there is no healing in my flesh (ἐν τῇ σαρκί μου). (Ps 37:8)
>
> My heart (καρδία) was disturbed, my strength (ἰσχύς) failed me, and the light of my eyes also was not with me. (Ps 37:11)

The terms σάρξ, ὀστέον, ψύα, καρδία, and ἰσχύς all point to the bodily and psychological locale of the lamenter's pain. The affliction takes place within the physical body and mental psyche of the lamenter. These two locations are in fact indissolubly linked as indicated in the complaint "I was in misery (ἐταλαιπώρησα) and I was bent down (κατεκάμφθην) completely, all day long I was going looking sullen" (Ps 37:7). Terrein recognizes how the complaint links the lamenter's mental and physical anguish "The verb 'I am bent down' links the patient's physical condition to his psychological

---

17 Jewett notes "An extensive TLG search indicates that the expression 'sold under sin' (πεπραμένος ὑπὸ τὴν ἁμαρτίαν) appears here for the first time in Greek literature, and thereafter is entirely restricted to patristic writers dependent on this verse." Jewett, *Romans*, 461.

18 For Ps 37 (38 MT) as an individual lament, see Anderson, *Out of the Depths*, 240.

disturbance."[19] Pain afflicts the lamenter within his body and mind. This physical and psychological disturbance within the lamenter stems from a "thematic trilogy" of affliction.[20]

The "trilogy" of affliction consists of sickness, sin, and enemies that disturb the lamenter's body and mind. The affliction caused by all three, specifically within the mind and body of the lamenter, is evident in the requests and complaints of Psalm 37:

> Lord, do not convict me in your anger (τῷ θυμῷ σου) nor discipline me in your wrath (τῇ ὀργῇ σου). For your arrows were stuck to me and you rested your hand upon me; there is no healing in my flesh because of your wrath (ἀπὸ προσώπου τῆς ὀργῆς σου), there is no peace in my bones because of my sins (ἀπὸ προσώπου τῶν ἁμαρτιῶν μου). (Ps 37:2–4)

> But my enemies (ἐχθροί μου) live and they have prevailed against me, and those who hate me without cause have multiplied. (Ps 37:20)

The Lord's anger for the lamenter's sin afflicts him within his "bones," and he also suffers from multiple enemies. The lynchpin of this trilogy is divine wrath. While suffering stems from an overwhelming flood of sin and human enemies, it is God's anger that stands behind them both and ultimately causes pain in the lamenter's body and mind.[21] The lamenter is aware that sin incurs God's wrath which is often manifested in human enemies. This same trilogy afflicts the mind and body of the "I" in Romans 7:7–25. We will return to this feature of Paul's argument below.

Echoes of a Miserable State

The climactic moment in Romans 7:7–25 is the cry of distress "I am a wretched (ταλαίπωρος) man; who will deliver me from the body of this death?" (7:24). The adjective ταλαίπωρος, along with its surrounding context, echoes the "miserable state" of the lamenter in OT lament. It is a state that, like Paul's "I," results from the combinations of overpowering enemies and fear of divine wrath that takes a huge toll on the lamenter's body and mind. In OT lament, terms such as ταλαίπωρος, ταλαιπωρία, and

---

19 Terrien, *The Psalms*, 326. Of course, Terrein is referring to the MT's use of עוה.
20 Ibid., 328.
21 For sin as an overwhelming flood and a complaint about human enemies, see Ps 37:5–6, 13–22.

ταλαιπωρέω signal the outcome of an oppressive experience.[22] The experience can be described in various ways, but the result is the same, namely "misery." Misery is shorthand for the lamenter's experience at the hands of enemies and even before God.

References to "misery" at the hands of enemies are frequent in the lamenters' complaints and requests:

> Destruction and misery (ταλαιπωρία) are in their paths. (Isa 59:7)
>
> Keep me as the apple of your eye; in the protection of your wings shelter me from before the ungodly who made me miserable (ταλαιπωρησάντων). My enemies encompassed my soul. (Ps 16:8–9)
>
> And he brought me up from the pit of misery (λάκκου ταλαιπωρίας) and from the mud of the mire and set my feet upon the rock and he directed my steps. (Ps 39:3)

We should take note of the images associated with ταλαιπωρία and ταλαιπωρέω in these examples, because they contribute to our understanding of "misery" in OT lament and, consequently, in Romans 7:24. The lamenter in Isaiah 59 describes enemies who walk in "paths" of misery. In other words, the enemies' deeds destroy, even kill, and thereby make the lamenter miserable.[23] The imagery in Psalm 16:8–9 indicates that the enemy made the lamenter miserable by "encompassing" or "surrounding" (περιέσχον) him. As mentioned a number of times already, OT lament uses the image of wild animals, armies, and others who surround the lamenter in order to inflict pain and or kill their victim.[24] Therefore, the outcome of being surrounded is "misery." Similarly, in Psalm 39, the lamenter links misery with a pit (λάκκος). Enemies afflict their victims and place them in a λάκκος.[25] Lamenters play on the literal meaning of λάκκος and liken misery at the hands of enemies to being thrown in a pit out of which one cannot climb.[26]

---

22. Giesen, "ταλαίπωρος," EDNT 3:332; BDAG, 988. Additionally, for "misery" in OT lament, see chapter 2.

23 The noun σύντριμμα parallels ταλαιπωρία in Isa 59:7. As noted in the previous chapter, the wider context of Isa 59 describes enemies who afflict their prey through deceitful speech and violent deeds. See Isa 59:3–8.

24 See e.g., Pss 17:5; 21:13, 17.

25 The literal sense of the noun λάκκος is a reservoir, dungeon, or pit. LEH 364. The metaphorical sense of the word in the LXX is often associated with Sheol/Hades or death itself. See e.g., Pss 27:1; 39:3.

26 The noun βόθρος is in the same semantic domain as λάκκος, and it is also found

There are also instances in OT lament where personified enemies such as wickedness (κακός) and lawlessness (ἀνομία) leave their victims in "misery." Psalms 37 and 39 are particularly helpful here:

> My lawless deeds (ἀνομίαι) rose over my head, like a heavy load they were made heavy on me. My wounds smelt and decayed because of my foolishness. I was in misery (ἐταλαιπώρησα) and I was bent down completely, all day long I was going being sullen faced. (Ps 37:5–7)

> Because wickedness (κακά) surrounded me, of which there is no number, my lawless deeds (ἀνομίαι) seized me, and I was not able to see; they multiplied more than the hairs of my head, and my heart failed. (Ps 39:13)

These two texts personify evil and lawless enemies in the vein of political enemies who overpower, surround, and even cast the lamenter into a pit. The specific outcome of this work is described as misery (ἐταλαιπώρησα) (Ps 37:7). The lamenter in Psalm 39, before complaining about the misery caused by enemies such as lawlessness and wickedness, praises God for delivering him ἐκ λάκκου ταλαιπωρίας. Clearly, whether the opponent is a human being or evil personified, "misery" is shorthand for the lamenter's ultimate condition at the hands of enemies. It encapsulates the outcome of enemies surrounding, overwhelming, and even lowering the lamenter into a pit.

However, there is yet another layer to the "misery" that lamenters experience. Terms such as ταλαιπωρία and ταλαιπωρέω also occur in contexts where God is the agent of misery. Various complaints in OT lament bear this out:

> For day and night your hand was heavy on me, I was turned to misery (ταλαιπωρίαν) when the thorny bush had been fixed .(Ps 31:4)

> Woe is me, woe is me, because the day of the Lord is near and misery will go out from misery. (ταλαιπωρία ἐκ ταλαιπωρίας) (Joel 1:15)

The wider context of Psalm 31 indicates that God made the lamenter miserable because of the lamenter's sin. God orchestrated the ταλαιπωρία as indicated by the image of God's "hand" being heavy upon the lamenter. The "heaviness" is related to the lamenter's guilt. The "weight" of that guilt makes the lamenter miserable before God. Similarly, in the example from

---

in OT lament involving the affliction caused by enemies. See e.g., Ps 56:7.

Joel, the "day of the Lord" will result in a change from peace to misery.²⁷ The idiom ταλαιπωρία ἐκ ταλαιπωρίας accentuates the totality of the misery.²⁸ The one who is guilty before God can expect misery and nothing but misery on the "day of the Lord." Similarly, Jeremiah describes the "day of the Lord" as a day of misery "Their widows will be multiplied more than the sand of the sea; they bring upon the mother of a young man misery (ταλαιπωρίαν) in the midday, I suddenly thrown upon them trembling and anxiety" (Jer 15:8).²⁹ Thus, "misery" is also shorthand for the resultant pain caused by the lamenter's guilt before God.

When we test these echoes in Romans 7:7–25, we find that their volume, thematic coherence, and illumination of the surrounding context standout. The use of ταλαίπωρος in this context evokes the OT lamenter's miserable outcome stemming from enemies and divine wrath. This includes figurative references to being surrounded, overcome, and even thrown into a "pit" as we will see. The echoes of a miserable state cohere with the experience of the "I" in Romans 7. They also illuminate that experience as we will discuss below.

Echoes of a Cry of Distress

We discussed in chapter 2 that the most recognizable feature of lament is the cry of distress, especially the question which often accompanies it. While OT lament is more than simply a cry for help, such a request does in fact define the prayer form. One of the most explicit cries of distress in Paul's letter is "I am a wretched man; who will deliver me from the body of this death?" (Rom 7:24). This is both a complaint and a request. We considered how Romans 7:24 echoes OT complaints about a miserable state in the previous section. Here I want to deal with the request that comes in a classical idiom of OT lament, namely the request and the question.³⁰ The request and question of the ἐγώ in Romans 7 echoes those found in OT lament.

The verb ῥύομαι, used in Romans 7:24, is often found in requests of OT lament. It is most frequently part of a lamenter's request for deliverance or a statement of assurance that God will deliver:

---

27 On lament in Joel, see Dillard, *Joel*, 243; Ogden, "Joel 4 and Prophetic Responses to National Laments," 97–106; Hayes, "When None Repents, Earth Laments," 119–43.

28 See Dillard, *Joel*, 266.

29 Cf. the use of ταλαιπωρία in 2 Macc 6:9 to describe the "misery" caused by Seleucid oppression in Judea.

30 See chapter 2 for an extended discussion of questions in OT lament.

Deliver me (ῥῦσαί με) from all my lawlessness, you have given me as a reproach to the fool. (Ps 38:9)

Deliver me (ῥῦσαί με), because I am miserable and poor, and my heart has been disturbed within me. (Ps 108:22)

He himself will deliver me (ῥύσεταί με) from the trap of the hunters and from a terrifying word. (Ps 90:3)

The first two requests are accompanied by complaints about enemies and internal disturbances. Once again, in the case of Psalm 38, the lamenter specifically requests to be delivered from the enemy of lawlessness (ἀνομία).[31] This comes closest to the request of the "I" in Romans 7 who needs deliverance from a body of death caused by sin. In the example from Psalm 90, the future tense ῥύσεταί expresses the lamenter's confidence that God will deliver.[32] While the use of ῥύσεται in Romans 7:24 echoes these kinds of OT requests, it is also unique. The "I" does not indicate a confidence that God will deliver him. Rather, there is great uncertainty as we will discuss further in a moment. In any case, the presence of ῥύομαι alongside the lament form and idiom in the wider context echoes the OT lamenter's request to be delivered from enemies.

The cry in Romans 7:24 also echoes the kinds of questions that arise in OT lament. The question of the "I" is represented in the interrogative pronoun τίς. Yet, the more common OT lament questions are "why?" and "how long?" As I discussed in chapter 2, these kinds of questions contain an imbedded complaint, or protest, about the incongruity between what God promised and what the lamenter experiences. Patrick Miller explains, "The present circumstances of distress seem to indicate to the ones praying a terrible inconsistency on the part of God."[33] Consequently, lamenters ask questions that are ultimately not requests for information but protests and pleas for deliverance. Those questions are explicitly addressed to God as seen in the repeated uses of the vocative κύριε or θεός.[34] The lamenters know that only God can answer their questions/pleas for deliverance.

Romans 7:24 echoes such questions/pleas but not without qualification. The interrogative pronoun τίς replaces the vocatives κύριε or θεός. This indicates the degree of the "I's" pain and sense of uncertainty in the face of sin and divine wrath. The question echoes OT lamenters in the sense of

---

31. See also the use of ῥύομαι in the requests found in Pss 6:5; 7:2; 16:13; 21:21; 24:20; 30:2, 16; 42:1; 50:16; 58:3; 68:19; 70:2, 4; 78:9.

32 For other uses of ῥύσεταί in expressions of assurance see e.g., Pss 17:18, 20; 33:8, 20; 36:40; 40:2; 88:49; 96:10.

33. Miller, *They Cried to the Lord*, 70.

34 See e.g., Pss 7:2; 11:2; 16:13; 37:23; 84:8; 85:2.

expressing a protest and plea for deliverance. In this way, in terms of testing the echoes of a lamenter's question, there is both thematic coherence and illumination of the surrounding discourse. However, the question in 7:24 is also unique in that the "I" is doubtful about "who" can deliver him from sin and divine wrath. We will come back to this in a moment.

READING ROMANS 7:7–25 IN LIGHT OF ITS ECHOES AND PATTERN OF LAMENT

It is clear that Romans 7:7–25 echoes various individual features of OT lament. Yet, those individual features can only be understood in light of the larger pattern of lament that shapes the structure of Paul's argument. The five-fold pattern discussed in chapter 2 is on display in this portion of the letter. The "I" describes an experience that involves promise, suffering, cry of distress, deliverance, and praise. Each part echoes the lament idiom identified above. As Paul describes the suffering of the "I" caused by sin's use of the law, OT lament provides him with an idiom and pattern to describe the entire experience. We will examine each part of the pattern in light of its OT echoes. There are two sets of echoes at work here. We will hear the OT lament echoes previously identified, but we will also hear echoes of various figures that the "I" represents. Their experiences are echoed through the idiom and pattern of lament.

Promise of Life (Rom 7:7–11)

Oswald Bayer observes "Without promise there is no cause for lamentation."[35] In previous chapters, I have discussed the symbiotic relationship between God's prior promise, suffering, and the cry of distress. A cry arises when suffering threatens or contradicts a prior promise. The latter is either axiomatic or explicitly stated in the pattern of lament. The promise is not necessarily stated first within the pattern, but in the lamenter's experience it precedes suffering and the cry of distress. This begs the question. What prior promise did the "I" receive in Romans 7:7–25? The answer lies in hearing the echoes of Adam and Israel in the experience of the "I." Romans 7:7–25 echoes Adam's and Israel's experience with sin, the law, and the promise of life attached to it. Their experiences are representative of all who are plagued by sin's use of the law. We begin with the echoes of Adam's experience and the prior promise of life.

---

35 Bayer, *Living By Faith*, 69.

The loudest echo of Adam's experience is heard in the complaint "Sin having seized an opportunity through the commandment deceived me (ἐξηπάτησέν με) and through it killed me" (Rom 7:11). The complaint of the "I" echoes Eve's complaint in Genesis 3:13, "The serpent (ὄφις) deceived me (ἐξηπάτησέν με), and I ate." The larger context of Genesis 2–3 reveals that the serpent deceived Adam and Even by using God's command and prior promise:

> And the Lord God commanded (ἐνετείλατο) Adam saying "From every tree which is in the garden for eating you shall eat, but from the tree which is to know good and evil, you shall not eat from it; but in whatever day you eat from it, you will surely die (θανάτῳ ἀποθανεῖσθε)." (Gen 2:16–17)

God commanded Adam and Eve not to eat from the tree of the knowledge of good and evil and promised them death if they did. The serpent used the divine command not to eat and the promise of death to deceive Adam and Eve craftily saying, "You certainly shall not die (οὐ θανάτῳ ἀποθανεῖσθε)" (Gen 3:4). With respect to the echoes of this narrative in Romans 7, the ὄφις is replaced with ἁμαρτία and the command "you shall not eat" is replaced with "you shall not covet."[36] The command not to covet is already implied in the Genesis narrative "And the woman saw that the tree was good for eating and that it was pleasing to look at with the eyes and it is beautiful to observe, and having taken the fruit she ate it" (Gen 3:6). The serpent tempted Adam and Eve to covet the very thing God commanded them not to eat, and they "died." In Romans 7, sin tempts the "I," who is Adam, to covet, contrary to God's command that would result in life, and the result is death.

Along similar lines, Dunn argues that the "I" in Romans 7 should be identified as Adam. Dunn posits that "The use of the Adam story once again to speak of the general condition of humankind seems clear beyond dispute."[37] He explains that Paul evokes the Adamic narrative in order to "pin the blame for human subjection to death firmly on the power of sin."[38] The serpent is the "representation of sin" in Romans 7. However, for Dunn, Paul does more than connect the "I" to Adam in order to describe the condition of humanity. Paul also employs the Adamic narrative in order to explain an overlap between the experience of "I" before and after Christ. As Dunn puts it, "Notwithstanding the decisiveness of the beginning of

---

36 This echo raises questions about how Paul viewed the relationship between "sin" and "Satan." Interpreters have wrestled with this question for quite some time. See e.g., Aquinas' comments on Rom 7:7–12 in Levy, *The Letter to the Romans*, 158.

37 Dunn, *The Theology of Paul*, 99.

38 Ibid., 98.

salvation, there was still an unavoidable and marked continuity with what had gone before."[39] This means that the Adamic reading does not limit the identity of the "I" to Adam.

In fact, Adam's experience is recapitulated in Israel. God gives Israel a command not to covet, along with several others, and the command is accompanied by a promise of life for obedience and death for disobedience. This reflected in the Pentateuch:

> And you shall keep my commandments and all my judgments and you shall do them, which a man having done them will live (ζήσεται) by them; I am the Lord your God. (Lev 18:5)[40]
>
> I call as a witness against you today both heaven and earth that I have put before you life and death, a blessing and curse; choose life, in order that you and your offspring might live. (Deut 30:19)[41]

God promised ancient Israel that in Canaan life and death rested upon obedience or disobedience to the Mosaic commands.[42] Like Adam, Israel covets what God forbids. They intermarry and worship foreign deities with the belief that it will result in life. The Pentateuch and other OT narrative do not identify sin or Satan as the agent who deceived Israel, but Paul does. He echoes the command not to covet through the citation of Exodus 20:17, "You shall not covet" (Rom 7:7). This in turn evokes the kinds of promises cited above, namely that obedience results in life and disobedience results in death.

N. T. Wright is the most notable proponent of identifying the "I" as Israel. In his recent tome on Paul, Wright notes "The whole chapter (i.e. Rom 7) has been a close and careful account of what happens when Torah arrives in Israel and when Israel then lives with it."[43] Yet, Wright does not limit the identity of the "I" to Israel. He explains "The problem is not Torah; the problem is not the vocation to be Torah-people; the problem is the Adamic humanity, 'the body of this death.'"[44] Israel, like the rest of humanity, is in Adam. What distinguishes Israel from the rest of Adamic humanity, so says Wright, is that Israel's plight has "salvific intent."[45] He explains "This is the

---

39 Ibid., 476.
40 Cf. Rom 10:5; Gal 3:12.
41 See also Deut 27:26.
42 See Deut 4:1; 6:24; 8:1; 16:20; 30:6.
43 Wright, *Paul and the Faithfulness of God*, 1017.
44 Ibid., 1018.
45 Ibid., 1017.

divine purpose: that sin be drawn onto this one place, onto Israel, so that it can be dealt with conclusively by the covenant God himself in the person, in the flesh, of Israel's Messiah, the son of this very God."[46] Consequently, for Wright, the "I" in Romans 7 is Israel who "bore the 'messianic woes' all the way up to the Messiah's coming."[47]

For my purposes here, the take away from Dunn and Wright is that they both recognize the polyvalent nature of the "I."[48] What we have with the "I" is a figure whose experience echoes that of both Adam and Israel. Even more, it is an experience that is representative of anyone who suffers from sin's deceitful and deadly use of the law. Paul has already portrayed Israel and Adam as representatives of humanity in Romans 3:1–20 and 5:12–21 respectively. It is not surprising that something similar takes places in Romans 7 with the "I."

We can now return to the idiom and pattern of lament that shapes the experience of the "I," particularly the prior promise of life. In Romans 7:7–11, we find a figure who hears God's promise that obedience to his command would result in life.[49] Sin uses that command and its concomitant promise of life to deceive and kill the "I" (Rom 7:10–11). Paul identifies the specific command as "you shall not covet," something Adam and Israel both did. Sin uses that command to produce coveting, and thereby death, rather than obedience, and thereby life, "But sin having seized the opportunity through the commandment produced in me all coveting" (Rom 7:8). Like the enemies in OT lament discussed earlier, sin's deceptive speech masks its deadly intention.[50] We can hear echoes bemoaning deceitful enemies such as "And they deceived (ἠπάτησαν) him with their mouth and with their tongue they lied (ἐψεύσαντο) to him (Ps 77:36)." What is particularly hurtful to the lamenting "I" is that sin uses the prior promise of life attached to the law as the very means of death. This was true for Adam, Israel, and thereby, at least in retrospect, Paul. Moreover, if sin uses the prior promise of life found in the law to kill these figures, it afflicts all others in the same way. The law provides knowledge of sin, but it is not the means to the life God promised (Rom 7:7).[51] Yet, sin deceptively tells the "I" that the law leads to life before God. In reality, sin uses the law to produce more disobedience, in this case

---

46 Ibid., 1015.

47 Ibid., 1019.

48 However, I do not necessarily agree with specific points of their Adamic and Israelite readings.

49 The promise of life to Adam is negatively stated in Gen 2:16–17. Similarly, the promise of life to Israel is positively stated in texts such as Lev 18:5.

50 See chapter 2.

51 Cf. Rom 3:20; Gal 3:21.

coveting, and thereby death (Rom 7:8–11). Sin, like the serpent, twists the law and the prior promise of life in order to kill the "I." So, the pattern of lament in Romans 7:7–25 contains a prior promise of life attached to the law which sin, the enemy, uses to kill the "I."

Suffering Death "Within" (Rom 7:13–23)

Suffering is the second element of the lament pattern in Romans 7. The suffering of the "I" stems in part from the incongruity between the prior promise of life and the death which the ἐγώ experiences. Death (θάνατος) is the epitome of the suffering of the "I."[52] The θάνατος described here is transcendent and has eternal implications.[53] Although there is no explicit reference to God in Romans 7:7–25, death in this context is the antithesis of life before him. Death and condemnation before God are the outcome of sin's deceitful use of the prior promise. Sin causes the incongruity between the prior promise of life and the current experience of death. Therefore, the suffering of the "I" has two sources: sin and condemnation before God. Paul calls this entire experience "death" and uses OT lament to describe it.

As I noted earlier in the chapter, Paul's description of sin in Romans 7 echoes the description of enemies in OT lament. In addition to their deception, those enemies launch an overpowering barrage against their victims, and the victims often suffer within their own bodies and minds. Such is the experience of the "I" in Romans 7:13–23. The overpowering nature of sin is evident in phrases such as "having been sold under sin," "another law warring in my members," and "taking me captive in the law of sin" (Rom 7:14, 23). I noted already that Israel's history is littered with complaints against enemies who overpowered them.[54] The "I" is Israel whose most overbearing opponent is sin. Yet, to reiterate, the identity of the "I" is not limited to Israel. Their experience is indicative of anyone who suffers at the hands of sin. All are "overpowered" by it. Moreover, like enemies in OT lament, sin defeats the "I" constantly and internally. Paul's description of sin echoes complaints against enemies such as "They surrounded me like water all day long (ὅλην τὴν ἡμέραν), they encompassed me together" (Ps 87:18). In the same vein, the "I" complains "So I find the law, in me the one who wants to

---

52 The verbs ἀποθνῄσκω and ἀποκτείνω both occur once (Rom 7:10, 11), and θάνατος occurs four times (Rom 7:10, 13, 24).

53 BDAG 442–43.

54 E.g., Exod 2:23–24; 3:9; Ps 105:40–45; Ezra 9:7.

do good, that evil is ready (παράκειται) in me" (Rom 7:21).⁵⁵ Sin is "ready" to overpower "all day long."

Romans 7:13–23 also echoes the internal affliction caused by the enemies described in OT lament. We can hear in the "I" complaints such as "There is no healing in my flesh from before your anger, there is no peace in my bones from before my sins" (Ps 37:4).⁵⁶ Similar complaints are heard in the constant references to sin's affliction within the σάρξ, μέλος, and νοῦς of the "I":

> But now I am no longer doing it but sin which dwells in me (οἰκοῦσα ἐν ἐμοί). (Rom 7:17)

> For I know that there does not dwell in me, that is in my flesh (ἐν τῇ σαρκί μου), good. (Rom 7:18)

> But if that which I do not want this I do, I am no longer doing it but sin which dwells in me (οἰκοῦσα ἐν ἐμοί). (Rom 7:20)

> But I see another law warring in my members (ἐν τοῖς μέλεσίν μου) in the law of my mind (τοῦ νοός μοθ) and taking me captive in the law of sin which is in my members (ἐν τοῖς μέλεσίν μου). (Rom 7:23)

Like OT lamenters, the "I" complains that sin causes affliction "within." Death is suffered in the body and the psyche. Moreover, the echoes from Psalm 37 indicate that part of this internal angst is fear of divine wrath. Paul does not explicitly mention condemnation in 7:13–23, but it is clearly a concern of the "I" as indicated in 8:1 "So now there is no condemnation" (κατάκριμα). This statement at the conclusion of the lament indicates that suffering death ultimately means suffering condemnation. Like OT lamenters, that suffering, that death, presently takes place "within" and takes a toll on the entire person (i.e. σῶμα and νοῦς). This is clearly articulated in the "I's" cry of distress.

Cry for Deliverance from the Body (Rom 7:24)

We have already seen that the cry of distress in Romans 7:24 echoes similar cries in OT lament, but it is also unique. Given the larger idiom and pattern of lament, the use of ῥύσεται could evoke the image of being surrounded by

---

55 BDAG 766. See also Rom 7:18.

56 See the previous discussion regarding echoes of psychological and bodily affliction.

enemies or thrown into a pit and left for dead.[57] The cry for deliverance is preceded by the complaint that sin wars against and takes the "I" captive. All of this is an internal experience, but it is likened to the trauma of being surrounded, captured, and tossed into a pit. Paul's shorthand phrase for this experience, just as in OT lament, is "misery." The "I" cries out "I am a miserable/wretched (ταλαίπωρος) man; who will deliver me from the body of this death" (Rom 7:24). This cry echoes cries of distress such as "I am miserable (ἐταλαιπώρησα) and bent down completely" (Ps 37:7a). As I noted previously, the enemy in Psalm 37 is also sin personified.[58] Yet, the echo of Psalm 37 in Romans 7:24 not only evokes the depiction of sin as an enemy but also concerns about divine judgment. Misery emanates from the activity of sin and guilt before God. This duel threat is what elicits the cry to be delivered from misery in Romans 7:24. It is a misery that Paul calls "the body of this death." We can understand this phrase by reading it in light of its lament echoes. The "I" is in a state of misery like one surrounded and tossed down into a pit. It is a kind of death that takes place within the person (mind and body) of the "I." Whether the "I" is Adam, Israelites, Paul, or anyone else afflicted by sin, the suffering takes places within the body. Therefore, a cry arises to be delivered from the "body of this death."

Yet, there is also something unique about the cry of distress in Romans 7:24 in comparison to OT lament. I noted earlier that cries of distress in OT lament usually contain a vocative phrase such as κύριε or θεός, but this is replaced in 7:24 with τίς. The interrogative pronoun that replaces the divine vocative indicates the severity of the lamenter's suffering. Sin bewilders the "I" so much that the "I" does not know where to find help. There is no help in the law of God, because sin has used that law to kill the "I." Consequently, since the law is broken, there is no salvation in God but rather death and condemnation before him. Therefore, the lamenting "I" cannot find deliverance in God. If there is no help in God, "who" can deliver? Who could really help Adam, Israel, Paul, and anyone else who is deceived, overpowered, and killed by sin? OT lamenters feared the prospect of Sheol/Hades, but held out hope that they would be delivered from it.[59] The "I" in Romans 7, in a certain sense, is already there—already in the ultimate misery of death. There is a hellish and fatal experience of condemnation now and the prospect of final judgment later.

---

57 See previous discussion regarding echoes of a miserable state.
58 See Ps 37:4–6.
59 See e.g., Ps 88:49.

Deliverance in the Body (Rom 8:1–4)

Deliverance is a key element in any OT pattern of lament. Yet, in Romans 7:7–25, there is no explicit reference to it. Instead, there is a terse shout of praise in 7:25a followed by a summation of the "I"s experience in 7:25b. The explication of deliverance is delayed until 8:1–4, where we find an answer to the cry from 7:24. These four verses show some important connections with 7:7–25.

To begin, Romans 8:1–4 provides relief from the condemnation that afflicts the "I." Paul famously announces in 8:1, "So there is now no condemnation (κατάκριμα) for those who are in Christ Jesus." The noun κατάκριμα abbreviates the experience of the "I" both presently and eschatologically.[60] It is ultimately the fear of κατάκριμα that elicits the cry in 7:24. For all of sin's deceit and deadly affliction, it is divine condemnation that plagues the "I" the most. That is the ultimate cause of "misery" in the body of death. Yet, the τίς of deliverance turns out to be θεός after all. Paul asserts that for those who are "in Christ Jesus," there is not the kind of condemnation lamented by the ἐγώ in Romans 7. That does not mean God simply set aside the condemnation experienced in the body of the "I," nor did he condemn the "I." Instead, he condemned the enemy of the "I," sin, in the death of Jesus (Rom 8:3).

Romans 8:1–4 also answers the cry from 7:24 by announcing "freedom" from the enemy who deceives, overpowers, and kills the "I." Paul explains "For the law of the spirit of life in Christ Jesus freed (ἠλευθέρωσέν) you from the law of sin and death" (Rom 8:2). The cry in 7:24 is "who will deliver," and the divine response in 8:2 is basically "Jesus." Of course, Paul's phrasing here is finely nuanced. The subject of ἠλευθέρωσέν is actually "the law (νόμος) of the spirit of life in Christ Jesus," and the enemy of sin is described as "the law (νόμος) of sin and death." Νόμος, as it appears in 8:2, frees and gives life, but it is also linked to sin and death. Obviously, there is a great deal of theological abbreviation in the phrases "the law of the Spirit of life in Christ Jesus" and the "law of sin and death." Why does Paul answer the cry from 7:24 in such a nuanced way?

The answer is that these theological abbreviations encapsulate a whole complex of ideas that are at work in Romans 7 and 8. The suffering lamented in Romans 7 revolves around sin using the law to deceive and kill the "I" in its σῶμα. Even worse, sin's deceptive use of the law results in condemnation before God. This experience of suffering is condensed in the phrase "law of sin and death" in 8:2. Similarly, the abbreviation "the law of the Spirit of life

---

60 Paul's use of κατάκριμα and its cognates throughout the letter indicate an eschatological scenario in which God doles out both the sentence and punishment against those guilty of sin. See e.g., Rom 2:1–11.

in Christ Jesus" refers to the condemned and resurrected Jesus who provides life beyond the internal death and condemnation described so vividly in Romans 7. The reference to πνεῦμα signals not only the Spirit-led walk of the believer but also the eschatological work of the Spirit described in the broader context of Romans 8. Additionally, the πνεῦμα leads those who are in the crucified and risen Christ so that the δικαίωμα τοῦ νόμου might be fulfilled (Rom 8:4). Sin's use of the law in Romans 7, which leads to death and condemnation, is overcome by those who are led by the Spirit of Christ (Rom 8:9). Moreover, the "I" ultimately experiences freedom from sin's use of the law through the Spirit's redemption of the body. Paul explains:

> But if Christ is in you, the body is dead on account of sin but the Spirit is life on account of righteousness. And if the Spirit of the one who raised Jesus from the dead dwells in you, the one who raised Christ from the dead will also make alive your mortal bodies through the same Spirit who dwells in you. (Rom 8:10–11)

The assertion that the "body is dead on account of sin" but the "Spirit is life on account of righteousness" summarizes the situation of the "I" who is in Christ.[61] It is similar to Paul's statement in 7:25b "So then I myself in my mind serve the law of God but in my flesh the law of sin." Even the "I" who is in Christ continues to be afflicted in the body, because sin still dwells there. The "I" will finally experience freedom in Christ from the "body of this death" when the same Spirit who raised Christ from dead raises the "I" from the dead. Obviously, the phrase "the law of the Spirit of life in Christ Jesus" is densely packed. Only when we unpack the abbreviation do we understand how it serves as Paul's answer to the cry of distress in 7:24. In the Christ who had sin condemned in his body by God and was raised from the dead through the Spirit, there is the promise of the freedom that the "I" so desperately needs in his own body. As we will discuss further in the next chapter, Paul's answer to lament is a gospel that promises bodily resurrection from the dead.

---

61 See the reference to δικαιοσύνη in Rom 8:1

Praise for Deliverance in Christ (Rom 7:25)

Praise is a definitive element in the pattern of lament.[62] In Paul's pattern of lament, praise for deliverance precedes the explanation of it.[63] What immediately follows the cry of distress in Romans 7:24 is spontaneous doxology "But thanks (χάρις) be to God through Jesus Christ our Lord. So then I myself in my mind serve the law of God but in my flesh the law of sin."[64] The latter part of the doxology acknowledges that, despite this outburst of praise, the cry of distress is never entirely silenced. As long as the "I" is in the body, even an "I" who is in Christ, sin will continue to cause death and elicit cries of distress. The praise does indicate that God answers the cry for deliverance through the Lord Jesus Christ. Yet, the "I" does not fully experience redemption through the Lord Jesus apart from redemption of a body indwelled by sin. That is why the doxology is momentary and balanced by a return to lament in Romans 8:18–39, something we will explore in the next chapter. For the moment, it is worth noting that in Romans 8 redemption of the body is a key motif in the chapter (Rom 8:24). We find creation, God's children, and even the Holy Spirit crying out for that redemption. It is the kind of redemption the lamenting "I" of Romans 7 desperately needs.

SUMMARY

A brief summary is in order given all that has been covered in this chapter. The aim throughout has been to identify and analyze OT lament in Romans 7:7–25. What we have discovered is that the identity of the ἐγώ is polyvalent and its experience is relayed through the idiom and pattern of OT lament. The identity of the "I" is anyone who is plagued by sin's use of the law in the body. This means that proposed identities such as Adam, Israel, Paul, and the like are not mutually exclusive.

It also should be noted that my identification of the "I" does not necessarily fall under the category of a "rhetorical" reading, an approach made famous by Kümmel's seminal work.[65] Kümmel argued that Paul used a Greco-Roman style (*Stilform*) in which the writer or speaker could use ἐγώ without making any personal reference to oneself.[66] Subsequent interpreters

---

62. On the constant oscillation between lament and praise, see Villaneuva, *The Uncertainty of a Hearing*.
63. On the flexibility of the OT lament pattern, see chapter 2.
64. Cf. doxology in Rom 1:25; 9:5; 11:33–36.
65. See Kümmel, Röm 7 und die Bekehrung des Paulus.
66. On this point, see Moo, *The Epistle to the Romans*, 427 fn. 12.

have built upon Kümmel's reading. It opened the door to a wide array of philosophical and rhetorical interpretations.[67] One notable example is the work of Stanley Stowers. He argues that "Rom 7:7–25 resembles tragic soliloquy and *prosopopoiia* of the person in a tragic situation in several ways."[68] Stowers explains that *prosopopoiia* is a "speech-in-character" that ancient writers such as Celsus and Origen were familiar with and would have recognized in Romans 7.[69] With this background in mind, Stowers asserts that Paul combined *prosopopoiia* with Greek philosophy's concern over a "lack of self-mastery" (ἀκρασία).[70] He cites a number of ancient philosophers, both Stoic and Platonic, who gave much thought to the "Greek-Roman ethic of self-mastery." As an example, Stowers points to the "famous Medean saying" in Euripides "I am being overcome by evils. I know that what I am about to do is evil, but passion is stronger than my reasoned reflection; and this is the cause of the worst evils for humans."[71] Paul then uses these features of Greek rhetoric in Romans 7 in order to "characterize not every human or every human who is not a Christian but rather gentiles, especially those who try to live by works of the law."[72]

I do not wish to deny the interpretive impact of Kümmel and those such as Stowers who have followed him. However, Kümmel wrongly downplays Paul's personal involvement in the experience of the "I." I would agree that the identity should not be reduced to a pre- or post-Damascus Paul. However, it does not follow that Paul is entirely absent from the suffering and cry of distress articulated in Romans 7. We should not allow a proposed rhetorical strategy to eclipse the theological argumentation of Romans 7–8. Paul has to be included among those whose bodies are "dead on account of sin" and thereby subject in some way to the experience of the "I" (Rom 8:10). Moreover, following Stowers, it is possible that Paul's language in Romans 7 is shaped in some way by Greco-Roman rhetoric. However, given Paul's pervasive use of the OT in Romans and his Jewish heritage, the influence of Greco-Roman rhetoric on Romans 7 would have to be secondary to OT lament.

In light of what we have already seen in chapters 3 and 4, it is better to describe the "I" in Romans 7 as "figural" rather than narratival, Pauline,

---

67 See e.g., Huttunen, *Paul and Epictetus on Law*, 101–26.

68 Stowers, *A Reading of Romans*, 271.

69 Ibid., 264. For further discussion on Paul's use of *prosopopoiia*, see Collins, *The Power of Images in Paul*, 259–60.

70 Stowers, *A Reading of Romans*, 260.

71 As cited in Longenecker, *Introducing Romans*, 370.

72 Stowers, *A Reading of Romans*, 273.

rhetorical, and the like.[73] Specifically, the "I" is a figure who laments like those who suffer at the hands of enemies and in the face of divine judgment in OT lament. Echoes of the lament idiom can be heard in Paul's description of sin. The text not only echoes the idiom of lament but also the pattern of lament. The movement from promise to praise and everything in between echoes the experiences of Adam, Israel, Paul, and anyone like them who are plagued by sin's work within the body. To some extent, at least in retrospect, Paul describes the experience of the unbeliever and believer. The main difference with the latter is that his or her cry of distress is answered in the promise of the gospel.

---

[73] On figural reading in general, see Auerbach, *Mimesis*; Hays, *Reading Backwards*, 1–16.

6

The Gospel as Answer to Groans and Inexplicable Rejection (Romans 8:18–39)

IT SHOULD BE CLEAR by now that Romans contains a number of OT lament echoes that illuminate Paul's argument in a number of ways. As a reminder, the ultimate aim in reading Romans as lament is to understand what it tells us about Paul's theology of suffering in the letter.[1] That will be our task in the conclusion. In the meanwhile, it is necessary to identify the lament echoes in another portion of Romans and assess how they impact the interpretation of Paul's argument. In this chapter, we will consider the echoes present in Romans 8:18–39.

The overarching thesis in what follows is that when one reads Romans 8:18–39 in light of its OT lament echoes two features of the text emerge that might otherwise go unnoticed: (1) the echoes in 8:18–27 provide the background story as to why creation, God's children, and the Holy Spirit are involved in a collective lament in which they "groan" for the resurrection of the dead; and (2) the citation of Psalm 43, along with other echoes, indicates that Paul is addressing an underlying question about the apparent divine condemnation and rejection of the elect. There is a distinct idiom and form of OT lament here that needs to be identified and analyzed in its original context. We can then assess how these echoes affect our exegesis of the text. There are two major sections in Romans 8:18–39 that contain OT lament echoes. The echoes in Romans 8:18–30 involve the participants and pattern of OT lament. Romans 8:31–39 echoes a number of OT texts,

1 See chapter 1.

most prominently Psalm 43, a classic lament psalm. We will consider each of these in turn.

IDENTIFYING THE ECHOES OF LAMENT IN ROMANS 8:18–30

What stands out about the lament language in Romans 8:18–30 is the mutual involvement of three likeminded participants: creation, God's children, and the Holy Spirit. Their laments need to be read in light of the OT echoes they contain. There is a cluster of echoes present here from a wide variety of OT texts. We need to analyze those echoes in their original contexts in order to full appreciate their impact on the reading of Romans 8:18–30.

Echoes of "Groaning" by God's People

As a reminder, the participants of OT lament are "I/we" (lamenter), "you" (God), and "them" (enemies).[2] Lament always involves an interchange between these three participants whether implicitly or explicitly. The three explicit participants in Romans 8:18–30 fall into the first slot of "I/we." The "I/we" participants are creation, the sons of God, and the Holy Spirit. Paul tethers together the cries of all three through the use of συστενάζω, στενάζω, and στεναγμός (Rom 8:22, 23, 26). Hahne is right to note that the use of "groaning" is a structural device in Romans 8, but it is more than that.[3] Specifically, we need to consider how this "groaning" echoes various OT lament passages.

The verb στενάζω and its cognates often appear in the LXX to describe the inarticulate groaning and sobbing of a lamenter.[4] "Groaning" speaks to the intensity of the lamenter's pain, but also their enduring hope that God would hear them.[5] There are a number of examples that span various genres of the OT, but they all involve participants who cry out in pain and await their deliverance.

Groaning is often associated with childbirth in the OT. In fact, God's judgment against the woman in Genesis 3 involves groaning at childbirth,

---

2 For a discussion on the participants of OT lament, see chapter 2.

3 See Hahne, *The Corruption and Redemption of Creation*, 201; Crump, *Knocking on Heaven's Door*, 200.

4 See e.g., στεναγμός in Pss 6:7; 11:6; 30:11; 37:9–10; 78:11; 101:6, 21.

5 For a brief discussion of words associated with crying or lament in the NT, see Öhler, "To Mourn, Weep, Lament and Groan," 150–51. On στενάζω in the LXX and Rom 8:22, see Braaten, "All Creation Groans," 131–59.

"And he said to the woman, 'I will certainly multiply your grief (λύπας) and your groaning (στεναγμόν), in grief (λύπαις) you will bear children" (Gen 3:16). The parallelism between λύπη and στεναγμός indicates the interplay between physical and emotional trauma involved in childbirth. Moreover, the wider context of Genesis 3 indicates that pain in childbirth is ultimately rooted in God's judgment for human rebellion. The στεναγμός conveys more than physical pain. The groaning acknowledges God's judgment against humanity and creation.

We should also consider the sons of Israel who "groan" as slaves in Egypt. Their groans are noted a few different times in the Exodus narrative:

> Now after those many days the king of Egypt died. And the sons of Israel groaned (κατεστέναξαν) because of their works and they cried out, and their cry ascended to God because of their works. And God heard their groaning (στεναγμόν), and God remembered his covenant to Abraham and Isaac and Jacob. (Exod 2:23–24)

> And I heard the groaning (στεναγμόν) of the sons of Israel, whom the Egyptians oppress them, and I remembered your covenant. (Exod 6:5)

Israel's "groaning" at a critical stage of her history should not be overlooked. Westermann reminds us that "The cry to God out of deep anguish accompanies Israel throughout her history."[6] When Israel's history is recounted elsewhere, their "groaning" to God is included in the account. For example, in Stephen's retelling of Moses' call to deliver Israel, his version of Exodus 3:7 reads "I have certainly seen the affliction of my people in Egypt and I have heard their groaning (στεναγμοῦ), and I went down to deliver them; and come now I will send you to Egypt" (Acts 7:34).[7] As recognized in Stephen's speech, Israel's στεναγμός in Egypt was part of a larger pattern. Their slavery in Egypt was at the same time predictable and yet incongruent with the prior promise to Abraham, namely that his descendants would dwell in their own land but also suffer oppression (Gen 12:1–3; 15:13).[8] Therefore, they cried out, or groaned, and God sent Moses to deliver them.

---

6. Westermann, "The Role of Lament," 20–21.

7 In Exod 3:7 LXX, the translator uses κραυγή rather than στεναγμός. They are in the same semantic domain, but my concern here is with the specific use of στεναγμός and its echoes in Rom 8:18–30.

8 Abraham was also promised that his descendants would be enslaved and mistreated for 400 years. See Gen 15:13.

Individual laments employ στεναγμός and cognates to express the pain they feel. The language appears in complaints about various kinds of suffering:

> My life is left in pain and my years in groaning (στεναγμοῖς); my strength weakened in poverty, and my bones were disturbed. (Ps 30:11)

> For before my food groaning (στεναγμός) comes near to me, and I cry while being gripped with fear. (Job 3:24)

> I was mistreated and lowered exceedingly, I was roaring from the groaning (στεναγμοῦ) of my heart. (Ps 37:9)

These examples demonstrate that groaning takes places within the body and the heart. It can be caused by physical factors such as hunger and poverty as well as personal guilt.[9] Yet, as always in lament, it is the tension between the prior promise and the lamenter's suffering that elicits the groan. There are even explicit promises that God will answer when he hears the στεναγμός. For example, in Psalm 11:6, κύριος is the speaker who promises "Because of the misery of the poor and because of the groaning (στεναγμοῦ) of the needy now I will rise, says the Lord, I will set him in salvation, I will deal openly with him." Therefore, a lamenter's groan not only expresses pain. It also evokes the promise that God will answer the lamenter's στεναγμός.

We must also consider the link between the "groaning" of God's people and the metaphor of child birth (ὠδίνω). As we will discuss below, Romans 8:19–23 echoes this metaphor as it is found in Isaiah:

> And as one who suffers birth pangs (ὠδίνουσα) so as to give birth and she cries out (ἐκέκραξεν) because of the labor pain (ὠδῖνι), in this way we have been to your beloved on account of fear of you, Lord. In the womb we conceived and we suffered birth pangs (ὠδινήσαμεν) and we gave birth. (Isa 26:17–18)

There is obviously groaning and crying involved in child birth, but there is more to the metaphor than the expression of pain. The metaphor of childbirth also holds pain and hope in perfect tension. Beyond the pain, there is the hope and expectation of what is to come. In the wider context of Isaiah 26, there is a blend of pain and hope indicative of childbirth. The pain stems from divine judgment at the hands of foreign invaders, and the result is death (Isa 26:5–6, 20). Yet, there is also hope for new life. Following the statement "we gave birth" (ἐτέκομεν) in 26:18, Isaiah explains "The dead will rise, and those who are in tombs will be raised, and those who are in the

---

9 See also Pss 6:7; 37:10; 78:11; 101:6, 21.

earth will rejoice; for your healing is like dew to them, but the land of the ungodly will fall" (Isa 26:19). The result of the crying and the birth pangs is resurrection from the dead. It is the shift from groaning to new birth that is echoed in Romans 8:19–25.

Echoes of "Groaning" by Creation

The OT also describes creation as something that "groans" in the face of pain and prior promise. For example, at the close of Job's final defense/complaint he personifies the land as something that could testify or "groan" against him, "If the land (ἡ γῆ) has groaned (ἐστέναξεν) against me, and if its furrows have wept together" (Job 31:38). The phrase indicates a link between human injustice and the abuse of the land. It is abuse that could cause the land to "groan" and "weep." Hartley interprets Job's statement in light of Mosaic regulations related to the land such as not sowing with two kinds of seeds or allowing the land to "rest" every seven years (Lev 19:19; Exod 23:10–11).[10] The OT connects occupation of the land to its inhabitants' moral behavior.[11] As Hartley puts it, "When the people are disobedient, the land withers and mourns beneath the weight of their sins. Conversely, when the people obeyed God's laws, he blessed the land so that it yielded abundantly."[12] The land not only mourns when its occupants disobey agricultural laws. It cries out against human on human violence. This is demonstrated in the narrative of Genesis 4 in which God tells Cain that the "voice of the blood of your brother cries out (βοᾷ) to me from the ground (ἐκ τῆς γῆς)" (Gen 4:10). According to the Mosaic Law, this kind of action defiles the land and requires God to cleanse it.[13]

Various passages in the OT indicate how this kind of lawbreaking directly impacts the earth. In short, God curses the earth for the misdeeds of its inhabitants, a judgment that began in Genesis 3.[14] Therefore, creation "mourns" or "groans." This scenario is recognized by the writer of Isaiah who observes:

> The earth mourns (ἐπένθησεν), the world has been ruined, the heights of the earth mourn (ἐπένθησαν). And the earth has been corrupted on account of those who dwell in it, because they have

10 Hartley, *The Book of Job*, 422.
11 Ibid.
12 Ibid., 422–23.
13 See e.g., Num 35:33.
14 See Gen 3:17.

transgressed the law and changed the law, the eternal covenant. On account of this a curse will consume the earth, because those who dwell in it sinned; on account of this those who dwell in the earth will be poor and few people will be left. (Isa 24:4–6)

The earth mourns because it has to suffer judgment for the sins of its habitants. Earth's cry against the announcement of divine judgment is also heard in Jeremiah 4:28, "Let the earth mourn (πενθείτω), and let the sky above be darkened, because I have spoken and I will not relent, I have sworn and I will not turn from it." Here earth expresses her mourning through darkened skies.[15] As Freitheim puts it, "Verse 28 portrays the dirge-like response of the (still existent!) heavens and earth to what has occurred—a mourning and a 'wearing' of funeral black."[16]

To summarize up to this point, "groaning" is lament language that evokes the interplay between pain and hope. The participants of this interplay are both God's people and creation. It evokes key moments in Israel's history in which the nation suffered, cried out to God, and either expected or experienced deliverance. The whole experience is sometimes likened to childbirth. In the midst of pain there is hope for the birth of something new. As we will see, this same interplay is echoed in Romans 8:18–30.

READING ROMANS 8:18-30 IN LIGHT OF ITS ECHOES

We have identified a number of OT lament echoes, especially those related to Paul's use of στεναγμός and other cognates. But how do these echoes impact the reading of Romans 8:18–30? To answer this question, we need to examine each participant individually. Then we will consider how they act in concert with one another.

Echoes of Creation Groaning (Rom 8:19–22)

In Romans 8:19–22, Paul personifies all creation (κτίσις) as an expectant mother who groans and suffers child pangs with (σύν) the children of God.[17] She is caught between futility and eschatological hope; therefore, she cries out like an OT lamenter. Key parts of the lament pattern are echoed in Paul's personification, namely promise, suffering, cry, and deliverance.

---

15 Cf. Amos 8:8–10.
16 Freitheim, *Jeremiah*, 101.
17. See Dodson, *The 'Powers' of Personification*, 162–77.

Creation suffers from her God-given futility that is exacerbated by hope. It is hope created by a prior promise. Paul explains that creation eagerly awaits the revelation of God's sons, because (γάρ) "creation was subjected (ὑπετάγη) to futility (ματαιότητι), not willingly but on account of the one who subjected it, in hope (ἐφ' ἐλπίδι)" (Rom 8:20). The term ματαιότης summarizes the essence of creation's suffering. It echoes a number of OT texts which, when heard, shed light on what Paul thinks ails creation and causes it to groan. Three echoes come from Genesis 3:17–19, Ecclesiastes 1:2–11, and Isaiah 24:4–6. All three passages speak to creation's pain from varying perspectives, but their common denominator is the disobedience of humanity. In Genesis 3:17–19, God curses the earth on account of Adam's transgression.[18] One result of the transgression is that it becomes more difficult for people to extract produce from the earth (Gen 3:18–19). Moreover, rather than reigning over the earth people die and return to the ground from which they came, "for you are dirt and you will return to the dirt" (Gen 3:19). This is the kind of ματαιότης that the writer of Ecclesiastes has in mind. He reflects on the futility/meaninglessness of creation given the fact that "[a] generation comes and a generation goes, and the earth stands forever" (Eccl 1:4). A person "toils under the sun," but death makes such work meaningless (ματαιότης). This also makes creation meaningless, because it continues while humanity dies. Consequently, creation is not only meaningless but also "ruined" (φθορά) by its inhabitants. This is Isaiah's point, "The earth will certainly be ruined (φθαρήσεται), and it will certainly be spoiled; for the mouth of the Lord spoke these things" (Isa 24:3). He connects the earth's ruin to the sin of its inhabitants:

> And the earth is corrupted on account of those who dwell in it, because they have transgressed the law and changed the law, the eternal covenant. On account of this a curse will consume the earth, because those who dwell in it sinned (ἡμάρτοσαν); on account of this those who dwell in the earth will be poor, and a few men will be left. (Isa 24:5–6)

The violence of the earth's inhabitants results in divine judgment against them. But that judgment often has a traumatic impact on creation such as famine, invasion, and the like. Therefore, Romans 8:19–22 echoes the suffering of creation as it is described in Genesis 3, Ecclesiastes 1, and Isaiah 24. In short, creation is cursed, meaningless, and ruined.

Paul describes the suffering described in Genesis, Ecclesiastes, and Isaiah and labels it "slavery." He writes, "For creation was subjected (ὑπετάγη) to futility, no willingly but on account of the one who subjected it, in hope;

---

18 See Gen 3:17, "Cursed (ἐπικατάρατος) is the ground because of your works."

because creation itself will be freed from the slavery (δουλείας) to ruin (φθορᾶς) in the freedom of the glory of the children of God" (Rom 8:20–21). Terms such as ὑποτάσσω, ἐλευθερόω, and δουλεία indicate the slavery motif. God enslaved creation to futility and ruin which, in light of Genesis, Ecclesiastes, and Isaiah, is a metonymy for divine judgment against humanity that traumatizes creation. Creation is enslaved to ruin, because its inhabitants are disobedient to the creator. Yet, God subjected creation to futility and ruin with a hope (ἐλπίς) of deliverance (Rom 8:20). Fulfillment of this hope hinges upon the revelation of the sons of God (Rom 8:19, 21).

Thus far we can hear two key parts of the lament pattern, prior promise and suffering. The friction between these two parts elicits a cry of distress which Paul describes in 8:22, "For we know that all creation groans together (συστενάζει) and suffers births pangs (συνωδίνει) until now." The verbs συστενάζω and συνωδίνω echo the OT lament identified above. The στεναγμός of Israel and various individuals is now put on the "lips" of creation. Of course, this is not without OT precedent. As I noted earlier, both Isaiah and Jeremiah describe creation as mourning or groaning.[19] The wider contexts of Isaiah 24 and Jeremiah 4 reveal that the earth groans because of God's judgment against rebellious people. This explains, at least in part, what Paul means when he describes creation as groaning. It groans because it is traumatized by the judgment God pours out on humanity. However, there is also an echo of creation's hope beyond the judgment through the use of συνωδίνω. Once again, the metaphor of child birth captures the interplay between pain and hope. Creation cries out like a woman suffering through childbirth, but in the midst of the pain there is hope for something new. Creation's cry began in Genesis 3 and continues at the time of Paul's letter.[20] Altogether, in the cosmology of Romans 8:19–22, creation cries out because it is suspended between suffering and hope like a lamenter in Israel's scriptures.

Finally, Romans 8:19–22 also echoes the fourth part of the lament pattern which is deliverance. Paul indicates that creation's deliverance is contingent upon what happens to its inhabitants. Creation eagerly awaits the "revelation of the sons of God" or the "freedom of the glory of the children of God" (Rom 8:19, 21). The terms ἀποκάλυψις and ἐλευθερία are shorthand references to the resurrection of the dead. The hope of creation and the hope of God's children are one in the same. Creation's futility only ends

---

19. See Isa 24:5–6; Jer 4:28.

20. This is indicated by the present tense verbs συστενάζει and συνωδίνει as well as the phrase ἄχρι τοῦ νῦν in Rom 8:22.

when its inhabitants, at least the righteous children of God, no longer die. This brings us to the echoes of lament by God's children.

Echoes of God's Children Groaning (Rom 8:23–25)

Creation is not the only one who anxiously groans in hope. Paul explains, "But not only this, but also we ourselves having the first fruits of the Spirit, we ourselves groan (στενάζομεν) in ourselves eagerly awaiting (ἀπεκδεχόμενοι) adoption, the redemption of our body" (Rom 8:23). The intensive pronouns and catchwords (στενάζω and ἀπεκδέχομαι) clearly indicate that Paul sees the children of God and creation as participating in the same lamenting actions.[21] Both cry out in hope, "For we were saved in hope (ἐλπίδι)" (Rom 8:24).[22] The substance of their hope is also the same, resurrection from the dead. Furthermore, the groaning of God's children also echoes the pattern of lament.

Like OT lamenters, and creation, God's children struggle with the relationship between the prior promise they heard and the pain they experience. The children's prior promise is undoubtedly found in the gospel of God that Paul preaches. For Paul, the message that Jesus was raised from the dead is at the same time a promise that those who believe in him will also be raised. Paul made this point earlier in the chapter, "But if the Spirit of the one who raised Jesus from the dead dwells in you, the one who raised Christ from the dead will also make alive your mortal bodies through the same Spirit who dwells in you" (Rom 8:11).[23] The children stand to inherit the same resurrection that Jesus experienced. As Paul puts it in 8:17, "But if children, we are also heirs; heirs of God and coheirs with Christ, if indeed we suffer with him (συμπάσχομεν) in order that we might also be glorified with him (συνδοξασθῶμεν)." The children must suffer with Christ, but that suffering comes with the promise of being glorified with Christ, or raised from the dead. Romans 7:7–25 and 8:12–17 indicate that the children suffer, at least in part, because of their ongoing struggle with sin in the body. Additionally, as we will discuss further below, the indication in 8:31–39 is that they are pained by the seeming absence/rejection of God. The ultimate solution is redemption from the body where are all of this pain transpires. The hope they have and the suffering they experience go hand in hand.

---

21. Cf. ἀπεκδέχομαι and συστενάζω in Rom 8:19, 22.

22 Cf. ἐλπίδι Rom 8:20. For a discussion regarding the interpretive options for ἐλπίδι, see Gieniusz, *Romans 8:18–30*, 200–202.

23 Cf. 1 Cor 6:14; 15:45.

The result of this tension, as is common in lament, is the cry of distress. In this instance, Paul describes the cry as "groaning." Once again, the use of στενάζω links the children's cry with that of creation, but it also echoes a few other OT lamenters. First, there are echoes of Israel's groaning in Egypt which I outlined above. They groaned because God promised them oppression for 400 years and freedom in Canaan, but they are languishing in Egypt.[24] In Romans 8:23–25, God's children have the promise of suffering with Jesus and being glorified with him, but they are currently languishing in Rome and elsewhere.[25] The tension between suffering and hope elicits the groan. Like Israel's groaning in Egypt, the children's groaning expresses pain and hope all at the same time. Neither reality is eclipsed by the other. That is not how the language of στενάζω works. Therefore, it is not appropriate to downplay the intensity of the suffering described in Romans 8:18–39 as commentators sometimes do.[26]

Second, Romans 8:23–25 also echoes individual laments in the OT.[27] I surveyed several of these already. Both Job and the Psalms of Lament describe figures who "groan" because what they hope for is not the reality the experience. Especially enlightening are some particular echoes of Job:

> Who were thrown out from the city and their own houses, and the great soul of the young children (νηπίων) groaned (ἐστέναξεν), but why does he not do visitation (ἐπισκοπήν). (Job 24:12)

> And because of every powerless one I wept, and I groaned (ἐστέναξα) having seen a man in distress. (Job 30:25)

The wider contexts of Job 24 and 30 contain further cries of distress that are echoed in Romans 8:23–25. Job complains that God allows the ungodly to afflict the needy without hindrance.[28] They are left without shelter and food. Job notes that the needy are forced to "lie down unjustly without clothing" (Job 24:10). The ungodly have thrown the needy out of their city and homes. They are hungry, thirsty, and naked; therefore, the children

---

24 See the previous discussion on Gen 15:13; Exod 2:23–24; 6:5.

25 This is not to suggest some kind of Exodus motif in Paul's thought here.

26 E.g., Moo, reflecting on Rom 8:18–30, notes "We must, Paul suggest, weigh suffering in the balance with the glory that is the final state of every believer; and so 'weighty,' so transcendently wonderful, is this glory that suffering flies in the air as if it had no weight at all." Moo, *Romans*, 511. Respectively, this kind of comment runs the risk of eclipsing the lament laden tenor of this section in the letter.

27 By "individual," I mean both lamenters who cry out for themselves and as representatives of others.

28 See e.g., Job 24:1–11. The needy in Job 24 include the poor, orphans, and widows.

(νήπιοί) groan (Job 24:12). The question that lingers is why God does not come to punish (ἐπισκοπή) those who afflict him.²⁹ In Romans 8:23–25, God's children (τέκνα) groan, because like the children in Job 24 they are afflicted, as indicated in Paul's catalogue of hardships in 8:31–39.³⁰ The echo from Job 24 indicates that the children in Romans 8 groan, because they are afflicted by sin and various forces. They too groan for God's ἐπισκοπή in which judgment will be doled out in the resurrection of the dead. They are like the orphans described in Job 24 who "eagerly await adoption (υἱοθεσία), the redemption of the body" (Rom 8:23).³¹ Similarly, in Job 30:9–31, Job complains that the ungodly have afflicted him. He focuses especially upon the pain within his body, "At night my bones have been burned up and my inward parts have broken up" (Job 30:17). Even more, Job holds God responsible for his condition (Job 30:19–23). He cries out that in the past he "groaned" for those who were powerless as he now finds himself. Once again, Job 30 anticipates the language of Romans 8:31–39 where suffering is linked to things such as hunger, nakedness, and enemies but ultimately to God's absence. The children groan to be vindicated before such enemies at the resurrection. Yet, there is another catalyst for the children's groaning besides the tension between the hope they have and the pain they experience. Paul points to that catalyst in 8:23 in the causal clause "because we having (ἔχοντες) the first fruits of the Spirit, we also groan in ourselves eagerly awaiting the adoption."³² It is the Spirit who also elicits the children's groaning.

Echoes of the Spirit Groaning (Rom 8:26–27)

We come now to the third participant in the laments of Romans 8:18–27, the Holy Spirit. Paul's use of OT lament is unique here. While two of the main participants in lament are normally the human "I" and the divine "You," in Romans 8:26–27 the Holy Spirit fills the first slot. The Spirit takes up the lament of the "I" or "we." In this context, the Spirit takes up the hopeful cry

---

29 On the use of ἐπισκοπή as indicating divine visitation and judgment, see Isa 24:22; 1 Pet 2:12. See also LEH 235.

30 The subject of στενάζομεν in Rom 8:24 is the "sons of God" or "children of God" mentioned in Rom 8:19, 21.

31 For Paul's other uses of υἱοθεσία, see Rom 8:15; 9:4; Gal 4:5; Eph 1:5.

32 The participle ἔχοντες is causal in its syntactical function. See, Schreiner, *Romans*, 438.

of creation and God's children. It is a cry that has OT echoes of its own.[33] Specifically, the Spirit's groaning echoes the "lament of the mediator."[34]

The Spirit's mediating function is indicated through two verbs in 8:26, "And likewise the Spirit helps (συναντιλαμβάνεται) in our weakness; for we do not know what we should pray as we ought to, but the Spirit himself intercedes (ὑπερεντυγχάνει) with inexpressible groaning." The verb συναντιλαμβάνομαι only occurs three times in the LXX.[35] The first of the three occurrences involve Jethro's advice to Moses that he should appoint elders who can help (συναντιλήμψονταί) settle minor disputes in the nation (Exod 18:22). The second use in Numbers 11:17 is especially interesting, "And I will go down and I will speak there with you and I will take from the spirit (πνεύματος) which is upon you and I will place it upon them and they will help (συναντιλήμψονται) with you the burden of the people, and you will not bear them alone." This instruction is God's response to Moses' cry regarding the people's request for meat. Moses' cry is riddled with questions indicative of lament:

> Why have you mistreated your servant, and why have I not found favor before you so as to place the rage of this people upon me? I did not conceive all these people in the womb, or did I bear them, that you say to me "Take him into your bosom, like a nurse lifts up the one who nurses, into the land, which you swore to their fathers?" From where is there meat for me to give to this people? For they cry out against me saying, "Give meat to us, in order that we might eat." I alone will not be able to bear this, because this matter is too burdensome for me. But if you do in this way to me, he will certainly kill me, if I have found mercy with you, in order that I might not see my affliction. (Num 11:11–15)

Moses would rather die than bear the burden of feeding meat to the entire nation. He laments the impossibility of the task. Part of God's response is that the spirit which is on Moses will be on the elders of Israel, so that he will not bear the burden alone. God also asks Moses, "Will the hand

---

33 The adverb ὡσαύτως in Rom 8:26 links the activity of the Spirit with the children of God in 8:23–25.

34 For a discussion of the mediator's lament, see chapter 2. As Westermann explains it, the mediator's lament "first appears in the lament of Moses, recurs in the lament of Elisha and reaches a high point in the lament (or confessions) of Jeremiah, which then in turn point to the songs of the Suffering Servant in Deutero-Isaiah." Westermann, "The Role of Lament," 34.

35 The rarity of συναντιλαμβάνομαι elsewhere increases the volume of the echo in Rom 8:26.

of the Lord not be sufficient? Now you will know if my word will overtake you or not" (Num 11:23).

The echoes of this narrative in Romans 8:26–27 revolve around the following: Moses' lament that he is weak, that he is faced with an impossible task, God's help through the spirit, and the announcement that God's word will not fail. For Paul, God's children face an impossible task of their own. They must suffer until the resurrection from the dead. Like Moses, they cry out, and they are helped through the work of the Spirit. Of course, the Spirit's work for the children of God in Romans 8 exceeds what Moses and the Israelites experience in Numbers 11. The Spirit will raise the children from the dead, lead them, put the deeds of sin within them to death, testify within them that they belong to God, and pray for them (Rom 8:9–17). The latter work is Paul's focus in 8:26–27. The Spirit helps (συναντιλαμβάνεται) in the children's weakness (ἀσθένια) and their specific weakness is that they do not know what (τί) to pray. They are groaning until the resurrection, but they do not know what they ought (δεῖ) to pray until that time. Therefore, the Spirit intercedes (ὑπερεντυγχανει) with "groaning" (στεναγμοῖς) of its own.

It is groaning that is ἀλαλήτος. This adjective has generated various proposals among interpreters.[36] Yet, this much is clear. Given the fact that both creation and the children groan, and that groaning is understood in light of OT lament, the Spirit's groaning should be interpreted in the same way. To this extent, ἀλάλητος includes a cry that pleads for the resurrection just as creation and the children of God do. Nevertheless, there is an element to the Spirit's cry, or groaning, that is inexpressible. It is unknown to creation and the children of God. There is a lament for the children that only the Spirit can utter, because "he intercedes (ἐντυγχάνει) for the saints according to God" (Rom 8:27). The interplay between hope and pain makes it impossible for creation and the children of God to pray, or more exactly lament, as they should. Circumstances arise that are inexplicable, as we shall see in Romans 8:31–39. In those moments, when the pain is most poignant, only the Spirit really knows how to cry out to God. That is because only the Spirit knows how God works the hope of the resurrection and present pain for the good of those who love him.

---

36. Käsemann proposed that it referred to *glossolia*. See Käsemann, *Perspectives on Paul*, 122–37. For a brief discussion of the various interpretations, see Crump, *Knocking on Heaven's Door*, 202–4; Schreiner, *Romans*, 444–45.

Hidden Deliverance For Those Who Groan (Rom 8:28–30)

The lament pattern reflected in 8:18–27 includes promise, suffering, and the cry of distress. Creation, the children of God, and the Spirit are all three involved in the interplay between the hope of the resurrection and present suffering. They groan for deliverance. In response, and in step with the OT lament pattern echoed throughout this section, Paul highlights a particular aspect of that deliverance which is intended to comfort those who groan.

Interpreters often point out that Paul is accentuating God's sovereignty here in a way that downplays the pain Paul has in view.[37] However, the echoes of lament in 8:18–27 and 8:31–39 indicate a more nuanced point. The response to the tripartite groaning of creation, God's children, and the Spirit is not merely that "God is in control." Instead, as often happens in OT lament, deliverance comes in the form of evoking the prior promise.[38] Not only does Paul evoke the prior promise of the gospel in 8:28–30. He explicates it in a way that does after all accentuate divine sovereignty but in a manner that is indissolubly bound up with lament. For Paul, God's sovereignty is not an abstract panacea for the pain which elicits groaning. Instead, those who groan find sovereign deliverance hidden in their pain and hope.

Paul follows his discussion of the Spirit's groaning by acknowledging what he and his readers already know, "And we know (οἴδαμεν) that all things (πάντα) work together for good for those who love God, for those who are called according to his purpose" (Rom 8:28). Paul's statement is often misunderstood and abstracted because of the failure to properly identify the referents of key expressions. They need to be identified in light of the motif of suffering which dominates Paul's wider argument. First, the referent of πάντα is the suffering that is explicitly mentioned in 8:17–18 (συμπάσχω; πάθημα) as well as the suffering that is implied in the groaning language and echoes of lament in 8:19–27.[39] Inferred from the prior promise of the gospel and yet hidden in present pain is the assurance that the outcome of such circumstances will be good. Second, such good (ἀγαθόν) is ultimately the resurrection and not some general notion of goodness. But the "good" only applies to those "who love God" and to those who are "called (κλητοῖς)

---

37. E.g., Calvin, commenting on Rom 8:29, notes "There is therefore no reason for us to be grieved, or to think it hard and grievous that we are afflicted, unless we disapprove of the Lord's election, by which we have been foreordained to life, and unless we are unwilling to bear the image of the Son of God, by which we are prepared for celestial glory." Calvin, *Romans*, 317.

38. On this feature of OT lament, see chapter 2.

39. I take πάντα to be the subject nominative in Rom 8:28 although some witnesses (e.g., P46, A, B) contain ὁ θεός. Either way, the sense of the statement is surely that God works all things for good. On this textual variant, see Schreiner, *Romans*, 455.

according to his purpose (πρόθεσιν)." The use of κλητός evokes statements from the letter's introduction where Paul refers to the Romans as those who are "called (κλητοί) of Jesus Christ" and "called saints (κλητοῖς ἁγίοις)" (Rom 1:6–7). In the phrase κλητοί Ἰησοῦ Χριστοῦ, the genitive noun is subjective so that it is Jesus who "calls" the Romans to salvation in the gospel.[40] Therefore, to be "called according to his purpose (πρόθεσιν)," is to be called to the salvation that is promised and accomplished in Christ but ultimately experienced in the resurrection of God's children. Third, the referent of πρόθεσις, just as with ἀγαθόν, is not some abstract, philosophical, or pragmatic notion of finding meaning to one's life. It refers to God's sovereign purpose of raising his children from the dead so that they might truly be conformed to the image of his Son (Rom 8:29).

In Romans 8:29–30, Paul continues to describe the sovereign nature of deliverance that is hidden in pain and for which creation, the children, and the Spirit groan. He essentially explains that those who are called to resurrection and groan for that moment already have it. This indicated in the conclusion of 8:30 "And those whom he justified, these he also glorified (ἐδόξασεν)." In moving towards that conclusion, Paul explicates the divine actions that precede it:

> For those whom he foreknew, he also predestined to be conformed to the image of his son, in order for him to be the firstborn (πρωτότοκον) among many brethren; and those whom he predestined, these he also called; and those whom he called, these he also justified; and those whom he justified, these he also glorified (ἐδόξασεν). (Rom 8:29–30)

Paul's theological vocabulary is obviously dense. God foreknows, predestines, justifies, and glorifies. Yet, it is the latter action that I want to highlight here, because I believe it hits on Paul's main focus in 8:17–30. We have established that everyone who groans in 8:19–27 groans because of the interplay between hope for the resurrection and the reality of pain. The tripartite groaning echoes the promise, suffering, and cry of the lament pattern. Moreover, the deliverance within that pattern must respond directly to the lamenters' cry, or groaning. Such a response is evident in the reference to Jesus as πρωτότοκος and the verb ἐδόξασεν. The children of God are already

---

40 Wallace does not consider the possibility of a subjective genitive reading in Rom 1:6. See Wallace, *Greek Grammar*, 127. However, κλητός definitely conveys a verbal idea. Either Jesus "calls" the Romans, or they are "called" by him just as Paul says he was "called" by God as an apostle which he received through Christ in Rom 1:1, 5 (genitive of agency). In either reading, Jesus is the one doing the calling. Cf. Rom 9:12; 1 Cor 1:24.

raised, or glorified (ἐδόξασεν), through Jesus the "first born" (πρωτότοκος) from the dead.[41] While they do not yet experience that resurrection, it is assured to them through the resurrection of Jesus which is proclaimed in the gospel. This is consistent with the experience of deliverance in the OT lament pattern. It comes in the form of evoking and explicating the promise as Paul does in Romans 8:28–30.

IDENTIFYING THE ECHOES OF LAMENT IN ROMANS 8:31–39

Clearly, a number of OT lament echoes are present in Romans 8:18–30 that have a significant impact on the way we interpret Paul's argument. As the argument continues, 8:18–30 and 8:31–39 are not only linked grammatically but also through echoes of lament.[42] The suffering underlying 8:31–39 is a concern with divine abandonment, or rejection. It is a concern that often arises when the activity of enemies goes unchecked by God. The lamenter begins to wonder and complain about divine rejection. This concern is echoed through Psalm 43:23 which is cited in Romans 8:36, "Just as it is written, 'On account of you we face death all day long, we were reckoned as sheep for slaughter.'" Some interpreters fail to appreciate the implications of this citation given the psalm's original context.[43] Therefore, we will assess the citation in light of its larger context in Psalm 43.

In OT lament, divine rejection often elicits complaints by God's people.[44] The cause and nature of the rejection varies, but it normally involves enemies and the result is consistently separation from God and the deliverance he supplies. Romans 8:31–39 contains various echoes of this lament motif, but the dominate echo emanates from Psalm 43 as we shall see.

Echoes of Enemies

The first lament echo in 8:31–39 can be heard in Paul's question "If God is for us (ὑπέρ ἡμῶν), who is against us?" (Rom 8:31). Paul's question echoes the lamenter's question in Psalm 55:5b "I hoped in God, I will not fear; what will flesh do to me?"[45] The implied answer to both questions is "no

---

41. Cf. Col 1:18.
42. The grammatical link in indicated in 8:31 through τί οὖν.
43. See e.g., Moo, *Romans*, 543–44.
44. On this issue, see chapter 2.
45. The same exact phrase occurs in Ps 55:12.

one." The psalmist is confident that God will not allow his enemies to harm him. Various references to enemy activity are scattered throughout Psalm 55 and include: trampling, warring, plotting evil, and lurching to attack.[46] Additionally, their affliction is "all day long" (ὅλην τὴν ἡμέραν) (Ps 55:2, 6). Nevertheless, the lamenter is resolved in his hope that God will both see his affliction and deliver him, "You have set my tears before you even as it is in your promise. My enemies will turn backwards, in whatever day I should call on you; behold I have known that you are my God" (Ps 55:9b–10). The psalmist is confident that God is on his side, or "for him," even as enemies assail him.

Paul's questions in Romans 8:33–34 also contain echoes of enemies common to OT lament:

> Who will bring a charge against (ἐγκαλέσει) God's elect?
>
> Who is the one who condemns (ὁ κατακρινῶν)?
>
> Who will separate (χωρίσει) us from the love of Christ?

It is not clear if Paul is describing specific people, but we do find these kinds of enemies in OT lament. The descriptions there shed light on the kinds of people Paul has in mind. We have discussed in previous chapters that enemies, especially those in the Psalms of Lament, falsely accuse the righteous in order to harm or even kill them. For example, the lamenter complains "For the mouth of the sinner and the mouth of the deceiver (δολίου) was opened against me, they spoke against me with a deceitful (δολίᾳ) tongue" (Ps 108:2). Similarly, in Psalm 30:19 the request is "Let the deceitful tongues (χείλη τὰ δόλια) be mute those who speak lawlessness against the righteous one (δικαίου) in arrogance and contempt."[47] The false accusations by the unrighteous are meant to bring condemnation upon the righteous. We find this aim in the complaint of Psalm 93:21, "They will hunt for the life of the righteous (δικαίου) and they will condemn (καταδικάσονται) innocent blood."[48] We see a similar aim by the enemies in Psalm 36:32–33, "The sinner observes the righteous one (δίκαιον) and seeks to kill him, but the Lord certainly shall not abandon him into his hands and he certainly shall not condemn (καταδικάσηται) him, whenever he should judge (κρίνηται) him." In this example, the enemies aim for the righteous to be condemned by God. That is the ultimate aim of their false accusations. Finally, the enemies' false accusations and condemnation result in

---

46 See Ps 55:2, 3, 6, 7.

47 Cf. Pss. Sol. 12:1.

48 The verb κατακρίνω used in Rom 8:34 and καταδικάζω in Ps 93:21 are in the same semantic domain. See LEH, 316; Louw-Nida, 56:1–56.38.

separation for the righteous. The separation can consist of distance between the righteous and his loved ones. We see this scenario in Psalm 68 where the lamenter complains that his enemies have dealt unjustly with him, even accusing him of stealing, "Those who hate me without cause have multiplied more than the hairs of my head, my enemies who pursue me unjustly have prevailed; things which I did not steal, then I would be paying for them" (Ps 68:5). The result is that the lamenter is separated from his loved ones, "I have been estranged (ἀπηλλοτριωμένος) from my brethren, and a stranger to the sons of my mother" (Ps 68:9).[49] A similar scenario in Psalm 21 results in the lamenter's separation from God, "Do not be far from me (μὴ ἀποστῇς), because tribulation is near, for there is no one who helps. Many bulls have surrounded me; they have opened their mouth against me like a lion who seizes and roars" (Ps 21:12–14). As I will discuss below, the echoes of Psalms 21 and 68 in Romans 8:33–34 indicate an echo of the crucifixion narrative.

Echoes of Divine Condemnation

Paul's question, "Who will separate us from the love of Christ?" is followed by a list of possibilities "Will tribulation or distress or persecution or famine or nakedness or danger or sword?" (Rom 8:35). The terms cataloged here include: θλῖψις, στενοχωρία, διωγμός, λιμός, γυμνότης, κίνδυνος, and μάχαιρα. Some interpreters, most notably Bultmann, have associated Paul's list with a Stoic *Peristasenkatalog* similar to those found in Epictetus and Seneca.[50] While Paul's list may parallel those penned by Stoic writers, the echoes in Romans 8:31–39 indicate that OT lament shapes Paul's thinking here. Specifically, the list of distressing experiences in 8:35 that threaten to separate God's elect from the love of Christ echo experiences in the OT often associated with divine condemnation.[51]

We begin with θλῖψις and στενοχωρία, two terms that should be read together since they appear as a pair elsewhere.[52] On the one hand, we do not want to over-interpret these two terms. They can be general descriptions of any number of distressing situations. Nevertheless, they are more

---

49 The term ἀπαλλοτριόω used in Ps 68:9 and χωρίζω in Rom 8:35 are in the same semantic domain. See LEH, 60, 671.

50 Fitzgerald notes, "Bultmann cited examples of Peristasenkataoge from Epictetus, Musonius Rufus, Horace, and Seneca, and pointed especially to Romans 8:35 as an example in Paul." Fitzgerald, *Cracks in an Earthen Vessel*, 11. For more on *Peristasenkataoge* in this portion of the letter, see chapter 9.

51 Two of the terms in 8:35, διωγμός and κίνδυνος, do not appear to echo a specific OT text as the other terms in the list do.

52 See e.g., Rom 2:9.

than generalities or allusions to Paul's apostolic suffering.⁵³ For example, the two terms appear together in Deuteronomy 28 and Isaiah 8 where God describes what awaits disobedient Israel:

> And you will eat the young of your womb, the meat of your sons and your daughters, as much as the Lord your God gave to you, in your tribulation (στενοχωρίᾳ) and in your distress (θλίψει), with which your enemy will afflict you. (Deut 28:53)⁵⁴

> And they will look downwards to the earth, and behold tribulation (θλῖψις) and distress (στενοχωρία) and darkness, constricting discomfort and darkness so as not to see. (Isa 8:22)

A common thread in the larger contexts of Deuteronomy 28 and Isaiah 8 is that God pours out tribulation and distress, because the people are disobedient to his law. The warning in Deuteronomy 28:15 is "And it will be that if you shall not listen to the voice of the Lord your God so as to keep and do all his commandments (πάσας τὰς ἐντολάς), as much as I am commanding you today, all these curses will come upon you and seize you." The author then lists a variety of curses that include two more terms found in Romans 8:35, λιμός and γυμνότης. They appear in one of the author's conclusions "And you shall serve your enemies, whom the Lord will send upon you, in famine (λιμῷ) and in thirst and in nakedness (γυμνότητι) and in abandonment of all things; and he will place an iron yoke upon your neck, until he should destroy you" (Deut 28:48). Similarly, in Isaiah 8:21 λιμός indicates divine condemnation, "And a harsh famine (λιμός) will come upon them." Therefore, in both Deuteronomy 28 and Isaiah 8 we find the infrequent combination of θλῖψις and στενοχωρία as well as other terms that appear in Paul's list.⁵⁵ This is not mere coincidence, but an indication that the volume of the echoes from these texts in Romans 8:35 is significantly high. We will return to the interpretive implications of these echoes in a moment.⁵⁶

---

53 E.g., Moo comments on Rom 8:35 noting "The list of difficulties that follows requires little comment, except to note that all the items except the last are found in 2 Cor 11:26–27 and 12:10, where Paul lists some of those hazards he himself has encountered in his apostolic labors." Moo, *The Epistle to the Romans*, 543.

54 See also Deut 28:55, 57.

55 The two terms appear together in the following LXX passages: Deut 28:53, 55, 57; Esth 1:1; Isa 30:6.

56 The noun ὁδός occurs three times and τρίβος once in these two verses thereby emphasizing the conduct or "way" of the people. Oswalt notes that words for "way" and "highway" are prominent throughout Isaiah. See Oswalt, *Isaiah*, 516.

The terms λιμός and μάχαιρα, also cited in Romans 8:35, echo other OT texts involving the revelation of divine condemnation. For example, the lamenter in Lamentations 2:21 complains, "They have fallen asleep in the street, young and old; my virgins and young men went into captivity; with sword (ῥομφαία) and famine (λιμῷ) you killed them, in the day of your wrath you mangled them, you did not spare." The speaker interprets the sword and famine of the Babylonians in Jerusalem as the revelation of God's wrath (ὀργή).[57] The pairing of sword and famine also occurs in Jeremiah's lament language:

> They lied to their own Lord and said, "These things are not; calamities will not come upon us, and we will not see sword and famine (μάχαιραν καὶ λιμόν)." (Jer 5:12)

> Behold I will visit them; their young men will be killed by the sword (μάχαιρᾳ), both their sons and daughters will die by famine (λιμῷ). (Jer 11:22)

In these examples, and elsewhere in Jeremiah, λιμός and μάχαιρα are paired together to express God's condemnation of his people.[58] There is no doubt that God ultimately stands behind such condemnation as punishment for his people's lawlessness. As God says through Jeremiah, "I will send famine (λιμόν) to them and death and the sword (μάχαιραν) until they should cease from the earth" (Jer 24:10). A similar ominous tone is struck in the announcement, "Upon every passage in the desert destroyers have come, the sword of the Lord (μάχαιρα τοῦ κυρίου) will devour from one end of the land to the other, there is no peace to all flesh."[59] Clearly, in Lamentations and Jeremiah, famine and sword signal God's condemnation of his people. They experience a lack of sustenance and violence at the hands of enemies, because God is condemning them for their lawlessness.

We will examine Romans 8:31–35 in light of the OT echoes below. It is sufficient to note here that five of the seven terms in Paul's list echo the same kinds of OT texts, namely those which interpret experiences of loss, violence, and hunger by God's people as an indication of divine condemnation. The connection between such experiences and divine condemnation is an underlying question that Paul addresses in Romans 8:31–35.

---

57 For a similar complaint about "hunger" and "sword" in the book, see Lam 4:9; 5:10.

58 See Jer 14:12, 16; 16:4; and 18:21.

59 On the tone of lament in Jer 12, see Baumgartner, *Jeremiah's Poems of Lament*, 86.

Echoes of Divine Rejection

The most definitive OT echo in Romans 8:31–39 is Paul's citation from Psalm 43:23, "On account of you we face death all day long, we were reckoned as sheep for slaughter." As we have discussed throughout this work, the interpretive significance of the citation can only be understood in light of its wider context. Psalm 43 is a classic lament that has received a great deal of attention from OT interpreters.[60] It contains a clear pattern and idiom of lament which I discussed in chapter 2. Here I want to focus on three features that are most pertinent to Romans 8:36: (1) the nature of the rejection in Psalm 43; (2) the reason for the community's rejection; and (3) the function of Ps 43:23 within the structure of the entire psalm.

By "nature of the rejection," I am referring to how the community reached the conclusion that God had rejected them. In short, their conclusion stems from the incongruence between the experience of past deliverance and present affliction at the hands of enemies. Psalm 43:1–9 praises both the report that God delivered Israel from its enemies in the past and that the current community had even experienced deliverance.[61] The lamenter confesses, "For you saved us from those who afflict us and you put to shame those who hate us" (Ps 43:8). Nevertheless, despite this confession, the lamenter abruptly shifts to the complaint "But now you have rejected (ἀπώσω) and put us to shame and you will not go out with our armies" (Ps 43:10).[62] The lamenter proceeds to complain about this rejection and request deliverance from 43:11 to the end of the psalm. The complaints and requests further indicate the nature of the community's rejection. It is defined by the thought that God handed the community over to its enemies for no apparent benefit to himself and through no fault of the community itself.[63] They are inexplicably and persistently taunted and accosted by their enemies.[64] Yet, the pain caused by enemies is secondary to the thought that God had rejected the community without cause.

Interpreters of Psalm 43 (44 MT) continue to debate the real cause behind the community's apparent rejection. The two major options are usually couched as either mystery or martyrdom. For example, Terrien concludes that the community's suffering in this psalm remains "a total

---

60 For recent treatments, see Basson, *Divine Metaphors*, 161–86; Melancthon, *Rejection by God*; Waltke, *The Psalms as Christian Lament*, 175–215.

61 There is no consensus on the historical circumstances underlying Ps 43. For a discussion of the issue, see Berlin, "Psalms and the Literature of Exile," 71–75.

62 Cf. Rom 11.1.

63 See Ps 43:13.

64 See ὅλην τὴν ἡμέραν in Ps 43:16.

enigma."⁶⁵ Contrastively, Kraus argues "Suffering comes to the community because it belongs to Yahweh. It is experiencing martyrdom."⁶⁶ However, these two views should not be separated from one another. The lamenter twice acknowledges that the community is suffering some kind of unspecified martyrdom, but that does not mute the lamenters' cries of distress (Ps 43:12, 23). The acknowledgment offers no real explanation as to why they are suffering martyrdom. That remains a mystery. The assumption would be that the community had disobeyed God. The lamenter's complaint about God "hiding," or "turning" (ἀποστρέφω) indicates divine rejection, "Why do you turn your face (τὸ πρόσωπόν σου ἀποστρέφεις), have you forgotten our poverty and affliction?" (Ps 43:25). As I have mentioned several times already, the "turning" of God's face evokes Deuteronomic warnings about what will happen when Israel breaks the covenant:

> I will be extremely angry with them in that day and I will leave them and I will turn my face (ἀποστρέψω τὸ πρόσωπόν μου) from them, and it will be a devouring, and many evils and tribulations will find him, and he will say in that day, "Because my Lord is not with me, these evils have found me. And I will certainly turn my face (ἀποστροφῇ ἀποστρέψω τὸ πρόσωπόν μου) from them in that day because of their wickedness, which they did, because they turned to strange gods." (Deut 31:17–18)

Yet, this warning does not explain the turning of God's face in Psalm 43. The lamenter insists on the community's innocence "All these things have come upon us, and we have not forgotten you and we did not mistreat your covenant" (Ps 43:18). Therefore, the turning of God's face, his rejection, at least in this instance, cannot be due to the community's violation of the Mosaic covenant. Moreover, if the lamenter really knew the reason for the rejection, he would strike a more penitential tone. Instead, we find complaints that God's rejection is inexplicable and pleas for him to deliver.

All this brings us back to the lamenter's complaint cited by Paul, "For on account of you we face death all day long, we have been reckoned as sheep for the slaughter" (Ps 43:23). Structurally, the complaint comes directly after the lamenter's confession that the community is innocent and the challenge that God "search these things out" (Ps 43:22). The initial ὅτι in verse 23 indicates an explanation of the lamenter's challenge. God should search and see that the community is innocent, because they are suffering as if they are his enemies. Specifically, they persistently (ὅλην τὴν ἡμέραν) face the prospect of death like sheep. They have been reckoned, or classed, as

---

65 Terrien, *The Psalms*, 360.
66 Kraus, *Psalms*, 448.

sheep for slaughter (πρόβατα σφαγῆς). The agent implied in the passive verb ἐλογίσθημεν is θεός. The complaint is not that others have counted the community as sheep but that God has. This is clear from Psalm 43:12, "You gave (ἔδωκας) us as sheep for eating (πρόβατα βρώσεως). The subject of ἔδωκας is clearly God. It follows then that he is also the implied agent of ἐλογίσθημεν in 43:23. God has inexplicably treated the community as his enemies by handing them over to military-political opponents. Indeed, as the emphatic position of ἕνεκα σοῦ indicates, God is ultimately responsible for the community's suffering. He has rejected (ἀπωθέω) them. That is why the request in 43:24 is "Be awakened; why do you sleep, Lord? Rise and do not reject (μὴ ἀπώσῃ) forever." This is the original context and function of Paul's citation.

READING ROMANS 8:31–39 IN LIGHT OF ITS ECHOES

This section of Paul's argument, like so many others in Romans, contains echoes of OT lament that impact our reading of the text. In this particular instance, the echoes indicate an underlying question or experience that Paul is addressing. It involves the possibility that God has rejected his elect given the fact that their enemies seek, without divine impediment, to condemn and separate them from God. Historically, Paul is probably not addressing one particular event.[67] Instead, the question of divine rejection arises through a broader reflection on the shared experiences of God's elect in Paul's day. It is quite probable that their pain would elicit questions, like the psalmist's, about whether or not God had rejected them. Therefore, his poetic words, especially in light of their OT echoes, are meant to reassure those who are suffering rather than triumphantly (ὑπερνικῶμεν) gloss over their pain, or minimize their affliction as a mere lesson about what to expect as the people of God. What I offer here aims to avoid those kinds of exegetical missteps by reading 8:31–39 in light of its OT lament echoes.

The Assurance of Love in Rejection (Rom 8:31–36)

As I mentioned already, the OT echoes in Romans 8:31–36 involve enemies, condemnation, and rejection. The specific scenario is that enemies falsely accuse the righteous in order that they might be condemned and rejected by God. The false accusers are unimpeded in their affliction of the righteous

---

67 Jewett points to the persecution suffered by Jewish Christians in Rome due to Claudius' edict. See Jewett, *Romans*, 546. However, Meeks points out that many Jews viewed Rome quite favorably, even as a "Protector," given the evidence from Josephus, Philo, and others. See Meeks, *The First Urban Christians*, 38.

which elicits the cry/question to God, namely "Why have you rejected us?" As we have seen, it is a scenario played out often in the Psalms of Lament.⁶⁸ It is also the scenario underlying Romans 8:31–36. To hear the echoes of that scenario, one must obviously give great attention to Psalm 43, but there are other echoes at work here as well. Paul responds to all of this by assuring the afflicted that God loves them in the crucified and risen Christ rather than rejects them.

Paul begins in 8:31 by drawing a conclusion from his previous discussion where he laid out the interplay between pain and the tripartite groaning for the resurrection of the dead, a hope grounded in God's hidden yet sovereign deliverance (Rom 8:28–30). Paul concludes that "If God is for us, who is against us?" (Rom 8:31). The paraphrase of the rhetorical question τίς καθ' ἡμῶν is not merely "Who really stands a chance against us?" Given the underlying scenario evoked from OT lament echoes, and the surrounding argument, the paraphrase is more accurately "If God has not rejected or condemned us, as evidenced by his work in Christ, who (τίς) really can do such a thing?" The interrogative τίς is a key catchword in this section.⁶⁹ Although the specific historical identity of the τίς might vary for Paul and his readers, the aim of the "τίς" is the same. Those who afflict the elect are like enemies in OT lament who attempt to accuse (ἐγκαλέω), condemn (κατακρίνω), and thereby separate (χωρίζω) them from God. Once again, there are a cluster of OT echoes in Paul's rhetorical questions marked by τίς. Each question marks a specific action of the enemies that is followed by an explanation of how God responds. The divine response is thoroughly grounded in the death and resurrection of Jesus Christ. That is in fact how Paul answers his initial query "If God is for us, who is against us?" He answers in 8:32 with another question "He who did not spare his own son, but handed him over for us all, how will he not also with him graciously give to us all things?" We will come back to this in a moment.

As noted above, the questions "Who will bring a charge against God's elect?" and "Who is the one who condemns?" evoke a number of OT lament echoes in which enemies hurl false accusations against the righteous and seek their condemnation.⁷⁰ The questions echo the lamenter's complaint and request that God would respond to them:

> They will hunt for the life of the righteous (δικαίου) and they will condemn (καταδικάσονται) innocent blood. (Ps 93:21)

---

68. See chapter 2.
69 It occurs four times in Rom 8:31–35.
70 See Pss 30:19; 93:21; 108:2.

> The sinner observes the righteous one (δίκαιον) and seeks to kill him, but the Lord certainly shall not abandon him into his hands and he certainly shall not condemn (καταδικάσηται) him, whenever he should judge (κρίνηται) him. (Ps 36:32–33)

In Romans 8:33–34, these complaints and requests are echoed by the elect as they suffer. Yet, Paul assures them of God's answer in his terse but theologically dense statements:

> God is the one who justifies. (Rom 8:33b)

> Christ Jesus is the one who died, but rather was raised, who also is at the right hand of God, who also intercedes for us. (Rom 8:34)

Cries against enemies who falsely accuse the elect and seek their condemnation are answered by the God "who justifies (ὁ δικαιῶν)" as well as the crucified and risen Christ "who intercedes (ἐντυγχάνει)" for the elect. God's justification or condemnation of the elect is not impacted by the false accusations hurled against them. Rather, God listens to Christ's intercession on behalf of the elect (ἐντυγχάνει ὑπὲρ ἡμῶν). When ἐντυγχάνει is rendered as "intercede," it tends to obscure the contrast Paul is drawing.[71] The enemies falsely accuse the elect, but Jesus "pleads" (ἐντυγχάνει) for them. Jesus' death and exalted position (raised to God's right hand) provide an assurance to the elect whose voice God will hear when it comes to their election or condemnation.[72] However, this does not answer the elect's underlying complaint entirely, as Romans 8:35–36 indicates.

Paul asks another question in 8:35, "Who will separate (χωρίσει) us from the love of Christ?" He expects the answer "no one." The verb χωρίζω is shorthand for the enemies' false accusations and condemnation that is thwarted by God in Christ. Their attempt to separate the elect from God fails. However, the OT echoes in Romans 8:35b–36 evoke further concerns about divine condemnation and rejection. Here the underlying question shifts from concerns over false accusations by enemies to God's inexplicable aloofness in the face of pain. As I explained above, the inexplicable condemnation is echoed in the items cataloged in Romans 8:35. In the OT, tribulation and distress, as well as the other five items listed in 8:35, are often indicators of God's judgment against his disobedient people. Paul's list echoes this divine action, particularly as it is discussed in Deuteronomy 28, Isaiah 8, and various passages in Lamentations and Jeremiah. Therefore,

---

71 See e.g., the renderings in ESV, NASB. See also BDAG, 341; Balz, "ἐντυγχάνω," in *EDNT* 3:461–62.

72 Cf. Rom 1:3–4; Heb 1:3.

if Paul and his readers are experiencing these things, it could indicate that they stand under God's judgment for disobedience. However, this would be entirely inexplicable, a thought echoed through Paul's citation of Psalm 43:23 in Romans 8:36.

The citation formula καθώς γέγραπται in 8:36 links the list of divine punishments to the psalmist's complaint "On account of you we face death all day long, we were reckoned as sheep for slaughter."[73] As we discussed already, in the broader context of Psalm 43, the psalmist's cry follows reflection on past deliverance (43:1–9), a complaint that God has rejected his people in war (43:10–17), and a protest that the people are innocent (43:17–22). For no apparent reason, and in contrast to his past saving work, God has handed them over to their enemies like sheep for the slaughter. In the psalms, sheep are either those whom God protects or those who are headed for death.[74] The latter applies in both Psalm 43 and Romans. The agent of the passive verb ἐλογίσθημεν is God in 43:23, and it is still God in Romans 8:36.[75] In short, the underlying concern of the elect, expressed through the OT echoes in 8:35–36, is that their tribulation and distress suggest God has rejected them. What else are they to conclude given the pain that they experience? Like the Israelite community in Psalm 43, the elect have a difficult time reconciling the prior promise of God's saving work in Christ with the seemingly divine rejection they now face. If they are in fact justified before God through Christ as the gospel promises, why has God rejected them as if they were his lawless enemies? If God handed Jesus over to death for the elect (Rom 8:32), why do the elect sense that God has handed them over like sheep to be slaughtered?

While this underlying question is never completely answered in Romans, Paul assures that no one can separate the elect from "the love of Christ" (Rom 8:36).[76] Unidentified enemies fail in their false accusations and their attempt to condemn the elect. Moreover, even what seems to be divine rejection in the vein of covenant curses and the complaints of Psalm 43 cannot separate the elect from Christ's love. The suffering is inexplicable, but the elect still overcome it as Paul explains in 8:37–39.

---

73 On Paul's citation formulas, see Watson, *Paul and the Hermeneutics of Faith*, 43–47.

74 Kuntz points to Pss 49:15; 74:1; 77:21; 78:52; 79:13; 80:2; 95:7; 100:3; 107:41; 114:4, 6. See Kuntz, "Growling Dogs and Thirsty Deer," 51.

75 Once again, for the divine agent in Ps 43:2 cf. 43:12.

76 We will return to this point in chapter 9.

The Assurance of Victory in the Face of Rejection (Rom 8:37–39)

The initial conjunction ἀλλά in Romans 8:37 indicates that Paul is drawing a contrast between the complaint that God has rejected his elect like sheep for the slaughter and their "super-triumph" in Christ.[77] Paul explains, "But in all these things we overwhelmingly conquer (ὑπερνικῶμεν) through the one who loved (ἀγαπήσαντος) us" (Rom 8:37). The referent of ἀγαπάω is the death of Jesus.[78] His death, propelled by love, provides the impetus for the emphatic nature of the victory indicated in ὑπερνικάω. It is a term that matches the cosmic scale of the forces that threaten to separate the elect from God's love in Christ.[79] The forces described in 8:37–39 are all created and controlled by God; therefore, the concern with divine rejection continues. Either the elect overcome these forces or they are overcome by them thereby separating them from God. If the latter occurs, it means God has rejected the elect, because he creates and controls such forces. Therefore, Paul assures them of their victory through God's love for them in Christ.

The forces in 8:37–39 make up four pairs of enemies who could potentially separate God's people from him: existence (life and death), supernatural agents (angels and rulers), time (things present and things to come), powers, and spatial dimensions (height and depth).[80] To reiterate, these forces could not oppose the elect unless God rejected them. The assurance of their acceptance by God is measured by whether or not these forces defeat them. Additionally, Paul's list echoes OT texts that describe God has having these forces under his control.

Paul begins the list with death and life: "For I am convinced that neither death (θάνατος) nor life (ζωή)" (Rom 8:37). Neither death nor life is able to separate the elect from God's love in Christ. Death is the "fiercest enemy of God," the "separator par excellence," and life is almost as wearisome.[81] Yet, as Israel's scriptures indicate, God controls both:

---

77 Seifrid reflects on Paul's use ὑπερνικάω and glosses Rom 8:37 as "Through 'the one who loved' we super-triumph'"; Seifrid, *Romans*, 637. Similarly, Jewett renders it as "supervictors." He points to uses in Greek literature that bear the sense of "crushing one's enemies completely." See Jewett, *Romans*, 548.

78 For the link between ἀγαπάω, or ἀγάπη, and Jesus' death, see e.g., Rom 5:8; 2 Cor 5:14; Gal 2:20; Eph 5:2.

79 On ὑπερνικάω, see BDAG, 1034; Bauernfeind, "νικάω, νίκη, νῖκος, ὑπερνικάω." *TDNT* 4:942–45.

80 The only force that is not paired with something else is δύναμις. It could be paired with "angels" and "rulers." Some interpreters lump these three together. See e.g., Schreiner, *Romans*, 465.

81 Stuhlmacher, *Paul's Letter to the Romans*, 140–41. Black, "Pauline Perspectives on Death," 429.

> Behold, behold because I am, and there is no God beside me; I will kill (ἀποκτενῶ) and I will give life (ζῆν ποίησω), I will strike and I will also heal, and there is no one who will deliver from my hands. (Deut 32:39)
>
> The Lord kills (θανατοῖ) and makes alive (ζωογονεῖ), he brings down to Hades and brings up. (1 Sam 2:6)[82]

This recognition is echoed in Romans 8:38. Since the believing community lives in a world subjected to futility and decay, God can use life or death to separate people from him.[83] Yet, Paul assures the elect that "through the one who loved" them they have overcome both.

Paul next pairs together angels and rulers, "For I am convinced that . . . neither angels (ἄγελλοι) nor rulers (ἀρχαί)" (Rom 8:38). The ἄγελλοι and ἀρχαί could refer to "fallen angels and principalities."[84] Paul frequently uses ἄγγελλος to refer to both godly and demonic agents.[85] He often employs ἀρχή to denote hostile spiritual forces.[86] The experience of angels and rulers who afflict the elect could have been felt through societal and political opposition.[87]

Yet, even then, Paul is clear about the forces that stand behind such entities.[88] There is no sharp bifurcation between political and spiritual forces in Paul's thought. Evil is at work in political leaders, but they remain unwitting servants of God.[89] In this context, angels and rulers are simply part of a pantheon of cosmic forces that God has at his disposal to reject his enemies. Again, Paul is convinced that the elect overcome this threat of rejection through the one who loved them.

The sequence of pairs is interrupted by the phrase δυνάμεις. The "powers" cannot separate the elect from the love of God present in the crucified Christ. Interpreters have struggled to explain why Paul places this lone term

---

82 See also Ps 67:21.

83 Cf. 1 Cor 15:54–57.

84. Stuhlmacher, *Paul's Letter to the Romans*, 141. For an alternative reading of the phrase "angels and rulers" in the Pauline corpus, see Carr, *Angels and Principalities*.

85 See e.g., 2 Cor 11:13; 12:17; Gal 1:8; 3:19; 4:14.

86 See e.g., Eph 3:10; 6:12; Col 1:16, 18; 2:15.

87 Jewett, *Romans*, 552.

88 See, e.g. 1 Cor 2:6–8; Col 2:15. For "angels" of nations, Keener points to the following: Dan 10:20–21; Deut 32:8 LXX; Jub 15:30–32; 1 En. 40:9; 61:10; 89:59—90:19; 1QM 14:15–16; 15:13—14; Mek. Shir. 2:112. He also notes texts that indicate "angels" over nature. See e.g. Jub 2:2; 1 En. 20:2; 60:12–22; 66:1–2; 2 En. 19:3–4; 1QM 10:11–12. See Keener, *Romans*, 113 fn. 57.

89 See Rom 13:1–6.

in the midst of so many pairs.⁹⁰ It is possible that the phrase should be read with "things present" and "things to come."⁹¹ However, a better explanation is found in the term's OT echoes. The use of δυνάμεις echoes two psalms:

> Bless the Lord all his angels (οἱ ἄγελλοι), the powers (δυνατοί) in strength doing his word so as to hear the voice of his words. Bless the Lord, all his powers (αἱ δυνάμεις), his servants (λειτουργοί) who do his will. (Ps 102:20-21)

> Praise him, all his angels (ἄγγελλοι); praise him, all his powers (δυνάμεις). (Ps 148:2)

Both psalms contain parallelisms involving ἄγελλοι and δυνατοί. The "angels" and "powers" are servants (λειτουργοί) who do what the Lord commands. They do his will (θέλημα). These echoes shed light on a few things in Romans 8:37-39. The seemingly misplaced δυνάμεις in 8:38 should probably be paired with "angels and rulers." Moreover, the echoes are commiserate with the underlying concern of the elect in Romans that God is inexplicably using various forces to reject them. Psalms 102 and 148 indicate that God commands these δυνάμεις, and the serve him in whatever way he directs them. Yet, Paul assures the elect that, despite all appearances, God's rejection manifested through the δυνάμεις that serve him has been overcome through the love of God in Christ.

Paul continues with his pairs explaining "neither things present nor things to come" can separate the elect from God's love in the crucified Christ. Interpretive suggestions for ἐνεστῶτα and μέλλοντα include "astrological powers" and "the power of the present age in contrast to a future utopia."⁹² However, given the lament echoes we have been examining, the ultimate sense of the phrases is that neither the affliction presently caused by enemies (political, spiritual, etc.) nor the affliction they will perpetrate can cause separation. We are helped by Paul's use of the same phrases in 1 Corinthians 3:22-23, "Whether Paul or Apollos or Cephas, whether the world or life or death, whether things present (ἐνεστῶτα) or the things to come (μέλλοντα); all things are yours, and you are of Christ, and Christ is of God." In Christ, all things belong to the Corinthians, even "things present" and "things to come." The sense is the same in Romans 8:38. The very things that could presently, or in the future, separate the elect from God actually

---

90 Interpreters have explained the insertion of δυνάμεις as an "emendation," an "afterthought," or "spontaneous dictation." See e.g., Jewett, *Romans*, 552.

91 Weiss, *Der Brief an die Römer*, 388. As noted by Jewett, *Romans*, 553.

92 See Barrett, *1 Corinthians*, 174; Jewett, *Romans*, 553; Schlier, *Der Römerbrief*, 280.

belong to the elect. Even if they do not experience such control over those things, the promise in Christ remains.[93]

The final pair is "neither height (ὕψωμα) nor depth (βάθος) ... will be able to separate us." Paul likens the threat of separation to diametrically opposed spatial dimensions.[94] Some have suggested that the contrast between ὕψωμα and βάθος signals "astrological fates" or forces.[95] However, the terms are better understood as spatial metaphors related to the created order.[96] There is no place that God has created, from the greatest height to the lowest depth, which results in separation from his love. We can hear an echo of certain Psalms of Lament where divine rejection is expressed as locative separation from God:

> Look, Lord, do not be silent, Lord, do not draw away (ἀποστῇς) from me. (Ps 34:22)
>
> Do not abandon me, Lord; my God, do not draw away from me. (Ps 37:22)[97]

Paul's underlying concern with divine rejection echoes the psalmist's spatial metaphor. Yet, we can also hear an echo of the psalmist who, like Paul, is certain about God's presence even in the remotest parts, "If I should go up to heaven (εἰς τὸν οὐρανόν), you are there; if I should go down to Hades (εἰς τὸν ᾅδην), you are present" (Ps 138:8). There is no place created by God where the elect will be separated from his love.

Paul closes his assurance with "nor any other created thing (τις κτίσις ἑτέρα) will be able to separate us from the love of God which is in Christ our Lord." The phrase τις κτίσις ἑτέρα accentuates the fact that every item listed in 8:38–39 is something God created and thereby placed under his control. They are created things that he could use to punish and separate the elect from him. Yet, Paul assures the elect that they have more than triumphed (ὑπερνικῶμεν) over the threat of separation "through the one who loved us." Therefore, the elect's suffering, though ultimately left unexplained, should not be interpreted as inexplicable rejection. The death and resurrection of

---

93 As Witherington puts it, "Since all things are now Christ's, in him they belong to believers as well, though at present this is so mainly in principle, and only in part is it a present experience." Witherington, *Conflict & Community in Corinth*, 135.

94 Paul uses similar spatial dimensions in Eph 3:18 where he also includes "width and height." Arnold suggests that the four dimensions could indicate a concern with supernatural powers connected to the practice of magic. However, this does not seem to be applicable to Rom 8:39. See Arnold, *Ephesians*, 216.

95 Jewett, *Romans*, 553.

96 Schreiner, *Romans*, 465.

97 See also Pss 9:22; 21:2; 79:19.

Christ, God's love, is the assurance of victory in the face of what seems to be divine rejection.

SUMMARY

Romans 8:18–39 is saturated with OT lament echoes that add depth of meaning to Paul's argument. We have seen that στενάζω, as well as its cognates, is a catchword that links the thought of 8:18–27 together. Creation, God's children, and the Holy Spirit "groan" for the same hope, namely the resurrection of the dead. The interplay between this hope and the experience of pain elicits a groan which in turn echoes an entire matrix of OT lament texts where creation, God's people, and various intercessors/mediators cry out to God. Romans 8:19–22 echoes a combination of texts from Genesis, Isaiah, Jeremiah, and Ecclesiastes that provide the background story as to why creation groans and how such groaning should be understood. In short, creation groans because it is cursed to futility. The futility is reflected in the fact that creation outlives it inhabitants. Yet, creation also has the hope that God's children will be raised from the dead thereby ending its futility. This interplay between pain and hope is why creation groans like an expectant mother whose pain in childbirth is only eclipsed by the new life she brings forth. God's children also join in this groaning, and their groans echo a number of OT lament texts as well. Israel's groaning in Egypt (Exod 2), as well as the Psalms of Lament and Job are especially prominent. Like creation, the children also hope for resurrection of the dead. Yet, their suffering has the tendency to weaken their ability to groan/lament/pray in the way they should. That is why the Holy Spirit joins in the groaning. The Spirit can help through groaning according to God's will even though such things are veiled to his children. Despite the implicit mystery in the Spirit's groaning, Paul does answer the tripartite groaning of 8:18–27 with a densely packed assurance that God's deliverance is hidden but certain in Christ.

Paul's assurance in 8:28–30 is followed by his poetic doxology in 8:31–39 which contains an underlying question about God's rejection of his elect. The echoes from Psalm 43 and a slew of other OT texts evoke a complaint that the elect take up, because they are afflicted by unidentified enemies. The nature of the pain could be interpreted as divine rejection. Paul catalogs a number of items that Israel's scriptures associated with God's condemnation against the unrighteous. Such condemnation would be inexplicable to the elect, and the citation from Psalm 43:23 articulates the elect's complaint that God has unjustly handed them over to be slaughtered. Yet, Paul gives the assurance throughout 8:31–39 that God has not condemned or rejected them.

The elect cannot be separated from God by enemies or forces that he could employ to reject them. His assurance is continually grounded in the death, resurrection, and exaltation of Christ. However, Paul's doxology of assurance still does not answer all lingering doubts about divine rejection. As we will see in the next chapter, the lament echoes in Romans 9:1–5 indicate an ongoing concern about Israel's unbelief and God's inexplicable rejection of his people.

7

The Gospel as the Answer to Israel's Intercessory Lamenter (Romans 9:1—11:36)

FOR ALL OF THE assurance that Paul offers in Romans 8:31-39 regarding inexplicable rejection by God, he strikes an equally dramatic, though starkly different, tone in 9:1-5. Paul's grief for Israel is undeniable. The echoes of lament in 9:1-5, and throughout chapters 9-11, indicate how profoundly Israel's unbelief hurts Paul. Their unbelief points to yet another underlying question about God's inexplicable rejection. Paul answers those questions in Romans 9-11, and the echoes of OT lament present in these chapters have a number of interpretive implications for the answer he provides.

The thesis of this chapter is that when we read Romans 9-11 in light of its OT lament echoes we find that Paul sounds like an intercessory lamenter who receives a response to his cry of distress. His cry in Romans 9:1-3 echoes Moses' request in Exodus 32 that he be blotted out of the book of life if God had in fact rejected his people. Just as Moses received a response focused on the hiddenness of God's ways, Paul does as well.[1] Romans 9:6—11:32 lays out this response that effectively answers Paul's cry. The divine answer is so overwhelming to Paul that by the end of it his cry of distress has turned to praise (Rom 11:33-36). In this way, the entire structure of Romans 9-11 is shaped by the five-fold pattern of lament that we have discussed throughout this work.[2]

---

1. With respect to "hiddenness" in Rom 9-11, I am following Seifrid at many points. See, Seifrid, *Christ Our Righteousness*, 151-69.

2 The influence of the Psalms of Lament on the structure of Rom 9-11 has not been

We will begin by analyzing the lament echoes in Romans 9:1–5 where Paul cries out over Israel's unbelief. We will then assess the answer to Paul's cry in 9:6—11:32. Naturally, special attention will be given to the various echoes contained in this section. Finally, we will consider 11:33–36 in light of its echoes and its function as the culminating piece of the lament pattern. It should be noted that, unlike in previous chapters, I will combine the discussion on the identification of the echoes and their impact on reading this portion of the letter rather than separate them.[3]

IDENTIFYING AND READING THE ECHOES OF LAMENT IN ROMANS 9:1–5

The prayer report in Romans 9:1–3 is especially jarring to the reader, particularly in light of the immediately preceding doxology in 8:31–39 where Paul spoke so assuredly about not being separated from the love of God (ἀπό τῆς ἀγάπης τοῦ θεοῦ).[4] Paul briefly describes what he often prays:

> I speak the truth in Christ, I do not lie, while my conscience testifies in me in the Holy Spirit, that great grief (λύπη) and unceasing pain (ὀδύνη) is in my heart. For I myself was wishing (ηὐχόμην) to be accursed from Christ (ἀνάθεμα ἀπὸ τοῦ Χριστοῦ) for my brethren my fellow kinsmen according to the flesh. (Rom 9:1–3)

The language of the prayer report speaks to the depth of Paul's distress. It is also language that echoes OT lament on a few different levels. First, the phrase "great grief and unceasing pain is in my heart" echoes a classic psalm of lament. Second, Paul's request to be "accursed from Christ" echoes Exodus 32:32 and the larger narrative of 32–34 in which Moses intercedes on behalf of Israel. We will look at each of these in turn.

Echoes of Pain in the Heart

The phrase ὀδύνη καρδία in Romans 9:3 signals an echo from one of the classic Psalms of Lament, Psalm 12.[5] This psalm stands out in part, because the

---

entirely lost on interpreters. See e.g., Hays, *Echoes of Scripture*, 64; Wallace, *Election of the Lesser Son*, 235.

3 The large swath of verses being covered requires a more compact approach.

4 Once again, on the distinction between Paul's prayers and prayer reports, see Wiles, *Paul's Intercessory Prayers*.

5. See Janowski, "Das verbogene Angesicht Gottes," 25–53.

question "how long," a classic idiom of lament, occurs four times in quick succession:

> How long (ἕως πότε), O Lord, will you forget me forever? How long (ἕως πότε) will you turn your face from me? How long (ἕως πότε) will I set counsel in my soul, having sorrows in my heart (ὀδύνας ἐν καρδίᾳ) all day long? How long (ἕως πότε) will my enemy be exalted over me? (Ps 12:2–3)

As we discussed in chapter 2, the question ἕως πότε functions as both a complaint and request. What the lamenter really wants is for God to bring an end to his or her pain. We see other classic complaints here as well such as "will you forget me forever" and "how long will you turn your face from me?" The former question is an embedded petition for God to "remember" what he promised, and the latter is an idiom that contains another layer of intertextual echoes.[6] Specifically, as we have already seen, the turning of God's face echoes the Deuteronomic warnings about breaking the law and or suffering caused by God's inexplicable rejection of his people.[7] In this instance, as Terrien notes, the psalmist "reveals no sense of guilt that might have caused God's withdrawal."[8] It is not clear why God has withdrawn his favor and protection, or "turned his face." What is clear is that the psalmist is assailed by enemies, but God has inexplicably withdrawn from him.[9] The pain of the situation is felt "in the soul" and "in the heart." Such expressions point to thoughtful reflection on God's inexplicable rejection that is distressing to the mind and psyche of the lamenter. Despite such mental anguish, Psalm 12 ends with praise in the lamenter's heart "But I have hoped in your mercy, my heart (ἡ καρδία μου) will rejoice in your salvation" (Ps 12:6).

When we test the echo of Psalm 12 in Romans 9:1–5, a few things stand out. First, the volume of the echo is indicated through the phrase ἀδιάλειπτος ὀδύνη τῇ καρδίᾳ μου. It echoes the psalmist's complaint ὀδύνας ἐν καρδίᾳ μου ἡμέρας (Ps 12:3). The dative phrases are the same, and the psalmist's ἡμέρας is replaced with ἀδιάλειπτος. The latter phrases indicate the constancy of the speaker's internal pain. Next, there is thematic coherence between the two passages. The psalmist complains about God's inexplicable rejection, a rejection described as divine forgetfulness and the turning of God's face (Ps 12:2). The larger context of Romans 9–11 also contains the

---

6 See chapter 2.
7 See e.g., Deut 31:17, 18, 20; Ps 43:25.
8 Terrien, *The Psalms*, 160.
9 See Ps 12:3–5.

theme of inexplicable divine rejection. This theme can be heard in various statements scattered throughout the section:

> But it is not as though the word of God has failed. (Rom 9:6)
>
> What will we say to these things? There is not unrighteousness with God is there? (Rom 9:14)
>
> Therefore I say, God did not reject his people whom he foreknew did he? (Rom 11:1)

Obviously, these statements and questions arise in the course of Paul's larger argument. The point here is that the larger discussion about inexplicable divine rejection is already evoked in Romans 9:1–5 through the echo of Psalm 12. Finally, the echo from Psalm 12 illuminates the surrounding discourse by providing insight into the severity and nature of Paul's pain. Once again, the larger context of Psalms 12 shows that the pain in the lamenter's heart arises from God's inexplicable rejection as enemies assail him without hindrance. Nevertheless, the psalm ends with praise for God's mercy just as Paul will do.

When we read Romans 9:1–5 in light of the echoes from Psalm 12, we catch a glimpse of what Paul might have actually prayed regarding his kinsmen according to the flesh.[10] Paul acknowledges that he prays (ηὐχόμην) for his fellow Israelites, and it is clear that he requested to be separated from Christ on their behalf.[11] Yet, as is often the case in Paul's letters, we do not hear the actual content of his prayer. This is where the echo from Psalm 12 fills in the gap. As Paul reflects upon the interplay between Israel's continuous rejection of the gospel and God's prior promises, it is quite possible that he might have prayed like the psalmsit:

> How long, O Lord, will you forget me forever? How long will you turn your face from me? How long will I set counsel in my soul, while pain is in my heart all day? How long will my enemy be exalted over me? (Ps 12:2–3)

Such questions evoke the very prior promise that Paul wrestles with in Romans 9–11. The question "How long, O Lord, will you forget me forever?" is an embedded request for God to "remember" what he promised his people.[12] He promised to deliver them, and the lamenter wants God to act on that

---

10 See Crump, *Knocking on Heaven's Door*, 221.

11 The imperfect ηὐχόμην indicates Paul's customary prayer for his kinsmen. On the customary imperfect, See Wallace, *Greek Grammar*, 548.

12 On the petitionary aspect of the complaint in lament, see chapter 2.

promise.¹³ In the same way, Paul acknowledges that he prays for Israel's salvation in Romans 10:1, "The desire of my heart and prayer (δέησις) to God for them is for their salvation (σωτηρίαν)?" Additionally, the echo of "how long" also speaks to Paul's complaint/request about the duration of Israel's rejection. The answer to this question is heard later in Romans 11:25, "until (ἄχρι) the fullness of the Gentiles might enter in." It is then that Israel will finally experience God's prior promise to deliver them, because "the gifts and calling of God are irrevocable" (Rom 11:29). It is a promise that Paul hears in both Isaiah and Jeremiah:

> And in this way all Israel will be saved, just as it is written, "The deliverer will come from Zion, he will turn away ungodliness from Jacob. And this is the covenant from me with them, whenever I might take away their sins." (Rom 11:26–27)¹⁴

The Isaianic promise to "take away" Israel's sins explains how the enemies in Psalm 12 work in Paul's lament. Psalm 12:3 and 12:5 complain about political-military enemies. Yet, for Paul, the complaint is against the enemy of sin that continues to afflict his kinsmen.

Moses as Intercessor in Context

There is another lament echo that fills in the gap of what Paul prayed on behalf of his fellow Israelites. It is an echo that speaks to the depth of Paul's pain for Israel and the lengths he was willing to go to for their salvation.¹⁵ The specific echo comes from Exodus 32:32, and it is "loudest" in Romans 9:3:

> And now if you will forgive their sin, forgive; but if not, wipe me (ἐξάλειψον) out from your book, which you wrote.
>
> For I myself was wishing to be accursed (ἀνάθεμα) from Christ from my brothers my fellow kinsmen according to the flesh.

A number of interpreters have noted the connection between these two prayers.¹⁶ However, the echo of Moses' request in Romans 9:3 is not

---

13 This is clear in Ps 12:6, "But I hoped in your mercy, my heart will exalt in your salvation (σωτηρίῳ)."

14 Paul's citation in Rom 11:26–27 comes from Isa 27:9, 59:20; Jer 31:33.

15. On Paul's intercessory prayer language in general, see Longencker, "Prayer in the Pauline Letters," 205.

16 See e.g., Abasciano, *Paul's Use of the Old Testament in Romans 9.1–9*, 45–146; Dunn, *Romans 9–16*, 525; Jewett, *Romans*, 560–61; Lohse, *Der Brief an die Römer*,

limited to the prayer in Exodus 32:32. Instead, through the echo of Exodus 32:32, the larger narrative of Exodus 32–34 is evoked. Here we find further elements of lament that also illuminate Paul's prayer report and the rest of Romans 9–11.[17]

Moses' intercessory cry of distress in Exodus 32:32 is not the only such cry in the narrative. There are actually multiple intercessory cries that need to be assessed in light of the events surrounding them. First, Moses is distressed and cries out about God's wrath that threatens to destroy Israel.[18] His wrath stems from the nation's idolatrous act of fashioning and worshipping a golden calf (Exod 32:1–6). Aaron, who directed the fashioning of the calf, even credited it with delivering Israel from Egypt, "These are your gods (οἱ θεοί σου), Israel, who brought you up out the land Egypt" (Exod 32:4). Consequently, God threatens to destroy the nation telling Moses "And now, let me alone and having been greatly angered against them I will destroy them and make you into a great nation" (Exod 32:10). Moses responds with a cry of distress:

> And Moses prayed before the Lord God and said, "Why, O Lord, are you exceedingly angry against your people, who you brought out from the land of Egypt by great strength and by your exalted arm? Lest the Egyptians speaking might say, 'With wickedness he brought them out in order kill them in the mountains and to destroy them from the earth.' Cease the wrath of your anger and be merciful upon the wickedness of your people remembering Abraham and Isaac and Jacob your servants, to whom you swore against yourself and you spoke to them saying, 'I will surely multiply your seed like the stars of heaven in multitude, and all this land,' which you said you would give to your descendants, and they will possess it forever." (Exod 32:11–14)

Moses' cry is mixed with complaint and request. His question as to "why" the Lord is angry actually imbeds the request "Do not be angry with them," something he explicitly asks for later in the prayer. He grounds the

---

266–67; Sanday and Headlam, *A Critical and Exegetical Commentary*, 229; Stuhlmacher, *Paul's Letter to the Romans*, 145. Bratsiotis suggests that Rom 9:3 alludes to Mordecai's prayer in Esth 4:17d. See, Bratsiotis, "Eine Exegetische Notiz zu Rom. IX 3 and X.1," 299–300.

17 For Exod 32–34 as a distinct unit, see Davidson, *The Courage to Doubt*, 69–79; Wildmer, *Moses, God, and the Dynamics of Intercessory Prayer*, 89–225.

18 As Moberly explains, "It was this, as a basic part of the covenant relationship, that was jeopardized by Israel's sin, and it is for this that Moses urgently pleaded, that despite the people's sin Yahweh should yet go with the people in a movable shrine and be present in their midst." Moberly, *At the Mountain of God*, 110.

request for mercy (ἵλεως γενοῦ) in an appeal to God's reputation and remembrance of his prior promise. If God destroys Israel, the Egyptians will accuse him of wickedness. Moreover, Israel's destruction would mean that he had failed in his promise to the patriarchs. Moses specifically points to the promise of multitudinous descendants and a permanent land to dwell in.[19] As a result of Moses' intercession, the narrator tells us "The Lord was favorably inclined/propitiated (ἱλάσθη) about the evil, which he said he was going to do to his people" (Exod 32:14).[20] Moses' intercession somehow assuages God's wrath, though not entirely. As we see in 32:15-29, Moses also acts as an agent of God's wrath in slaying more than 3,000 Israelites with the help of the Levites.

Moses' second intercessory cry arises in Exodus 32:32. He informs the Israelites that he is going to intercede for them before God, "You have sinned greatly; and now I will go up to God, in order that I might propitiate (ἐξιλάσωμαι) for your sin" (Exod 32:30). Just as with the first cry of distress, Moses sees his intercessory task as propitiating (ἐξιλάσκομαι) God's wrath, or turning God's favor towards his people.[21] Moses confesses the nation's sin, and requests their forgiveness. His prayer is especially dramatic "And now if you will forgive their sin, forgive; but if not, wipe me out (ἐξάλειψόν) from your book, which you wrote" (Exod 32:32). Moses' request ἐξάλειψόν με is usually understood in one of two ways. Either Moses is offering himself in place of Israel, or he truly wants to perish with Israel if God will not forgive them.[22] The former interpretation is supported by the propitiatory terms (ἱλάσκομαι and ἐξιλάσκομαι) in Exodus 32:14 and 32:30 used to describe what Moses attempts in his intercession. However, if that attempt fails, it seems probable that Moses would rather perish with them than go on without them. Such a disposition is already evident in the fact that Moses rejects God's proposal to make him "into a great nation" (Exod 32:10). Therefore, the meaning behind Moses' request ἐξάλειψόν με is that he wants to offer himself in place of Israel, but if that fails he wants to perish with them. Either way, Moses expresses a willingness "to be cut off from his relationship with YHWH and thus would subject himself to curse and eventual death."[23] Of course, God's response indicates that such matters are ultimately out of Moses' hands, "If anyone has sinned before me, I will wipe

19 Cf. Gen 12:1-3.

20 The verb ἱλάσκομαι, in the passive voice, can bear the sense of be 'be merciful' or 'be propitious.' See LEH, 287.

21 Cf. use of ἱλάσκομαι in Exod 32:14.

22 On these interpretive options, see Davidson, *The Courage to Doubt*, 73; Widmer, *Moses*, 131-34.

23 Widmer, *Moses*, 130.

him out (ἐξαλείψω) from my book" (Exod 32:33). God will lead Israel as he promised, but he will also pour out his wrath on them in whatever day he visits (Exod 32:34–35).

The third intercessory cry arises after the golden calf incident and as Israel continues its trek to Canaan. Moses is concerned that God's presence will not go with them. He cries:

> Behold you say to me, "Bring up this people"; but you have not shown me whom you will send with me; but you said to me, "I know you more than all, and you have favor with me." Therefore, if I have found favor before you, reveal (ἐμφάνισον) yourself to me that I might clearly see, in order that I might find favor before you, and in order that I might know that this great nation is your people (Exod 33:12–13).

The cry continues after God promises to go before (προπορεύσομαί σου) the people (Exod 33:14). Moses prays:

> If you yourself certainly shall not go, do not bring me up from here. And how will it truly be known that I have found favor with you, both I and your people, unless you will go with us? And both I and your people will be glorified more than all the nations, as many as are upon the earth. (Exod 33:15–16)

Moses is once again willing to forfeit a great deal for the sake of the nation.[24] He would rather forego entrance into Canaan than go without God's presence. Moreover, Moses complains that God's absence in Israel would result in a lack of δόξα before other nations. The nations would not know that Israel had found favor with God; therefore, the prior promise to Israel would fail. This is another appeal to God's divine reputation.[25] If his people are not glorified through God bringing them into Canaan, God will not be glorified as the one who brought them out of Egypt and into the land he first promised to Abraham.[26] After God responds again, Moses asks to see his glory, presumably as confirmation of the promise (Exod 33:18). God reveals only a glimpse of his glory (Exod 33:19–23).

---

24. Cf. Exod 32:11–14, 32.

25. Cf. Exod 33:12.

26. The only uses of ἐνδοξάζω in the book are Exod 14:14, 17, 18; 33:16. The subject in the uses from Exod 14 is God, and it is related to God being glorified through his defeat of Pharaoh.

Echoes of Moses' Intercession in Romans 9:1–5

When we return to Romans 9:1–5, Paul's prayer report is now illuminated by Moses' three cries of distress and the larger narrative in Exodus 32–34. Moses' cries and willingness to suffer loss for Israel sheds light on what Paul means when he says "For I myself was wishing to be accursed from Christ (ἀνάθεμα ἀπὸ τοῦ Χριστοῦ) for my brethren my fellow kinsmen according to the flesh" (Rom 9:3). When we read the phrase ἀνάθεμα ἀπὸ τοῦ Χριστοῦ in light of its echoes from Exodus 32–34, a number of interpretive questions are answered.

First, the echoes from Exodus 32–34 help answer the question "Why is Paul so grieved in his heart?" The answer involves more than the fact that so many of his kinsmen were without salvation through faith in the gospel, something that clearly bothers Paul (Rom 10:1). It is the implications of this reality, implications that can be heard in the echoes from Exodus 32–34. As noted above, in his cries of distress, Moses attempts to assuage God's wrath against Israel by appealing to his divine reputation and prior promises. If Israel is destroyed, God's prior promises fail and his divine reputation is sullied before the nations. Paul has the same concerns. His prayer report is immediately followed by the assertion, "But it is not as though the word of God has failed" (Rom 9:6). Later, in Romans 11:1, Paul asks rhetorically "God did not reject his people did he?" Both statements point to an underlying concern with God's prior promise. Just as God responded to Moses when he appealed to the prior promise, Paul's argument throughout Romans 9–11 represents a similar response. However, the implications of Israel's rejection go beyond what is echoed from Exodus. Paul is also grieved by the fact that the resurrection of the dead is indissolubly linked to Israel's acceptance. He explains, "For if their rejection (ἀποβολή) is the reconciliation of the world, what will their acceptance (πρόσλημψις) be if not life from the dead?" (Rom 11:15). As we saw in the previous chapter, the hope for the resurrection of the dead lies at the heart of everyone's suffering. In summary, Paul is grieved by Israel's rejection, the impact of that rejection on the hope of the resurrection, and the impact of both on God's reputation.

Next, the echoes from Exodus 32–34 help answer the questions "What does Paul ask on behalf of Israel, and what is he willing to do on their behalf?" Here we are helped a great deal by the specific requests Moses makes. Once again they are:

> Cease the wrath of your anger and be merciful upon the wickedness of your people. (Exod 32:12)

> And now if you will forgive their sin, forgive; but if not, wipe me out (ἐξάλειψόν) from your book, which you wrote. (Exod 32:32)
>
> Therefore, if I have found favor before you, reveal (ἐμφάνισον) yourself to me that I might clearly see, in order that I might find favor before you, and in order that I might know that this great nation is your people. (Exod 33:13)
>
> If you yourself certainly shall not go, do not bring me up from here. (Exod 33:15)

In short, Moses asks for God to be merciful to disobedient Israel. He is willing to sever his relationship with God, even forego entrance into the promise land, and face divine wrath for/with Israel. Yet, he wants know that God has indeed heard his prayer. This fills in the gap for what we lack in Paul's prayer report. His request and willingness echoes that of Moses, and it is abbreviated in the expression ἀνάθεμα ἀπὸ τοῦ Χριστοῦ. To be "accursed from Christ," is tantamount to being wiped out from God's book.[27] As Jewett notes, "To pray to be ἀνάθεμα is an apt expression of being blotted out of the book of life."[28] Paul's use of ἀνάθεμα, as elsewhere in his writings, signals divine judgment and being cut off from the life God gives like a wicked person.[29] This is something Paul actually prayed.[30] It is worth noting that Paul specifically speaks of being accursed ἀπὸ τοῦ Χριστοῦ rather than ἀπὸ τοῦ θεοῦ. Moses was willing to be separated from God for Israel, but Paul is willing to be separated from Christ. There is no difference, because for Paul Christ is "God (θεός) over all blessed forever" (Rom 9:5).[31] Additionally, as

---

27. See Exod 32:32. For a discussion of the divine record book, see Widmer, *Moses*, 130.

28. Jewett, *Romans*, 560. See also, BDAG, 63; Kuhn, "ἀνάθεμα," 1:80–81.

29. See uses of ἀνάθεμα in Gal 1:8, 9; 1 Cor 16:22.

30. There are a number of interpreters who see Paul's statement as potential, or hypothetical, rather than actual. In other words, what Paul prayed was that "If I could be accursed for my kinsmen, I would." However, I find the absence of conditional particles telling. Moreover, a hypothetical reading tends to mitigate the depth of Paul's pain and ignore, or at least disfigure, the echoes of Moses' "actual" prayer for the Israelites. I am in agreement with Crump who notes, "In the heart of his letter to the Romans, Paul strikes a near-spiritual profligacy when he admits a willingness to surrender his own salvation in the cause of Israel's inclusion within the church. These words are more than rhetorical flourish; Paul vents a genuine desire expressed in real petitions to God"; Crump, *Knocking on Heaven's Door*, 221. For those who support a "potential" rather than "actual" prayer, see, e.g., Caragounis, *The Development of Greek and the New Testament*, 163; Moo, *Epistle the Romans*, 558; Wallace, *Greek Grammar Beyond the Basics*, 552; Schreiner, *Romans*, 480.

31. For a recent defense and explanation of reading ὁ ὢν ἐπί πάντων θεὸς in Rom 9:5 as a reference to Jesus, see Carraway, *Christ is God Over All*.

the larger context of Romans 9–11 indicates, Paul is willing to preach to the Gentiles on behalf of Israel.[32] His willingness to suffer for Israel is not just in word but in his deeds also.

Third, the echoes from Exodus 32–34 evoke the expectation that God will respond to Paul's cry of distress just as he did to Moses' cries. God's response to Moses is a mixture of mercy and wrath. Moses assuages God's wrath to some degree, but, in other ways, he has no real say in it.[33] God's response to Paul is along the same lines. I will address this further below. Here, I would simply note that we come up against the difficulty of understanding how Paul's prayer actually affects God's dealings with Israel. To put it another way, what do Moses and Paul think they will accomplish in their prayers of distress? God responds to both intercessors by pointing to his sovereignty over his dealings with Israel. Yet, if the cries have no real impact on God, they are superfluous. Obviously, God does not allow Moses or Paul to be separated from him on behalf of Israel. How, then, do their prayers make any difference? It should be kept in mind that the very act of intercession suggests "there is some freedom and openness within God's providence, which is nevertheless reliable and not capricious."[34] As Miler describes it, "God incorporates human prayers into the dynamic, nonstatic, purposive divine activity."[35] In other words, God's responsiveness to Moses' cry is built into the prior promises and purposes of God. He drives Moses to the point of offering himself in place of the nation. Paul most likely would have recognized this dynamic in his reading of Exodus 32–34. He finds himself in a similar situation, interceding for Israel according to the purposes of God.

Finally, the echoes from Exodus 32–34 raise the question "How does Paul know that God has answered his cry?" Moses needs assurance that God has heard him and will go with him and the people into Canaan. That is why he asks, "Reveal (ἐμφάνισον) yourself to me that I might clearly see, in order that I might find favor before you, and in order that I might know that this great nation is your people" (Exod 33:13). God responds by allowing Moses to catch a glimpse of his glory. In Paul's case, God reveals more than a glimpse. Romans 9:6—11:32 reveals a great deal about God's dealings with Israel that serves as an answer to Paul's cry of distress. Nevertheless, by the

---

32 See Rom 10:14–18; 11:13–14.

33 See Exod 32:14, 15–29, 30, 31–35.

34 Miller, *They Cried to the Lord*, 280. By "openness," Miller is in no way referring to the notion of open theism. Biblical lament is often marshalled as evidence of God's openness, but it is a false inference that misunderstands lament's form and theology. See e.g., Ellington, *Risking Truth*, 1–32.

35 Miller, *They Cried to the Lord*, 280.

end of that answer, Paul speaks as one who, like Moses, has only caught a glimpse of what God is doing (Rom 11:33–36).

Pattern of Lament *in Nuce*

Romans 9:1–3 echoes both Psalm 12 and Exodus 32–34. These OT passages evoke cries of distress that fill in the gap of Paul's prayer report. If the echoes are heard, we can hear Paul tearfully asking "how long" Israel will be rejected and interceding like Moses, even offering himself on their behalf. Despite this expression of heartfelt grief, there is a shift in the lamenter's, or Paul's, mood. After all, Romans 9:5 ends with ἀμήν thereby marking Paul's spontaneous doxology. The explanation for this shift is laid out methodically in 9:6—11:36. As a result, we find the entire pattern of lament represented in Romans 9–11.[36] However, Romans 9:1–5 already contains the entire pattern *in nuce*, which includes promise, suffering, cry of distress, deliverance, and praise.

I have already explained why Paul suffers and cries out. It is an explanation grounded in the echoes from Exodus 32–34. Paul is distressed by Israel's unbelief and divine rejection, because it is in tension with God's prior promise and brings into question God's reputation before the nations. This works on both a personal and theological level. We do not often consider the fact that pre-Damascus Paul had a number of Jewish contemporaries whom he cared about both before and after the revelation of Jesus. Although by his own admission he wanted to outdo them in the past, he now longs for their salvation.[37] At the risk of romanticizing the historical reconstruction of Paul's prayer, he likely "saw" names and faces of Jewish brethren and kinsmen when he cried out to God.[38] If before Damascus Paul wanted to use zeal in order to turn God's wrath away from Israel, he now wanted to offer himself to turn it away.[39] With that said, on a broader and theological level, Paul is concerned about God's prior promises and reputation before the na-

---

36 Seifrid notes, "Paul's opening lament provides the conceptual framework for the entire discourse, including the closing hymn of praise, which, according to the pattern of the psalms of lament, reaffirms the hope of the promises, contrary to all outward appearances." Seifrid, *Romans*, 638.

37. See Gal 1:13–14.

38 When the wider context of Paul's Jewish background is kept in view, the sense of ἀδελφός and συγγενής in Rom 9:3 have to bear a sense that is than more than merely "belonging to the same people group."

39 Hengel likens pre-Damascus Paul to Phinehas in Num 25:10–13 who was willing to "use force in order to turn God's wrath away from Israel." Hengel, *The Pre-Christian Paul*, 70.

tions. He must deliver Israel in order to make good on his prior promises. I want to focus our attention here on three parts of the lament pattern found in 9:1–5, specifically the prior promise, deliverance, and praise.

The prior promises and deliverance that Paul prays for as part of his lament are embedded in Romans 9:4–5. He describes his fellow kinsmen according to the flesh as those:

> Who are Israelites, whose are the adoption and the glory and the covenants and the instruction of the law and the service and the promises, whose are the fathers and from whom is the Christ that is according to the flesh, who is God over all blessed forever, amen.

These nine descriptive phrases evoke different facets of Israel's history, but collectively they are prior promises from God. As Seifrid observes, the phrases indicate that "Israel's history is itself promissory."[40] The specific referents of the promises vary, and some are more easily identifiable than others.

The first three referents indicate the "promissory" nature of Israel. The title "Israelites" recalls the "sacred name" given first to Jacob and then his descendants.[41] As Israelites, they are inheritors of the promises first given to Abraham.[42] The referent of υἱοθεσία is somewhat difficult to locate in Israel's history. It is not a term that appears in the LXX. Nevertheless, the concept of God adopting Israel as his son is not entirely foreign to the OT. For example, God commands Moses "And you will say to Pharaoh, 'Thus says the Lord, Israel is my firstborn (πρωτότοκος) son'" (Exod 4:22). Ezekiel has a colorful parable that recalls the birth/adoption of Israel:

> And I went through you and I saw you, and behold your time was a time of those being destroyed, and I spread out my wings over you and I covered your shame; and I swore (ὤμοσα) to you and I entered in a covenant (διαθήκη) with you, says the Lord, and you became mine (ἐγένου μοι). (Ezek 16:8)[43]

Ezekiel's parable implies the adoptive origin of Israel that Paul explicitly states. Moreover, the uses of ὄμνυμι and διαθήκη indicate the promissory nature of the adoption. The term δόξα evokes moments in Israel's history where God revealed his glorious presence to both individuals and the entire community. If we confine ourselves to moments in which the actual term

---

40. Seifrid, *Romans*, 639.
41 Dodd, *Romans*, 165.
42 Gen 12:1–3; 17:1–8.
43 See Ezek 16:1–14.

δόξα appears, we find the following: the supply of manna, the theophany at Sinai, God's presence in the tabernacle, the dedication of the temple, Isaiah's vision in the temple, and Ezekiel's vision of the divine glory returning to the temple.[44]

The fourth phrase in Paul's description, διαθῆκαι, calls to mind key figures and moments in Israel's history where God established covenants containing various promises. In the Abrahamic covenant, God promised to give Abraham many descendants, a land to live in, a great name, and to make Abraham's descendants a blessing to the nations.[45] Yet, the latter promise, along with Genesis 15:6 ("Abraham believed God, and it was reckoned to him as righteousness") are definitive for Paul's understanding of the promises that God gave to Abraham.[46] The Mosaic covenant promised God's blessing for those who obeyed the law and curse for those who broke it.[47] The Jeremiac covenant promised something new in comparison to the Mosaic covenant.[48] Specifically, it contained the promise of a law "written on the heart" (Jer 38:33; 31:33 MT). We should also include God's promise to David in 2 Samuel 7:11–13, even though the actual term διαθήκη does not occur there.

The term νομοθεσία suggests Mosaic legislation.[49] Such legislation is also promissory in nature. There is a promise of life for those who obey and death for those who do not.[50] Part of that legislation involves the priestly system which Paul refers to through the term λατρεία. The actual use of the term in Exodus 12:25–26 and 13:5 refers to the observance of Passover and the feast of unleavened bread respectively. Yet, the priestly service obviously involves many other things such as daily sacrifices, the Day of Atonement, and service in the temple.

The seventh phrase that describes Israel's promissory history is αἱ ἐπαγγελίαι. God's promises to Israel would obviously include the covenants mentioned already. In addition to those, the term could refer to more general promises often invoked in the Psalms of Lament. The psalmist often appeals to the promise of God's protection, deliverance, and vindication.

---

44 See Exod 16:7; 24:16–17; 40:34–35; 1 Kgs 8:11; 2 Chr 5:14; Isa 6:1, 3; Ezek 43:2, 4, 5.

45 Gen 12:1–3; 15:6; 17:1–8.

46 See e.g., Rom 4:3, 9, 23; Gal 3:6, 8.

47 See Deut 28:69.

48 Jer 38:31–34 (31:31–34 MT)

49 The only other appearances of the term are found in 2 Macc 6:23; 4 Macc 5:35; 4 Macc 17:16.

50 See e.g., Lev 18:5.

The final two phrases that Paul uses to describe the Israelites are ὧν οἱ πατέρες and ἐξ ὧν ὁ Χριστὸς τὸ κατὰ σάρκα. The patriarchs belong to the Israelites; therefore, the promises of the fathers do as well. Once again, the promises to Abraham are instructive with their assurance of countless descendants, land, a great name, and a blessing for all nations. With the latter likely in mind, as well as Genesis 15:6, Paul ends the list by describing the Israelites as those "from who is the Christ according to the flesh." The prepositional phrase "according to the flesh" stresses physical descent of the Christ from Abraham to Jesus. It is a fitting end, because Paul sees Israel's Messiah as "the one 'place' on earth in which all God's promises have come to fulfillment."[51] All the other promissory descriptions of Israel that Paul lists in Romans 9:4–5 "remain fragmentary and unanswered" apart from him.[52] It is no wonder that in Paul's spontaneous doxology he describes Jesus as "God who is over all blessed forever, amen."[53] Paul prepares the reader here for his Christological interpretation of Yahweh's action throughout Romans 9:6—11:32.[54]

When we put all the lament pieces together, the result is that Paul cries out in intercession for Israel because their separation from God is in tension with what he promised. For Paul, everything about Israel's history is defined by promise, from their title as "Israelites" to their Messiah and everything in between. God adopted Israel, revealed his glory to them repeatedly, entered into covenants with them, instructed them through the law, provided atoning sacrifices in the temple for them, and gave them countless promises, especially through the patriarchs. These phrases signal the abbreviated answer to Paul's cry of distress that he will subsequently unpack in 9:6—11:36. It is a response that will end in praise just as it does in 9:5 where Paul describes Jesus as "God over all (ἐπί πάντων)," both Jew and Gentile. The divine answer that turns lament to praise, whether it is uttered by Jew or Gentile,

---

51 Seifrid, *The Second Letter to the Corinthians*, 62. See 2 Cor 1:20.

52 Ibid., 62.

53 There is an ongoing debate surrounding how Rom 9:5 should be read. Either the verse should be punctuated in a way that Christ is not praised as God, or it is punctuated in such a way that he is. However, the discussion does not really turn on grammatical issues alone. Dunn admits grammatically the line should be punctuated in a way that reads "From them, according to the flesh, comes the Messiah, who is over all, God blessed forever, amen." Yet, his final conclusion is that historically and theologically Paul's list "would naturally end with a benediction to the God of Israel, just as the whole discussion climaxes with a doxology to God alone." Dunn, *The Theology of Paul the Apostle*, 256. For a convincing counter argument, see Carraway, *Christ is God Over All*.

54 As we will see, several of the OT citations in Rom 9–11 have Yahweh as their original referent. However, in Paul's use of them, Christ becomes the clear referent. See Bauckham, *Jesus and the God of Israel*, 189.

is found in Jesus alone. He is God's answer to Paul's cry of "how long," and "I wish to be accursed from Christ on behalf of my kinsmen." We now turn our attention to the specifics of that divine answer.

READING ROMANS 9:6—11:36 AS THE ANSWER TO PAUL'S CRY OF DISTRESS

The answer to Paul's cry of distress occurs in three major movements before ending with praise in Romans 11:33–36.[55] In these movements, Paul not only unpacks the divine response he abbreviated in 9:4–5. There are also echoes of other lamenters, particularly Elijah and David, which remind us of the oscillation between pain and praise that permeates the entire argument. Far from a philosophical discussion about divine sovereignty, and even more than a theodicy explaining God's ways with Israel, what we have here is a discussion birthed in Paul's prayers. It is the pain, cries of distress, and praise uttered by Paul before God that form the framework for 9:6—11:36. Therefore, what we will find is neither an appendix to the letter nor its main argument.[56] This is Paul working out before his readers how the revelation of God's righteousness in the crucified and risen Jesus can be squared with Israel's rejection of that Messiah. The opening lament in 9:1–5, like the rest of the lament language in the letter, reminds us that Paul is highly invested in and deeply pained by what he experiences as an apostle to the Gentile whose kinsmen are Israelites. He suffers and intercedes for them like Moses.

Moses' cries of distress and the divine answer he receives can be heard throughout 9:6—11:36. One way to describe God's overarching response to Moses' cries in Exodus 32–34 is that in judging Israel his mercy is both hidden and revealed. For example, in the aftermath of the golden calf incident, Moses intercedes and successfully propitiates God's wrath, "And the Lord was propitiated concerning the harm, which he said he was going to do to his people" (Exod 32:14). He will not wipe out Israel entirely and build a new nation through Moses. However, as Exodus 32:15–29 indicates, God still poured out judgment on Israel as 3,000 were slaughtered in one day. Similarly, as Moses intercedes again in Exodus 32:30–32, God promises to lead the people and yet strikes them for their transgression (Exod

---

55 Similarly, Seifrid's three part-structure for Rom 9–11 is: (1) 9:1–13; (2) 9:14—10:21; and (3) 11:1–36. See, Seifrid, *Christ Our Righteousness*, 152.

56 The notion that Rom 9–11 is a kind of appendix to the letter has long been disproven. There is evidence of coherence throughout. See, Dunn, "Formal and Theological Coherence," 245–50. However, it does not follow that these chapters are the letter's main point. They are certainly part of the main point, but they do not necessarily function as the "heart of the matter." See Hays, *Echoes of Scripture*, 63.

32:33–35). In this judgment, God both hides his mercy by slaughtering thousands but reveals it by not slaughtering all. This is how God responds to Moses' intercessory lament, and it is the same way he responds to Paul's own intercession. Divine mercy is both hidden and revealed in judgment. Israel's judgment in Romans 9–11 is intertwined with their rejection of Jesus. In rejecting the gospel of God, Israel is judged. Yet, in that judgment mercy is revealed to a remnant and to Gentiles.

The Answer to Paul's Cry in Romans 9:6–13

The first answer to Paul's cry of distress is that God always creates his people through a word of promise (ἐπαγγελία). If Israel's unbelief raises a question about the effectiveness of God's prior promise, it is immediately answered "But it is not as though the word of God (ὁ λόγος τοῦ θεοῦ) has failed (ἐκπέπτωκεν). For not all those from Israel are Israel" (Rom 9:6)." We must be clear about the referent of ὁ λόγος τοῦ θεοῦ. It is a broad sweeping phrase that defines the entire origin of Israel, yet one that Paul ultimately boils down to the "word of faith" which he preaches (Rom 10:9). In the present context, Paul demonstrates how God's word of promise created Israel from the very beginning. To make this point, he cites two promises made to Abraham from Genesis 21:12 and 18:10:

> In Isaac your descendant will be called. (Rom 9:7)
>
> According to this time I will come and Sarah will have a son. (Rom 9:9)

Paul explicitly refers to the latter citation as ὁ λόγος ἐπαγγελίας. The children of God, those who are really Israel, are not "children of the flesh" (τέκνα τῆς σαρκός) but "children of the promise (τέκνα τῆς ἐπαγγελίας)" (Rom 9:8). They are children who have always come from, or been produced by, a promise just like Isaac was.[57]

The effectiveness of God's promise for producing Israel is further evidenced in the offspring of Isaac and Rebecca (Rom 9:10–13). Paul explains that God purposed (πρόθεσις) to produce a people based on election (κατ' ἐκλογήν) (Rom 9:11). The interplay between God's elective purpose and the promise which created Israel, in this instance as it relates to Jacob, is seen in Paul's citations from Genesis 25:23 and Malachi 1:2:

---

57. In the phrase τέκνα τῆς ἐπαγγελίας, the genitive functions as a genitive of source (i.e. children from the promise) or a genitive of production (i.e. children produced by a promise). On both options, see Wallace, *Greek Grammar*, 104–5, 109.

> Not from works but from the one who calls (ἐκ τοῦ καλοῦντος), it was said to her "The older will serve the younger." (Rom 9:12).
>
> Just as it is written, "Jacob I loved, but Esau I hated." (Rom 9:13)

The purpose of election and the call that went to Rebecca are intertwined, so that "Paul has in view God's immediate choice of Jacob by his word, not a hidden divine purpose."[58] The call of Jacob naturally excludes Esau and is unexpected given that the custom of the day was for the younger to be subservient to the older not vice versa.

So then, the first movement of God's response to Paul's cry emphasizes that Israel is always created through a divine promise. The tension between the prior promise to save them and their rejection troubles Paul. Yet, the prior promise has not failed. The word of promise created Israel from the beginning, at least the Israel whom God purposes to effectively call. As Paul will make clear, the same phenomenon takes place with Israel in his own day. Paul's comments on the patriarchs, and his citations pertaining to them, are not merely an explanation of how God established Israel in the beginning. They indicate that God works the same way in Paul's present pain over Israel. Israel still comes through the word of promise.[59]

The Answer to Paul's Cry in Romans 9:14–29

Romans 9:14–29 is the second movement in God's answer to Paul's intercessory cry. In answering questions from his interlocutor, Paul also articulates the answer to his own cry of distress. The movement throughout emphasizes God's freedom to act in righteousness as he chooses. In this way, Paul's argument continues to echo the divine response to Moses' intercession in Exodus 32–34. In fact, Paul cites a portion of that response in this section (Exod 33:19; Rom 9:15). There are a number of exegetical points to consider here, but I will limit my comments to a brief synopsis of the argument and highlight their relationship to Paul's cry of distress.

The argument in 9:6–13 raises a question that Paul addresses in 9:14–29. Specifically, if Israel is created through the word of promise, and God chooses to effectively call one but not the other (e.g. Jacob rather than Esau), is God unrighteous? As Paul puts it, "What then shall we say? There is not unrighteousness (ἀδικία) with God is there?" (Rom 9:14). Paul's immediate

---

58 Seifrid, *Romans*, 640.

59 As Hanson explains about Paul's citation in Rom 9:6–13, "He is not saying: 'the lineage that begins with a promise is the one that counts.' He is saying something much more like John 1:13: 'who were born, not of blood nor of the will of the flesh nor of man, but of God'"; Hanson, *Studies in Paul's Technique and Theology*, 89.

response is "May it never be" (Rom 9:14). He then explains that God is free to "call," or, as he puts in this context, "have mercy" on whomever he wants.

Paul grounds his explanation in two citations from Exodus that not only answer the interlocutor's question in Rom 9:14 but are also linked to Paul's lament in 9:1–5. First, he cites a portion of Exodus 33:19, "For he says (λέγει) to Moses, 'I will have mercy on whom I have mercy and I will have compassion on whom I have compassion'" (Rom 9:15).[60] As noted above, Moses wants to know that God will go with them into Canaan.[61] In seeking assurance of the divine presence, Moses asks to see God's glory (Exod 33:18). God answers, "I will pass by you with my glory and I will call by name, the Lord, before you; And I will have mercy on whom I have mercy, and I will have compassion on whom I have compassion" (Exod 33:19). God reveals his glory, but he still asserts control over his mercy. The same response applies to Paul's cry of distress in Rom 9:3. Paul can wish to be accursed from Christ for his kinsmen, but God will have mercy on those whom he wants. As Paul puts it in Romans 9:16, the effective call of salvation to Israel is not "of the one who wants nor of the one who runs but of God who has mercy." Second, Paul also cites an earlier portion of the Exodus narrative. As he further explains God's control over the mercy he gives to Israel, he cites a portion of Exodus 9:16, "For scripture (ἡ γραφή) says to Pharaoh, 'For this very reason I have raised you up in order that I might demonstrate in you my power and in order that my name might be proclaimed in all the earth'" (Rom 9:17).[62] While in the original context of the previous Exodus citation God responds to Moses, the setting of this citation is God's address to Pharaoh. Nevertheless, Paul applies the statement to God's dealings with Israel. God raised up Israel, in order to demonstrate that he has the power to give mercy and to harden as he wants (Rom 9:18). This also answers Paul's cry to be "accursed for Christ for his kinsmen." God's answer to Paul, similar to what Moses received, is that he gives mercy, or hardens Israel, as he wishes.

A second objection to Paul's argument appears in Romans 9:19, "Therefore, you will say to me, 'Why then does he still find fault? For who has resisted his will?'" Once again, Paul's response not only answers the

---

60. The present tense λέγει in the citation's introductory formula helps to make the "scriptural statement a contemporary utterance." Watson, *Paul and the Hermeneutics of Faith*, 45.

61 See Exod 33:12–23.

62 Paul's version of Exod 9:16 and the LXX's version diverge in their opening phrase. While Paul's version contains the phrase εἰς αὐτὸ τοῦτο ἐξήγειρά, the LXX reads ἕνεκεν τούτου διετηρήθης.

interlocutor but, at least to some degree, his own cry of distress. Additionally, he takes up the complaint of the fallen before God.[63]

Before analyzing Paul's argument in 9:19–23, we must determine whether Paul is speaking here about God's dealings with Israel particularly or people universally. It is clear in 9:6–13 that Paul's focus is Israel. As his argument moves forward in 9:14–23, he does not explicitly indicate that he is now speaking about how God deals with both Jews and Gentiles.[64] It is difficult to say with certainty that he has both groups in mind. However, there are a few reasons to believe that Paul is describing how God deals with Israel specifically and humanity in general. For example, in 9:16, Paul describes God's original response to Moses in a gnomic sense, "So then it is not of the one who wills nor of the one who runs but of God who has mercy." As Bayer and Seifrid explain, Paul perceives in God's response to Moses "the pattern (type) of God's ways with all human beings."[65] This is also seen in the way Paul reflects on God's dealings with Pharaoh. The conclusion in 9:18 also bears a gnomic sense, "So then he has mercy on whom he wants, and he hardens whom he wants." Finally, in Romans 9:24, Paul clearly qualifies "objects of mercy" as those whom God chose "not only from Jews but also from Gentiles." Therefore, one might infer that Gentiles are also included in "objects of wrath" (Rom 9:22).[66]

In any case, while God's specific ways with Israel have universal implications, Paul's main focus in 9:19–23 remains God's freedom to act towards Israel as he chooses. Once again, this serves as an answer to the interlocutor and Paul's cry of distress. The outcome of any encounter with ὁ λόγος τοῦ θεοῦ (Rom 9:6) is mercy or judgment, but Paul is especially concerned at this point with Israel's encounter.[67] In continuing this point, Paul employs the prophetic image of the clay and its potter.[68] The clay has no real say in

---

63 Seifrid notes, "As in 3:5, Paul voices the protest of the fallen human being to divine judgment. There the protest arises from the world of God that announces human guilt. Here it arises from the saving will of God announced in his word, by which in freedom he judges and shows mercy. God's right as Creator is at stake in both instances." Seifrid, *Romans*, 644.

64 Commentators are not always clear on this point. Their language can shift from Israel to the more general "human beings" without explanation or justification for the change. See e.g., Schreiner, *Romans*, 513.

65 Seifrid, *Romans*, 643.

66 The use of σκεύη in 2 Tim 2:20–21 is similar to the use in Rom 9:21–23. In the former use, the vessels intended for "honor" or "dishonor" bear a clear universal stamp. See Mounce, *Pastoral Epistles*, 530–32.

67 Seifrid, *Romans*, 644.

68 See e.g., Isa 29:16; 45:9; Jer 18:6; 50:25. On Paul's use of this OT image, see Collins, *The Power of Images in Paul*, 208–9; Jewett, *Romans*, 594–95.

the potter's design and use of itself. Israel cannot successfully object to how God freely acts in his mercy. The potter has the ἐξουσία to make Israel into objects for honor and dishonor, or salvation and judgment (Rom 9:21).[69] As Paul articulates it in 9:22–23:

> Now (δέ) if God wanting (θέλων) to demonstrate his wrath and to make known his power, bore with much patience vessels prepared for destruction, and in order to make known the wealth of his glory upon objects of mercy which he prepared beforehand for glory?

The point of this grammatically awkward question is that God prepared two types of vessels in order to reveal his wrath and mercy.[70] As the wider context of 9:24—10:21 will show, the vessels of wrath prepared for destruction are those who reject the gospel, and the objects of mercy are those whose hearing produces faith in the message. Paul includes himself in the latter noting that the objects of mercy are those whom "God called (ἐκάλεσεν) us not only from Jews but also from Gentiles" (Rom 9:24). It is a calling indissolubly linked to the gospel. For both vessels, the full revelation of God's power, wrath, and mercy is reserved for the eschatological day.[71] The divine mercy promised in the gospel will be all the more glorious in the face of divine wrath on that day. This once again echoes God's response to Moses' intercessory cries in Exodus 32–34. The response to Paul's cry is similar. God answers Paul's intercession for Israel by asserting his freedom to act in both mercy and wrath. He can prepare vessels for destruction through their rejection of the gospel and effectively call vessels to glory through the same message.

In Romans 9:24–29, Paul describes the Jewish and Gentile vessels of mercy by appropriating OT citations from Hosea and Isaiah. The description is still part of the divine response to Paul's cries of "how long" as well as "I was wishing to be accursed for Christ for the sake of my brethren." God is already overcoming Israel's enemy, namely sin. Yet, as God revealed to Moses, he will act in his righteousness according to his own wisdom and authority. That includes the kind of people that God fashions, as the collection of citations here indicates. The common motif in these citations is that God

---

69. Seifrid, *Romans*, 645.

70 Rom 9:22–23 poses a few different grammatical challenges. To begin, as Jewett notes, "Verses 22 and 23 provide the 'if clause' of an incomplete sentence whose logical but ungrammatical conclusion is found in v. 24." Jewett, *Romans*, 595. Additionally, the participle θέλων could be rendered in a purposive, causal, or concessive sense.

71 On this point, see Johnson, *The Function of Apocalyptic and Wisdom Traditions*, 110–75.

calls out and creates his own people. Paul cites Hosea 2:25, "As also in Hosea he says, 'I will call a people not my people my people and not beloved (I will call) beloved'" (Rom 9:25).[72] He continues with a citation from Hosea 2:1, "And it will in the place where it was say to them, 'You are not my people,' there they will called sons of God" (Rom 9:26).

What is especially important for our purposes here is that Paul casts Isaiah as someone who, like Moses, cries out and intercedes on Israel's behalf. This is indicated in the citation formula that introduces Isaiah 10:22. Paul writes, "And Isaiah cries out (κράζει) for Israel" (Rom 9:27a). In the wider context of Isaiah 10, there is an oracle of woe and a hope of salvation. God will send Assyria, "the rod of his anger," to judge sinful Israel (Isa 10:5). The prophet also envisions a time beyond Israel's judgment when a "remnant (τὸ καταλειφθέν) will return" to God (Isa 10:21). Paul takes up the remnant motif scattered throughout Isaiah and cites the following in 9:27–29:

> If the number of the sons of Israel should be as the sand of the sea, a remnant (ὑπόλειμμα) will be saved. (Isa 10:22)
>
> For completing (συντελῶν) and cutting it short (συντέμνων) the Lord will do it upon the earth. (Isa 28:22)[73]
>
> Unless the Lord of Sabbath had left to us a posterity (σπέρμα), we would have been like Sodom and we have likened to Gomorrah. (Isa 1:9)

Although in the wider contexts of these citations Isaiah is not described as "crying out" (κράζει), it is how Paul portrays the prophet. Isaiah sees God's judgment of his people; therefore, he cries out for them (ὑπέρ τοῦ Ἰσραήλ). As is often the case with the Isaianic influence on Paul, the prophet even shapes the apostle's prayers for Israel.[74] Specifically, God's promise of an Israelite remnant to Isaiah becomes the divine response to Paul's cry of distress.

---

72 With the citation of Hos 2:25, Paul uses a divine statement originally directed towards Israel and applies it to Gentiles. On this hermeneutical move, see Seifrid, *Romans*, 647.

73 Paul does not follow the LXX exactly at this point. Isa 28:22 LXX reads, "Because I heard of matters having been completed (συντετελεσμένα) and cut short (συντετμημένα) from the Lord, things which he will upon all the earth."

74 See Wagner, *Heralds of the Good News*, 43–118.

The Answer to Paul's Cry in Romans 9:30—10:21

The response to Paul's cry continues in Romans 9:30—10:21 where the emphasis lies more on the "human cause of Israel's failure" than God's freedom.[75] Paul's second prayer report sheds further light on his intercessory cry and the divine response to it, "Brothers, the desire of my heart and prayer to God is for their salvation (σωτηρία)" (Rom 10:1).[76] Clearly, in his petitions and intercessions before God, Paul requests that Israel be saved. He asks that Israel be saved from God's eschatological wrath in a way similar to Moses and other intercessory lamenters. That request stems not only from God's freedom to save or destroy Israel (Rom 9:14–23). It also emanates from Israel's rejection of God's "righteousness by faith" by pursuing a "law of righteousness" (Rom 9:30–31). As Paul describes it, "they have stumbled at the stone (λίθον) of stumbling" (Rom 9:32). Paul culls the λίθος language from Isaiah. In Rom 9:33, he conflates Isaiah 8:14 and 28:16, "Behold I lay in Zion a stone (λίθον) of stumbling and a rock of offence, and the one who believes in him will be not be put to shame."[77] Paul's conflation simultaneously highlights the positive and negative aspects of the λίθος. For Paul, God has laid the λίθος (or πέτρα) before Israel, and the stone is Jesus Christ. If the Israelites believe (ὁ πιστεύων) in the stone, they will not be disappointed, or ashamed (καταισχυνθήσεται) in their hope.[78] This is yet another response to Pauls' initial cry in 9:1–3. The answer to "how long" and "I wish that I might be accursed form Christ" is that Israel will either believe in the "stone" and find protection from his wrath, or reject it and be crushed by it.

As Paul's argument continues in Romans 10, the divine response to his intercessory lament does as well. The response here revolves around the motif of stripping away all excuses from Paul's kinsmen for their rejection of the "stone." Paul acknowledges that Israel's zeal for God is not according to knowledge (Rom 10:2). They are ignorant of God's righteousness in Christ

---

75 Seifrid, *Romans*, 650. Additionally, Sanday and Headlam note, "St. Paul now passes to another aspect of the subject he is discussing. He has considered the rejection of Israel from the point of view of the Divine justice and power, he is not to approach it from the side of human responsibility." Sanday and Headlam, *Romans*, 278.

76 Wiles notes the connection, "In the second prayer-report Paul takes up again the burden of the first, but now more positively and with less vehemence." Wiles, *Paul's Intercessory Prayers*, 257.

77 The phrase "stone of stumbling" comes from Isaiah 8:14 while the assurance "the one who believes in him will not be put to shame" is found in 28:16. Wagner explains, "Paul's composite citation takes an A-B-A form, with a portion of 8:14 spliced into the middle of 28:16." Wagner, *Heralds of the Good News*, 127. See also, Moo, *Romans*, 630.

78 Cf. Rom 1:16; 10:13. On shame/disappointment language in OT lament, see chapter 3.

and seek to establish their own (Rom 10:3). Nevertheless, as Paul argues throughout this section, there are no excuses available to them.

To help make this point, Paul draws from the OT once again. He reworks Deuteronomy 30:12–14.[79] In their original context, these verses are part of a warning to Israel about the danger they face for rejecting God's commands. They face two choices with two corresponding consequences. Seifrid explains, "By them (i.e. commands) they will ensure their well-being and preserve their life in the land. Disobedience will bring destruction, exile, and servitude."[80] The nearness of the word, or commandments of the law, remind the Israelites of God's grace and their obligation to obey him. Similarly, Paul speaks about the proximity of the gospel to Israel. Like the Mosaic Law, the word Paul preaches is close by in their mouths and hearts. What is lacking is Israel's own cry to the Lord and faith in the message. Paul can intercede and cry out for their salvation, but they must call upon the Lord to be saved. He cites a portion of Joel 3:5, "For everyone who should call upon (ἐπικαλουμένος) the name of the Lord will be saved" (Rom 10:13). In the larger context of Joel, the prophet warns of impending judgment at the hands of foreign invaders. Israel's only hope in the face of such judgment is to "call upon" the Lord (κύριος) who, as the underlying Hebrew text makes clear, is Yahweh. However, Paul identifies the κύριος as Jesus in the immediate context. His confessional statement in Romans 10:9 is, "If you should confess with your mouth that Jesus is Lord (κύριον) and believe in your heart that God raised him from the dead you will be saved." Jews and Gentiles must call upon (ἐπικαλέω) the Lord Jesus Christ to be saved from eschatological judgment. They must take up their own cry to Jesus for deliverance.

In Romans 10:14–21, Paul continues to strip away Israel's excuses for not calling upon Jesus for salvation, and he employs Israel's scriptures to do so. Paul acknowledges that in order for Israel to call upon Jesus they must believe in him (Rom 10:14). Such faith requires that they hear the gospel (Rom 10:15). Furthermore, hearing the gospel, which produces faith, necessitates a preacher (Rom 10:15). Paul asserts that this entire chain of events has taken place on Israel's behalf, but "not all obeyed (ὑπήκουσαν) the gospel" (Rom 10:16). He sees Israel's rejection of the gospel in his own day as Isaiah saw it in his. Paul even takes up the prophet's question "Lord, who has believed our report?" (Isa 53:1). He then proceeds to anticipate and squash two objections. Israel's objections can be heard in two rhetorical questions:

---

79 On Paul's use of Deut 30:12–14, see Seifrid, "Paul's Approach to the Old Testament in Rom 10:6–8," 3–37; Ciampa, "Deuteronomy in Galatians and Romans," 106–10; Bekken, *The Word is Near You*.

80 Seifrid, *Christ Our Righteousness*, 122.

> But I say (ἀλλὰ λέγω), they certainly did not hear (μὴ οὐκ ἤκουσαν) did they? (Rom 10:18)
>
> But I say (ἀλλὰ λέγω), Israel certainly did not know (μὴ οὐκ ἔγνω) did they? (Rom 10:19)

Israel's scriptures answer both questions. With respect to "hearing" the gospel, Paul cites Psalm 18:5, "Their voice (φθόγγος) has gone out into all the earth and their words (τὰ ῥήματα) to the ends of the world." The psalmist praises God for revealing his glory through creation.[81] The heavens and the firmament "declare" (ἀναγγέλλει) God's glory everywhere. Paul applies the psalmist's praise to the manner in which the gospel has been declared to Israel. Israel has heard the gospel as loudly and widely as they have heard creation declaring God's glory. With respect to "understanding" the gospel, Paul cites three texts:

> I will make you jealous of those who are not a nation, I will make you angry with an unwise nation. (Deut 32:21)
>
> I was found by those who do not seek me, I became manifest to those who do not ask for me. (Isa 65:1)
>
> All day long I stretched out my hands to a disobedient and obstinate people. (Isa 65:2)

Moses and Isaiah both speak of other nations making Israel jealous, because those nations seek the God whom they reject. That is the very thing Israel is doing in Paul's day. Therefore, scripture itself will not allow Israel to say they have failed to understand the gospel.

Romans 9:33—10:21 contains the second movement of Paul's argument and, more importantly for our purposes, the second part of God's response to the apostle's intercessory cry. The answer to "how long" and "I wished that I were accursed from Christ for my kinsmen" is that Paul's Israelite brethren are responsible for failing to be delivered from God's wrath. They have rejected the "stone" in who they should believe. Although they have a zeal for God, it is not in accordance with knowledge about the righteousness of God. Yet, their "ignorance" is inexcusable. God strips away their excuses for failing to "call upon the name" of Jesus and be saved from eschatological wrath. The gospel is as close to them as the Mosaic Law. God has sent preachers of the gospel to them, so that they might hear, believe, and call upon Jesus. The message is as loud and wide as creation's declaration of God's glory. Even more, Gentile acceptance of the gospel, an acceptance meant to provoke Israel to jealousy, is both promised in scripture and being

---

81. See Ps 18:1–4.

realized in Paul's day. God persistently ("all day long") offers himself to Israel in the gospel, and they are disobedient to it. This is how Paul explains to Gentile Christians the way God is dealing with Israel, and it is also a main part of God's answer to the apostle's intercessory lament.

The Answer to Paul's Cry in Romans 11:1–32

For Paul, Israel's responsibility for their current circumstances does not preclude the fact that God is sovereign in his judgment and mercy. In fact, a question along these lines emerges from his previous discussion that Paul quickly dismisses is "Therefore, I say God did not reject (ἀπώσατο) his people did he? May it never be" (Rom 11:1). Israel's unbelief is inexcusable, but unbelief is not the end of their story. If it were, that would mean God had rejected his people. In Romans 11:1–32, Paul explains that Israel's unbelief in Jesus does not mean God has rejected his people. The explanation is also the final part of God's answer to Paul's intercessory lament.

Romans 11:1–6 begins the explanation, and like 9:1–5, it contains echoes of intercessory lament. Paul denies that God has rejected his people by seeing himself in the experience of Elijah.[82] Paul, an Israelite from the seed of Abraham and the tribe of Benjamin, is living proof that God has not rejected his people whom he foreknew (προέγνω) (Rom 11:1–2). Despite his distress over Israel's unbelief and the cry he utters, it does not follow that God rejected his people. He likens his situation to Elijah's intercession "against," rather than "for," Israel:

> God did not reject (ἀπώσατο) his people whom he foreknew or do you not know what the scripture (ἡ γραφή) says in Elijah, as he intercedes (ἐντυγχάνει) to God against (κατά) Israel? "Lord, they killed your prophets, they have torn down your altars, and I alone have been left and they seek my life." But what does the divine response (ὁ χρηματισμός) say to him? "I have left for myself 7,000 men, who have not bent the knee to Baal." (Rom 11:2–4)

Elijah's exchange with God originally transpired at Mt. Horeb where the prophet fled from Jezebel (1 Kgs 19:1–9).[83] Elijah is told that there will be

---

82 On Paul's use of 1 Kgs 19:10, 14, see Seifrid, *Romans*, 667–69.

83 God's response to Elijah resembles what he told Moses in Exod 32–34. They both catch a glimpse of God's glory on the mountain, and they both hear a response that mixes judgment and mercy. Cf. Exod 33:19–23; 1 Kgs 19:11–13. Davidson observes the similarities between Moses and Elijah, "The parallelism with Mosaic tradition is explicit and intentional—Moses who spent forty days and forty nights on the mountain,

great bloodshed in Israel, but God will preserve a remnant (1 Kgs 19:15–18). The wider context of 1 Kings 19 reveals that Elijah had a limited understanding of Israel's condition. He rightly recognized that they were rebellious, violent, and apostate. He rightly anticipated their impending judgment. However, what he could not see was the 7,000 member remnant God had preserved for himself beyond the judgment. Paul's sees this exchange in light of his own circumstances. He interprets Elijah's intercession (ἐντυγχάνω) as a prayer uttered against (κατά) Israel (Rom 11:3). It is possible that at some point Israel's unbelief prompted Paul to utter a similar kind of intercession against Israel. The response Elijah receives from God is the one Paul receives as well. We should note once again Paul's personification of γραφή and χρηματισμός, as well as the present tense λέγει. Paul finds the answer to his cry in Israel's Scriptures. In this instance, the answer to his concern over Israel's unbelief and its implications for divine rejection is found in God's response to Elijah's intercession. As Paul puts it in Romans 11:6, "Therefore, in this way and in the present time, there has been a remnant (λεῖμμα) according to the election of grace." Paul is part of that remnant (Rom 11:1). Just as Elijah was not the only one who kept from bending to Baal, Paul is not the only Jew who had accepted the gospel. Paul's own faith and Israel's Scriptures answer his cry for/against Israel. God graciously elects a remnant of Israel; therefore, God has not rejected Israel.[84]

Paul's argument and God's response to his intercessory cry continues in 11:7–11. Paul can conclude that Israel does not obtain the righteousness which it seeks, because it seeks that righteousness by works (Rom 11:6–7).[85] Only the remnant, or election (ἐκλογή), obtains it. They rest of Israel was hardened (ἐπωρώθησαν) by God, and such a divine response is in accordance with scripture (Rom 11:7–8). Paul tethers together Deuteronomy 29:4 and Isaiah 29:10 to make his point, "Just as it is written, 'God gave to them a spirit of stupor, eyes so as not to see and ears so as not to hear, until this day" (Rom 11:8).[86] Paul then cites Psalm 68:22–23 part of a well-known individual lament, "Let their table (τράπεζα) become a snare and a trap and a stumbling block and retribution for them, let their eyes be darkened so as not to see and bend their backs continually" (Rom 11:9–10). Originally, the lamenter is speaking about his enemies and requesting their punishment.

Moses who experienced his strange theophany as he sheltered in the crevice of a rock." Davidson, *The Courage to Doubt*, 97.

84 If any Israelite understood that God preserved a remnant based on grace, it had to be Paul. See e.g., 1 Cor 15:8–10; Gal 1:22–23.

85 Cf. Rom 9:31.

86 On Paul's use of Deut 29:4 and Isa 29:10, see Ciampa, "Deuteronomy in Galatians and Romans," 112; Watson, *Paul and the Hermeneutics of Faith*, 434–36.

He uses a hunting metaphor to describe what he is asking God to do to them. The Hebrew lying underneath the term τράπεζα (שֻׁלְחָן) could refer to an "outspread mat," or "open snare," upon which the hunter places food to catch his prey.[87] The lamenter wants God to trap his enemies and wipe them out (Ps 68:29). Somehow this applies to Israel in Paul's day.

The connection between the enemies in Psalm 68 and the rest (λοιποί) of Israel whom Paul has in view is grounded in the psalm's images of trapping and punishing. God traps Israel like a hunter through a τράπεζα that Paul probably sees as "Israel's exclusive table fellowship."[88] Table fellowship functioned as more than a "boundary marker" in Paul's day. It marked a "claim to true piety and godliness."[89] Such a claim results in Israel's rejection of the crucified and risen Christ. God punishes them with stupor, blindness, and deafness, essentially the very things the psalmist requests against his enemies. God's trapping and punishing of Israel in Paul's day is no more arbitrary than the actions taken against unrighteous enemies in the psalm. They are hardened, trapped, and punished for their claim to true piety and godliness, a claim which denies the righteousness of God revealed in the gospel.

Of course, God's response to Paul's cry does not end with "trapping and punishing." Paul's rhetorical question in Romans 11:11 indicates yet another shift in the argument and another piece of the response to his cry, "Therefore, I say (λέγω οὖν) they did not stumble in order that they might fall did they? May it never be." Paul denies the conclusion that God is trapping and punishing Israel so that they stumble and fall irrevocably from salvation. Instead, Israel's stumbling, or their transgression (παράπτωμα) of rejecting the gospel, is the divine means to Gentile salvation, Jewish jealousy, and ultimately resurrection from the dead. Paul explains:

> But by their transgression (παραπτώματι) salvation (σωτηρία) is to the Gentiles in order to make them jealous (παραζηλῶσαι). But if their (παράπτωμα) transgression is wealth for the world and their loss is wealth for the Gentiles, how much more their transgression. (Rom 11:11–12)

> For if their rejection (ἀποβολή) is the reconciliation of the world, what will their acceptance be if not life from the dead? (Rom 11:15)

---

87. Keel suggests, "The 'table,' consisting of an outspread mat, might very well be compared to an open snare . . . , and the foods placed on it could be compared to the trigger ('trap') which holds the bait." Keel, *The Symoblism of the Biblical World*, 91.

88 Seifrid, *Romans*, 671.

89 Ibid.

Here we find the catalyst for Paul's apostolic ministry and a major part of God's answer to his intercessory cry. Paul "glories" in preaching the gospel to Gentiles, because it will make his Jewish kinsmen jealous. That jealousy will lead to their acceptance of the gospel and their salvation which is the very thing Paul requests in Romans 9:3 and 10:1 (Rom 11:13–14). Yet, an answer to his cry for Israel will also answer the "groaning" of all creation, the children of God, and the Spirit (Rom 8:19–27). They all long for the resurrection of the dead, and God's answer to that longing is indissolubly bound up in Israel's faith in the gospel. Furthermore, Israel's faith in the gospel is indissolubly bound up with the jealousy created by Gentile faith in the Jewish Messiah. It is a faith created when Paul preaches to the Gentiles. In a certain sense, the answer to all of Paul's prayers, even those for his kinsmen, is found in preaching the gospel to the Gentiles.

In Romans 11:16–24, Paul further explains how God has not trapped and punished Israel so that they might irrevocably fall from salvation. Here he evokes the image of an olive tree. The image has a duel function of both assuring the reader that Israel can still be saved and warning Gentile Christians about boasting in their position. Paul begins with the olive tree's "first fruits" and "root," "But if the first fruit (ἀπαρχή) is holy (ἁγία), also the batch is holy; and if the root (ῥίζα) is holy (ἁγία), also the branches" (Rom 11:16). The holy ἀπαρχή and ῥίζα is a metaphorical reference to the patriarchs. They were ἁγία, or set apart by God to experience the blessing of deliverance.[90] Therefore, their "batch" or "branches" will experience the same. Paul explains that if wild branches were grafted into the tree, it follows that the natural branches, though cut off for the wild branches to be grafted in, can be grafted in once again into their own olive tree (Rom 11:24). Just as the wild branches were grafted in by faith, the natural branches will be grafted back in if they do not remain in unbelief (Rom 11:20, 23).

This leads to the final movement in Paul's argument and the final piece of God's response to his intercessory cry. In Romans 11:25–32, Paul labels all that he has been saying up to this point a μυστήριον. He explains, "For I do not want you to be ignorant, brothers, of this mystery (μυστήριον), in order that you might not be wise in yourselves, that a partial hardening has taken place with Israel until the fullness of the Gentiles might enter in" (Rom 11:25). After the allotted number of Gentiles has entered into the people of God, Paul says "all Israel will be saved" just as it is written in Israel's scriptures (Rom 11:26). The much debated reference "all Israel will be saved" is not an indication that all Israel from all historical periods will be saved irrespective of their faith in Jesus. That would make Paul's intercessory

---

90 See Havemann, "Cultivated Olive," 87–106.

lament in Romans 9:1–5 entirely superfluous.[91] Instead, Paul is thinking eschatologically about Israel's salvation. It is salvation marked by two eschatological moments: (1) the full number of Gentiles entering the people of God; and (2) the coming of Israel's deliver from Zion. Paul sees the latter moment discussed in the prophets, "The deliverer will come from Zion, he will turn ungodliness from Jacob. And this is the covenant with them from me, whenever I should take away their sins" (Rom 11:26–27). Paul conflates pieces from Isaiah 59:20, Jeremiah 38:31 (31:31 MT), and Isaiah 27:9.[92] As I discussed in chapter 4, the original context of Isaiah 59 speaks of God's judgment against Israel (59:1–8), their cry for help (59:9–15), and God's arrival like a warrior (59:16–20). Isaiah personifies sin like an enemy from whom Israel needs to be delivered. He will answer the cry of his people. For Paul, Israel's sin is unbelief in the gospel. Yet, when the deliverer comes from the heavenly Zion, they will believe and be delivered from that enemy.[93] Seifrid explains, "Israel will see and believe in him as the coming Redeemer, as Paul himself did. The final act in the drama of redemption is not the formation of a church that consists largely of Gentiles, but the creation of salvation for the people of Israel."[94] This is an eschatological moment of salvation for Israel. Until that moment, Paul continues to preach to Gentiles in order to make his kinsmen jealous. In this way, he hopes to save some, particularly those who will not be living when the deliver comes from "Zion" (Rom 11:14).

Paul finishes his thoughts on the "mystery" he has laid out in Romans 9–11, as well as the response he has received to his intercessory cry, by coming once again to the interplay between God's judgment and mercy. For the sake of the Gentiles, Paul's kinsmen are God's enemies (ἐχθροί) (Rom 11:28). Yet, in light of the promises made to the fathers, they are beloved (Rom 11:28). The promises to Israel which elicit Paul's original cry of distress in Romans 9:1–5 are described here as irrevocable, "For the gifts and the calling of God are irrevocable (ἀμεταμέλητα)" (Rom 11:29). God gives mercy to the Gentiles by means of Israel's rejection of the gospel (Rom 11:30–31). Yet, that rejection does not somehow undo God's prior promises and calling to Israel. Instead, both Gentiles and Jews have been disobedient (ἀπειθέω/

---

91 As Seifrid notes, "Paul's point here is not that every last member of Israel in all of time will be saved; if that were the case, his deep lament, with his willingness to suffer his own condemnation for Israel's sake would be pointless." Seifrid, *Romans*, 673. See also, Moo, *Romans*, 719–26.

92 On the conflation of Isa 59:20 and 27:9, see Shum, *Paul's Use of Isaiah in Romans*, 240.

93 On "heavenly Zion," see Schreiner, *Romans*, 619.

94 Seifrid, *Romans*, 673.

ἀπείθεια) to God (Rom 11:30–31). More precisely, "God has confined all to disobedience, in order that he might have mercy on all" (Rom 11:32).

To sum up the answer to Paul's cry in Romans 11:1–32, a few things should be kept in view. The answer to the echoes of "how long" and the cry "I was wishing to be accursed from Christ for my kinsmen" is personal, complex, and heavily reliant on Israel's Scriptures. The answer is found in Paul's own experience of God's grace which means Israel has not been entirely rejected (Rom 11:1). He is also told that there is a remnant just as Elijah was told when he cried out for/against Israel (Rom 11:2–6). Those outside the remnant are hardened and treated like the psalmist's enemies (11:7–11). Yet, it does not follow that Israel has irrevocably fallen from the possibility of salvation. Here the answer to Paul's cry is found in his own apostolic ministry to Gentiles, a ministry that makes Jews jealous to the point of faith in Christ. His preaching has the power to bring "natural branches" back into the people of God. Rather than be "accursed" for his kinsmen, he must preach to Gentiles to make his kinsmen jealous. Moreover, just as the lament in Isaiah 59 makes clear, the answer to Paul's cry on behalf of Israel is ultimately found in the arrival of the deliverer from the heavenly Zion. In that eschatological moment, Jesus will take away Israel's sin of unbelief. Finally, Paul's cry is answered in a mystery involving Jews and Gentiles. The former are hardened so that the latter might enter into the people of God. Yet, both have been confined to disobedience, in order that God might have mercy on all. In other words, the answer to Paul's cry of distress about unbelieving and rejected Israel is that God's mercy is hidden in his judgment. It is the very response given to Moses when he asked to be "wiped out" from the book if God were unwilling to forgive Israel. Paul indeed is Israel's intercessory lamenter, and, like anyone who laments in that way, there is a response from God. The impact of this response is not surprising. It is seen repeatedly in OT lament. God's answer turns heartfelt pain and cries of distress to praise. That is what we find in the final section of Romans 9–11.

The Shift from Lament to Praise in Romans 11:33–36

Although Paul began this section of the letter with a lament over Israel's unbelief and rejection, he ends with poignant doxology that is centered on God's incredible wisdom and judgment as creator.[95] OT lament is so often

---

95 Johnson observes a number of features in Rom 11:33–36 that indicate it is a hymn. She writes, "Its strophic structure of nine lines, the repetition of triads, the chiastic relationship among the divine attributes and rhetorical questions, the repeated pronominal references to God, and the doxological conclusion are all indications of

marked by the shift from cries of distress to praise, and that holds true here as well.[96] However, as is also true of OT lament, the shift here is not permanent. One should not assume that Paul ceases his intercessory lament after he receives the answer laid out in Romans 9:6—11:32. After all, the linchpin to the entire response is the return of Christ. Paul's intercession for Israel would certainly continue until that moment. Therefore, the echoes of "how long" could still be heard in Paul's requests. In any case, the praise in 11:33–36 evokes thoughts of God as the unfathomably wise creator. It is wisdom particularly related to how the creator deals with unbelieving Israel and wisdom that responds to Paul's cry of distress. There are three particular movements in the hymn that echo a number of OT texts.

First, Romans 11:33 contains the "threefold praise of God's riches, wisdom, and knowledge" in dealing with Israel and beyond.[97] As we have seen in Romans 9–11, God's dealings with Israel have implications for Gentiles and the resurrection of the dead. From this perspective, Paul exclaims "O the depth (βάθος) of the wealth and of the wisdom and of knowledge of God." In the LXX, βάθος often occurs in literal and figurative references to the immeasurable depth of the sea, waters, pit, or the earth.[98] Paul employs βάθος to describe the immeasurable wealth, wisdom, and knowledge that God does and will display in saving his kinsmen and Gentiles.[99] The final disclosure of the creator's mystery will result in wealth (πλοῦτος) that is difficult to measure. Paul especially extols God's σοφία and γνῶσις. His praise echoes the psalmist and Job:

> How great are your works, O Lord; you have done everything in wisdom (σοφίᾳ), the earth is filled with your creation. (Ps 103:24)

> With him is wisdom (σοφία) and power, with him is counsel (βουλὴ) and understanding (σύνεσις). (Job 12:13)

---

hymnic material"; Johnson, *The Function of Apocalyptic Wisdom Traditions in Romans 9–11*, 166.

96 See Villaneuva, *The Uncertainty of a Hearing*.

97 Seifrid, *Romans*, 678.

98 See, e.g. Job 28:11; Amos 9:3; Jon 2:4; Isa 7:11; Ezek 26:20; 31:14; 31:18; 32:24. Some uses occur in contexts where the speaker praises God for future forgiveness or deliverance. See, e.g. Isa 51:10; Mic 7:19; Zech 10:11. However, examples such as these are not echoed in Rom 11:33. In their original contexts, they do not speak directly about God but rather a figurative place to which he sends sin, or a place where he dries up waters to enable deliverance.

99 Paul employs βάθος in other doxological statements as well. See e.g., 1 Cor 2:10; Eph 3:18.

The praise of the creator's wisdom by the psalmist and Job comes from a place of pain. While the psalmist gushes over the creator for almost all of Psalm 103, the closing line is a request against sinners and the lawless.[100] Similarly, Job's acknowledgment of God's wisdom comes within the context of profound pain exacerbated by the "wisdom" of his "friends." These echoes are reminder that Paul's praise also comes from a place of pain. Israel's unbelief remains, as well as the causes of suffering discussed throughout the letter.

Next, Paul praises God's judgments and ways "how unsearchable are his judgments (κρίματα) and unfathomable are his ways (ὁδοί)" (Rom 11:33). Paul's praise for God's κρίματα echoes the psalmist, "Your righteousness is like the mountains of God, and your judgments (κρίματά) are a great abyss; men and beasts you will save, O Lord" (Ps 35:7).[101] In context, the psalmist complains against his enemies but shifts to praise in the midst of the complaint.[102] The psalmist likens God's judgments to a great abyss (ἄβυσσος πολλή). In other words, his judgments, or decisions, are difficult to comprehend. They are decisions that lead to salvation as the end of Psalm 35:7 indicates, "you will save" (σώσεις). This sheds light on what Paul means when he describes God's judgments as ἀνεξεραύνητα.[103] Echoing the psalmist, Paul praises the unsearchable decisions God makes in saving both Jew and Gentile. They are like an abyss in which the bottom cannot be reached. Despite the fact that Paul just "traced" God's dealings with Israel, and their implications for the whole cosmos, he praises God's judgments in this matter as being untraceable.

Parallel to God's "inscrutable judgments" in saving Jew and Gentile are his ἀνεξιχνίαστοι ὁδοί. Like κρίμα, the use of ὁδός is not abstract or general. Paul refers specifically to the "unfathomable ways" that God saves Jew and Gentile. The phrase echoes a few different OT texts that shed further light on Paul's praise. We begin with the psalmist who exclaims, "Your way (ὁδός) is in the sea, and your paths (τρίβοι) are in many waters, and your steps (ἴχνη) will not be known (Ps 76:20)." The wider context of Psalm 76 resembles some of the concerns expressed in Romans 9–11:

> The Lord will not reject (ἀπώσεται) forever will he? Will he not still delight? Or will he cut off his mercy forever, from generation

---

100 See Ps 103:35.

101 See also the use of κρῖμα in Pss 47:12; 96:8; 104:5; 118:62, 164.

102 See Ps 35:1–5.

103 The adjective ἀνεξεραύνητος is a *hapax legomenon* in the NT. It does not occur in the LXX.

to generation? Or will God forget to have compassion? Or will he withhold his compassion in his wrath? (Ps 76:8–10)[104]

Like the psalmist, Paul wrestles with whether or not God has rejected (ἀπωθέω) his kinsmen.[105] The psalmist questions whether God will ultimately act in mercy or wrath. His answer comes from remembering God's works and meditating upon them, "I will meditate (μελετήσω) on all your works and I will consider (ἀδολεσχήσω) your ways (ἐπιτηδεύμασίν σου)" (Ps 76:13).[106] The result is a shift from lament to praise for God's redemption (Ps 76:14-16). That redemptive work shakes creation as in the exodus (Ps 76:17-19, 21). Yet, despite the revelation of that salvation, God's saving ὁδός remains unseen, even like footprints in the sea.[107] Likewise, Paul cries out on behalf of Israel. He seeks an answer to his own questions, and he finds it through further meditation upon the gospel as it relates to Jew and Gentiles. His reflection does not result in praise that he now understands all that God is doing and will do. Paul recognizes that God is working to save, and he obviously has a great deal to say about it. Yet, he also confesses that God's ways (ὁδοί) of doing it are ultimately "not able to be tracked out."[108] That is the literal sense of Paul's modifier ἀνεξιχνίαστοι. Discerning God's saving ways with Jew and Gentile is like trying to track footprints in the sea.[109]

Paul's use of ἀνεξιχνίαστοι ὁδοί also echoes some statements made by Job about God's unfathomable ways:

> The one who does great and unfathomable (ἀνεξιχνίαστα) things, both glorious and praiseworthy of which there is no number. (Job 9:10)[110]

> Behold these are parts of his way (μέρη ὁδοῦ), and at the moisture of his word (ἰκμάδα λόγου) we will hear him; but the strength of his thunder who knows when he will do it? (Job 26:14)

Once again, Job speaks from a place of immense pain. His statements here, though bearing a doxological stamp, arise in the midst of many questions and profound suffering. Job wrestles to understand God's ways given the tension between what he knows about God and everything he is currently experiencing. In the first example, we find the actual term that Paul uses in

---

104 See e.g., Ps 76:1–4.
105 See the use of ἀπωθέω Rom 11:1.
106. See also Ps 76:12.
107 See Seifrid, "Storylines of Scripture," 88–106.
108 See BDAG, 691–692; Völkel, "ὁδός," in *TDNT* 2:491–93.
109 See Seifrid, "Storylines of Scripture," 88–106.
110 Cf. Job 5:9.

his doxology, ἀνεξιχνίαστα.[111] In the wider context of Job 9, Job laments the fact that he cannot really contend with his creator in a dispute, "For if he wished to be judged by him, he certainly would not listen to him, so that he would not answer back one word from a thousand" (Job 9:3).[112] Even worse, if God did answer Job's cry, Job is not sure if he would really discern it. The one who does "unfathomable things" (ἀνεξιχνίαστα) could pass by Job without him knowing it, "If he should pass, I certainly shall not see; and if he should go by me, not even then when I know it" (Job 9:11). Additionally, the lament in Job 26:14 strikes a slightly more positive note in terms of the ability to discern God's ways. Job sees "parts of his way" (μέρη ὁδοῦ), but it is likened to moisture (ἰκμάς) before a great storm. Both of these echoes shed light on Paul's praise that God's ὁδοί are ἀνεξιχνίαστοι. God answers Paul's cry, but his praise, which echoes Job 9:10, acknowledges that the response is almost imperceptible. This is surely an admission that Paul has a difficult time wrapping his mind around God's ways of saving Jew and Gentile. Even what God reveals is partial (Job 26:14). Partial knowledge of God's ways is something Paul explicitly acknowledges elsewhere.[113]

Paul's use of ἀνεξιχνίαστοι ὁδοί also echoes Isaiah 55 where God describes the unfathomable nature of his ways with Israel. He asserts, "'For my plans are not like your plans nor are your ways my ways (αἱ ὁδοί),' says the Lord; 'but as the heaven is distant from the earth, in this manner my way (ἡ ὁδός) is from your ways and your thoughts from my understanding'" (Isa 55:8–9). The wider context of Isaiah 55 contains thematic coherence with Romans 9–11. Most notably, there is mention made of foreign nations seeking refuge in Israel's God, "Nations (ἔθνη), who were not knowing you, they will call you, and peoples, who did not understand you, they will flee to you on account of your God the Holy One of Israel, because he glorified you" (Isa 55:5). As we saw at various points in Romans 9–11, part of God's response to Paul's cry involves the relationship between Israel and Gentiles. The disobedience of the former means mercy for the latter. From Paul's perspective, the nations are indeed coming to Israel's God as Isaiah prophesied. Yet, it is in an unfathomable manner. It is not the ὁδός that Paul, or any other person, would have chosen, just as Isaiah intimates. Nevertheless, the gospel remains God's power to save the Jew and Gentile who believes (Rom 1:16). It is a word that will not fail, and its effect on Jew and Gentile is as certain

---

111 There are only four uses of the term in the LXX, and Job contains three of them. Therefore, this increases the volume of the echo in Romans 11:33. See Ode 12:6; Job 5:9; 9:10; 34:24.

112 The emphasis on God as creator is clear in Job 9:6–9.

113 See, e.g. 1 Cor 2:6–9; 13:9–10.

as the produce that springs from the ground when it has been nurtured by rain (Isa 55:10–11).

Paul's doxology continues in Romans 11:34–35 which contain further uses of Isaiah and Job, "For who has known the mind of the Lord? Or who has been his counselor? Or who has given to him and it will be returned to him." These lines contain citations of Isaiah 40:13 and Job 41:3 respectively. In its original context, Isaiah 40:13 answers the question "Who can accurately comprehend the aspect of God and so tell him what to do?"[114] Both Isaiah and Paul praise God that his ways cannot be molded into manageable systems based on the input of fallen humanity.[115] Isaiah recognized that the creator would reveal himself to Israel and deal with the nations as he wished.[116] No one could advise God or be his σύμβουλος. In the same vein, Paul praises God's absolute autonomy and freedom to save both Jew and Gentile as he wished. For Paul, this is not something to be resented or resisted but praised. Moreover, it serves as yet another answer to his cries of "how long" and "I was wishing to be accursed." Just as God answered Moses in a way that asserted his wisdom and authority to act in judgment and mercy as he willed, the echoes from the citation of Isaiah 40:13 in Romans 11:34 evoke the same kind of response. This is also evident in Paul's citation of Job 41:3. Although Paul's citation diverges from the LXX version, conceptually they are very similar.[117] Job could not ultimately win a judgment against God, as the wider context demonstrates. Job presses God for an answer to his cries throughout the book. Yet, when God the creator finally answers in chapters 38–39, Job realizes that "the divine wisdom is beyond the ability of any human being to grasp."[118] Job cannot understand the profundity of the creator. He cannot accurately assess, nor counsel God, in his ways. Job provides no insight to God. Similarly, when God answers Paul's cries on behalf of Israel, he realizes that he too is unable to fathom the profundity of God's judgment and mercy. Paul cannot provide God with insight that would somehow obligate God to be indebted to him (Rom 11:35). To be sure,

---

114. Oswalt, *The Book of Isaiah*, 59.

115 Achtemeier notes, "The attempt to create a more manageable, visible God runs from the time of Israel's creation as a people to the post-exilic time when they still needed warning against such an attempt. Yet, there again, it was that very difference that made it possible for God to be deliverer and redeemer"; Achtemeier, *Romans*, 190.

116 See e.g., Isa 40:10–15.

117 Job 41:3 LXX reads, "Or who will resist my and endure, is not everything under heaven mine?" Stuhlmacher notes, "The apostle expresses this truth with words from an ancient Greek translation of Job 41:3, only the vestiges of which are still known to us." Stuhlmacher, *Paul's Letter to the Romans*, 176. To some degree, Paul's version is closer to the MT in this instance.

118 Hartley, *The Book of Job*, 536.

as Romans 9:6—11:32 demonstrates, Paul understands a great deal about God's dealings with Jew and Gentile alike. Nevertheless, as the echoes of this doxology make clear, Paul does not now claim to understand everything about God's ways. The praise suggests that like the psalmist, Isaiah, and Job Paul is well aware that the divine plan for Jew and Gentile is mysterious and can only be discerned to the degree which God chooses to reveal it.[119] No one can give to him in a way, not even if the offer is to be "accursed from Christ," that requires God to give back to him (ἀνταποδίδωμι) (Rom 11:35).

The final piece of the doxology in Romans 11:36 links Paul's answer to the preceding questions. The reason no one can counsel God in his ways, or give him instruction, is because "from him (ἐξ αὐτοῦ) and through him (δι' αὐτοῦ) and to him (εἰς αὐτόν) are all things." The string of prepositional phrases indicates that God is the source (ἐξ αὐτοῦ), agent (δι' αὐτοῦ), and purpose (εἰς αὐτόν) of all things.[120] He is especially the source, agent, and purpose of all things pertaining to how God fulfills his prior promises, the promises which Paul is deeply concerned about in Romans 9:1–5. Judgment and mercy are from God, through God, and the final goal is God. That is why Paul's intercessory lament can, and does, finally shift to praise.

SUMMARY

We have covered a great amount of exegetical ground in this chapter. The attempt to read Romans 9–11 as lament has proved challenging. The seemingly endless train of lament citations and echoes requires reading at the levels of Paul's argument, the original contexts of the OT usage, and the relationship between the former and the latter. When we ask what interpretive "gap" is filled by reading Romans 9–11 as lament at least two things stand out.

First, when Romans 9–11 is read as lament, Paul's entire argument becomes a divine response to his opening cry of distress. Collectively, the chapters contain the five-fold pattern of lament. Paul cries out on behalf of his Israelite kinsmen whose unbelief in the gospel has far reaching implications for them and for God. We catch a glimpse of how Paul prays for his brethren. The echoes of lament present in the text shed light on the possible content of that prayer. Specifically, the prayer report in Romans 9:1–5 echoes Psalm 12 and Exodus 32–34. These echoes indicate that Paul has two pressing complaints, or requests: (1) How long will God "hide his

---

119 Johnson notes that Isa 40:13 and Job 41:3 were often linked in rabbinic interpretation. See Johnson, *The Function of Apocalyptic and Wisdom Traditions*, 167.

120 See Sanday and Headlam, *Romans*, 340.

face," or reject his kinsmen? (2) If God is rejecting them, and unwilling to forgive them, Paul requests to be accursed from Christ in the same way Moses asked to be wiped out from God's "book." From 9:6—11:32, God responds to Paul's complaint in a way that echoes his response to Moses in Exodus 32–34.[121] The answer to Paul's complaint comes in four movements: (1) Rom 9:6–13; (2) 9:14–29; (3) 9:30—10:21; and (4) 11:1–32. In short, God always creates Israel through a promise. In this promissory act, God has the authority to act in his righteousness as he pleases in the same way that a potter can create different vessels for different purposes. It does not follow that Israel is without culpability for its rejection of the gospel. They have no excuses for their unbelief. Nevertheless, that is not the end of God's response to Paul's cry. Israel's rejection of the gospel is actually part of God's purposes and promises. It provides the platform for God to reveal his mercy to Gentiles and some of Israel now but to save "all Israel" in the end through the appearance of the Messiah. What all four parts of the answer share in common is that God's mercy is both hidden and revealed in judgment. The divine answer to Paul is something he can only call a "mystery." It is a mystery that moves Paul from crying out on behalf of Israel to praising God for the untraceable and unalterable ways he deals with them.

Second, reading Romans 9–11 as lament once again evokes the figure of a lamenter in the letter. In this instance, Paul is an intercessory lamenter. He echoes the cries of Moses, Isaiah, and Elijah. They all cried out for/against Israel, and their cries illuminate Paul's own pain and lament. Of course, neither their cries nor Paul's "changed" God's ways with Israel. The cries definitely affect the lamenters more so than God as the divine response to all four of them bears out. However, the sense of the divine response in Romans 9–11, just as the responses in the OT echoes, is not that Paul's cry is pointless. If none of the intercessors echoed in Romans 9–11 were told to stop "crying," it is safe to assume that neither was Paul. Instead, just as with Moses, Isaiah, and Elijah, the intercessory lament is something God purposes for Paul. He chooses for Paul to suffer as his apostle, and that suffering includes crying out on behalf of Israel. It is in such pain and in response to such cries that God's righteousness is revealed. In such distress, the gospel is the answer to Paul, Israel's intercessory lamenter.

---

121. To reiterate, the praise in Rom 11:33–36 helps to form an *inclusio* with the opening cry in 9:1–5. As Moo notes, "Rom. 9–11 is framed by an opening personal lament (9:1–5) and a closing doxology (11:33–36)." Moo, *Romans*, 553.

8

The Gospel as the Answer to the Church's Lament (Romans 15:1–6)

WE NEED TO EXAMINE one final echo of OT lament in Paul's most famous letter. It occurs in Romans 15:1–6 as Paul addresses a particular problem that had arisen between Jewish and Gentile Christians in Rome.[1] While exhorting the "strong" in faith to not please themselves, Paul cites a portion of Psalm 68:10, "The reproaches of those who reproach you fell upon me" (Rom 15:3). Paul's use of this psalm is intriguing on a few different levels. He puts the psalmist's words on the lips of Jesus and evokes the crucifixion scene, particularly the scorn and mocking Jesus had to endure. This seems like a drastic rhetorical move given the fact that Paul is addressing a dispute over observing certain holy days and dietary practices among Christians in Rome. The citation is even more perplexing when it is read in light of its original context. The psalmist describes enemies that Paul knows typify those who mocked Jesus. Yet, that does not prevent Paul from identifying those enemies with people in the church. Additionally, Paul follows his citation of Psalm 68 with the explanation "For as much as was written beforehand, it has been written for our instructions, in order that through endurance and the encouragement of the scriptures we might have hope" (Rom 15:4). The proximity between this explanation and the citation of a well-known lament psalm suggests that Paul recognizes how instructive OT lament is for the Christian experience. For these reasons and more, the

---

1. For various historical views on the "weak" and "strong" in Rom 14, see Barclay, "Do We Undermine the Law?" 287–308; Karris, "Romans 14:1—15:13," 65–85.

echoes of lament in Paul's argument in this section of the letter are both intriguing and worthy of consideration in the present study.

The overarching thesis in this chapter is two pronged. First, the echoes of Psalm 68 coupled with the narrative substructure of Jesus' crucifixion indicate that some believers in Rome were suffering intense pain at the hands of those within the church. Second, Paul's statement in Romans 15:4 highlights the didactic nature of OT lament for Christians in Rome and beyond. We will begin by examining Psalm 68 in its original context and then analyze how the echoes from this psalm impact the interpretation of Romans 15:1–6. We will then consider Paul's statement in Romans 15:4 as it relates to the didactic nature of OT lament.

ANALYZING AND READING THE ECHOES OF LAMENT IN ROMANS 15:1-6

The echoes of lament in Romans 15:1–6 resonate from Psalm 68 and Jesus' crucifixion.[2] The echoes here are not limited to the specific verse Paul cites but the wider contents of the psalm. In order to hear those wider echoes in the letter, we need to analyze Psalm 68:10 in its original context. We must also consider the use of Psalm 68 in the crucifixion narrative, because that makes up the narrative substructure of Romans 15:1–6. By analyzing the original context of Psalm 68, as well as the use of that psalm in the crucifixion narrative, we will be equipped to read Romans 15:1–6 in light of its echoes of lament.

Psalm 68 in Context

In Romans 15:3, Paul cites part of Psalm 68:10, "The reproaches of those who reproach you fell upon me." It originally functions as part of the psalmist's larger complaint to God against his enemies. The psalm oscillates between complaint and petition before ending with a word of confident praise.

The complaints in Psalm 68 revolve primarily around the activity of the speaker's enemies. The affliction they cause is colorfully described and far reaching. The psalmist complains that as a result of his enemies he is drowning, stuck in deep mud, and hoarse from crying out to God (Ps 68:2–5). He is at the point of losing hope, "My eyes have failed from hoping

---

2. For a different reading of the echoes in this portion of the letter, see Hays, "Christ Prays the Psalms," 101–18.

(ἐλπίζειν) in my God" (Ps 68:4). The psalmist has been driven to fasting and dressing in sackcloth, clear indicators that he is in mourning (Ps 68:11–12).

The psalmist especially emphasizes the pain caused by the verbal insults launched against him. Given his condition, the psalmist suffers reproach (ὀνειδισμός) from his enemies and has become a byword (παραβολή) to them (Ps 68:11–12). Those who sit in the gates of the city talk idly (ἀδολεσχέω) about the psalmist, and drunkards sing disparaging songs about him (Ps 68:13). The enemies sarcastically offer him gall for food and vinegar for his drink (Ps 68:22). God is well aware of the verbal affliction, "For you know my reproach (ὀνειδισμόν) and my shame (αἰσχύνην) and my humiliation (ἐντροπήν); all those who afflict me are before you" (Ps 68:20). The terms ὀνειδισμός, αἰσχύνη, and ἐντροπή share the same semantic domain. The language indicates that the psalmist is insulted by enemies resulting in shame and embarrassment. The shame and embarrassment is frequent as indicated by the psalmist's complaint that he has become a byword (παραβολή) to others and that people sing songs about him (Ps 68:11, 13). The ὀνειδισμός has even resulted in the psalmist's estrangement from his loved ones, "For on account of you I bear reproach (ὀνειδισμόν), humiliation has covered my face. I have been estranged from my brethren and a stranger to the sons of your mother" (Ps 68:8–9). Therefore, he finds no encouragement in his distress (Ps 68:21).

The petitions also reveal a great deal about the psalmist's suffering and the enemies who afflict him. The first petition is that his affliction might not lead to shame and disappointment on the part of those who look at him and seek God, "May those who wait on you not be disappointed by me, O Lord, Lord of powers, let not those who seek you be ashamed, O God of Israel" (Ps 68:7). This petition implies that the psalmist is worried that his suffering and shame could discourage others from seeking God. He also requests to be heard and thereby delivered from his enemies (Ps 68:14–15). The psalmist asks not to be swallowed up in the deep or in the pit at the hands of his opponents (68:16, 19). He requests that God see him rather than turn his face away (68:18). As we have seen elsewhere, references to the hiding of God's face echoes Deuteronmoic warnings about what would happen when Israel broke the Mosaic Law.[3] Instead, the psalmist requests that God see his affliction and entrap his enemies like a hunter seeking its prey (Ps 68:23–24).[4] The fiercest request is found in 68:28–29, "Pay attention to the lawlessness upon their lawlessness and let them not enter in your righteousness; let them be wiped out from the book of the living and let

---

3 See e.g., Deut 31:17–18.
4 Cf. Paul's use of Ps 68:23 in Rom 11:9.

them not be listed with the righteous."[5] Here the psalmist makes a clear and eschatological distinction between the righteous and the unrighteous. The psalmist is so pained by his opponents that he requests they be condemned in God's final judgment.

In Psalm 68:31–37, the psalmist's complaints and requests turn to a statement of certainty and praise. The psalmist recognizes that God is more pleased with his heartfelt praise than sacrifices, "And it will be more pleasing (ἀρέσει) to God than a new bull, horns and hoofs being brought forth" (Ps 68:32). He is also certain that God hears his cries (Ps 68:34). The psalmist encourages all of creation to join in praising God for the deliverance he gives to the righteous (Ps 68:35). He is certain that the cities of Judah will be built up despite their enemies and that those who love God's name will dwell in Zion (Ps 68:36–37).

It is in the midst of this oscillation between complaints, petition, and praise that the psalmist asserts, "Because zeal for you house (οἶκος) consumed me, and the reproaches of those who reproach you fell upon me" (Ps 68:10). The psalmist indicates a willingness to suffer at the hands of his enemies, because he is zealous for God's οἶκος. He also draws a connection between the verbal insult (ὀνειδισμός) that he endures and the insult of God. One is tantamount to the other. As the enemies insult the psalmist, they are actually insulting God. Yet, God does not receive that insult directly. It actually "falls upon" the psalmist.

Echoes of Psalm 68 in the Crucifixion of Jesus

The suffering of the lamenter in Psalm 68 is echoed in the Synoptic accounts of Jesus' crucifixion.[6] To begin, the Matthean account echoes the psalmist's complaint that his enemies gave him gall (χολή) to drink, "They gave him wine mixed with gall (χολῆς); and having tasted it he was not willing to drink it" (Matt 27:34).[7] Both in Psalm 68:22 and Matthew 27:34, the offer of something to drink are insults. Verbal insults that echo Psalm 68 are also present in the Synoptic accounts of Jesus' crucifixion. The psalmist complains that he has become a "byword" (παραβολή) to his enemies, and Jesus has a placard above him with the inscription "This is the king of the Jews"

---

5 Cf. Exod 32:32; Rom 9:3.

6. On the importance of this psalm in the early church, see Dodd, *According to the Scriptures*, 57–59. On the specific echoes of lament from the psalms in the Passion narrative, see Ahearne-Kroll, *The Psalms of Lament in Mark's Passion*, 68–71.

7 The parallel account in Mark 15:23 does not contain the noun χολή.

(Ps 68:12; Matt 27:37). Additionally, like the enemies of the psalmist who reproached him, Jesus' enemies do the same:

> Because on account of you I have borne reproach (ὀνειδισμόν), shame has covered my face. (Ps 68:8)

> "The Christ, the King of Israel, let him come down now from the cross, in order that we might and we might believe." And those who had been crucified with him were reproaching (ὠνείδιζον) him. (Mark 15:32)

Jesus is reviled by those being crucified with him, those who carry out the crucifixion, and those on the ground. Matthew contains a vivid account of the insults. He notes that people passing by Jesus were wagging (κινοῦντες) their heads at him. This is body language that indicates utter disgust with what is being witnessed.[8] The verbal insults include:

> The one who destroys the temple and in the three days rebuilds it, save yourself if you are the son of God and come down from the cross. (Matt 27:40)

> He saved others, is he not able to save himself; he is the king of Israel, let him come down now from the cross and we will believe in him. He has trusted in God, let him deliver him now if he wants him; for he has said "I am the son of God." (Matt 27:42–43)

These insults are uttered by those passing by, the chief priests, and the elders. They all believe that they are insulting a blasphemer or criminal. Yet, in these accounts, the Synoptic writers indicate that the insults are actually being hurled at God. For example, Matthew describes the insults as blasphemy, "And those passing by were blaspheming (ἐβλασφήμουν)" (Matt 27:39).[9] The centurion's confession indicates that the insults leveled against Jesus were actually leveled against God, "Truly this was the son of God" (Matt 27:54).[10] In the Lukan version, the centurion confesses, "Surely this man was righteous" (Luke 23:47). As he dies, Jesus' enemies revile him as being unrighteous. Yet, after he dies, the centurion reverses their insults and calls Jesus δίκαιος. The centurion is described as glorifying God rather than reviling him "And the centurion having seen the thing which happened was glorifying (ἐδόξαζεν) God" (Luke 23:47). The catalyst of the centurion's

---

8. The "wagging of heads" echoes what enemies do in Ps 21:8.
9 See also Mark 15:29.
10 See also Mark 15:39.

confession is witnessing the manner in which Jesus endured the insults and died.[11]

In recounting the insults Jesus endured at his crucifixion, the Synoptic writers do not cite Psalm 68:10b, "The reproaches of those who reproached you fell upon me." Yet, it is an apt description of what happens to Jesus. The Synoptic writers are well aware that the insults hurled against God actually "fell" on Jesus. Those passing by, chief priests, elders, and the criminals crucified with Jesus do not realize they are insulting God by insulting Jesus. Moreover, Jesus does not return insults with insults. He endures the verbal assaults and trusts that God will judge righteously. Later reflection on this feature of Jesus' crucifixion is found in 1 Peter 2:23, "Who although being reviled (λοιδορούμενος) was not reviling in return (ἀντελοιδόρει), while suffering he was not threatening, but he was handing himself over to the one who judges righteously." In the Petrine context, this dynamic of Jesus' crucifixion is evoked to instruct early Christians how to respond to insults from outside the church. Paul also evokes this feature of Jesus' crucifixion, but he does it through reflection on Psalm 68. Moreover, as we will see, he appeals to insults at the crucifixion in order to instruct a group of Christians how to respond to insults within the church.

Echoes of Psalm 68 and Jesus Crucifixion in Romans 15:1–6

We begin with testing the echoes from Psalm 68 in Romans 15:1–6. The echoes can be heard at a high "volume," and there is thematic coherence between the two passages. The volume is indicated by the repetition of the key term ἀρέσκω. Paul uses it three times in Romans 15:1–3:

> Now we who are strong are obligated to bear the weaknesses of the powerless and not to please (ἀρέσκειν) ourselves. Let each one of us please (ἀρεσκέτω) his neighbor for the good towards edification; for also Christ did not please (ἤρεσεν) himself, but just as it is written; the reproaches of those who reproach you fell upon me.

Contextually, ἀρέσκω conveys self-approving and self-satisfying conduct that Paul exhorts the "strong" in faith to avoid in their dealings with the weak in faith.[12] As an example, he points to Christ's conduct at his crucifixion focusing especially upon how he handled the verbal insults launched at him. He filters the evocation of Christ's conduct through Psalm 68 where

---

11 See Matt 27:54; Mar 15:39; Luke 23:47.
12 See BDAG, 129–30; LEH, 81; Schneider, "ἀρέσκω," *EDNT* 1:151.

we find ἀρέσκω.¹³ It occurs in the praise portion of the psalm as the speaker exclaims, "I will sing the name of God with an ode, I will magnify him with singing, and it will be more pleasing (ἀρέσει) to God than a new bull, horns and hoofs being brought forth" (Ps 68:31–32). The sense of ἀρέσκω here is that as the psalmist is afflicted by enemies what pleases God is heartfelt praise. For Paul, Jesus' endurance of insults at the crucifixion is an act of praise that pleases God. Christ did not please himself by hurling insults at his enemies. Rather, he endured the verbal assault and the crucifixion on their behalf. In this way, his sacrifice was pleasing to God. The enemies reproached God by reproaching Jesus, but Jesus praised him by enduring the insults. The "strong" in Rome can and must do the same by enduring the insults of the "weak."

We can also test the echoes of Psalm 68 through the thematic coherence with Romans 15:1–6. Here we must broaden the scope to Paul's argument in Romans 14. This is one of the most historically revealing passages of the entire letter.¹⁴ It points to a specific point of contention between two groups in Rome that Paul labels the "strong" (δυνατοί) and the "weak" (ἀσθενήματα). Paul never explicitly identifies the former as Gentile believers and the latter as Jewish. Nevertheless, this is surely part of the problem given the issues that Paul addresses in Romans 14.¹⁵ For example, there are differences of opinion regarding the spiritual importance of diet and the observance of days (Rom 14:1–9). The δυνατοί eat anything and regard one day as no more important than the next. The ἀσθενήματα take the opposite stance. Consequently, both groups judge one another and the basis of their judgment is the stance they take on these issues. This is what concerns Paul the most. He asks, "Who are you the one who judges another's servant? To his own Lord he stands or falls. But he will stand, for the Lord is able to make him stand" (Rom 14:4).

Paul recognizes the eschatological danger in their judgmentalism and disregard for the spiritual sensitivities of one another. It creates a stumbling block (πρόσκομμα) for some in the community (Rom 14:13). Specifically, the disregard of the strong for the weak is potentially damning for the latter, "For if your brother is grieved on account of food, you are no longer walking according to love; do not destroy (ἀπόλλυε) the one for whom Christ on account of your food" (Rom 14:15). The use of ἀπόλλυμι indicates the

---

13 This is the only occurrence of the verb in the Psalms.

14 See Jewett, *Romans*, 853–73.

15 Although, it does not necessarily follow that everyone in the "powerful" group were Gentiles and everyone in the "weak" were Jews. See Wright, *Romans*, 731.

eschatological wrath that accompanies the issue.[16] It is incumbent upon the "strong" to conduct themselves in a way that promotes peace and the building up of the community, particularly the weak (Rom 14:19). The stakes are extremely high. If the weak are encouraged by the strong to conduct themselves towards God in way that engenders doubt, it could lead to condemnation in the final judgment. Paul observes, "But the one who doubts (διακρινόμεος) if he should eat, has been condemned (κατακέκριται), because it is not from faith; and whatever is not from faith is sin" (Rom 14:23).

It is from this eschatological concern that we can see the thematic coherence between Psalm 68 and Romans 15:1–6. There are a few converging points here that illuminate Paul's argument. First, the suffering that the "strong" are to endure for the sake of the "weak" echoes one of the psalmist's requests:

> O God, you have known my foolishness, and my trespasses have not been hidden from you. Let not those who wait on you be disappointed because of me, O Lord, Lord of hosts, let not those who seek you be ashamed because of me, O God of Israel. (Ps 68:6–7)

The psalmist does not want to do anything that would cause those who are seeking the Lord to be ultimately disappointed in the Lord. Paul exhorts the "strong" in faith to make the same kind of request and live with a similar disposition. They must suffer like the psalmist, and in a certain way like Christ, so that the weak in faith are not ultimately disappointed in the Lord. Second, there is also thematic coherence in terms of the zeal (ζῆλος) that the strong must have for God's house (οἶκος). The psalmist cries out "I have become estranged from my brethren and a stranger to the sons of my mother, because zeal (ζῆλος) for your house (οἶκος) consumed me, and the reproaches of those who reproach you fell upon me" (Ps 68:9–10). Contextually, the psalmist is obviously speaking about the temple in Jerusalem. This zeal for God's οἶκος is echoed in Romans 14–15. Of course, Paul's concern is not the literal house of God but the church consisting of the "weak" and "strong" in faith. Temple language is one of Paul's favorite ecclesiastical metaphors, and it is implied in Romans 14:19–20:

> So then let us pursue the things of peace and the things of edification (οἰκοδομῆς) for one another. Do not destroy (κατάλυε) the work of God (τὸ ἔργον τοῦ θεοῦ) on account of food. All things are clean, but it is evil to the man who eats as through a stumbling block (προσκόματος).

---

16 See also the use of καταλύω in Rom 14:20.

The language of οἰκοδομῇ, κάταλυω, τὸ ἔργον τοῦ θεοῦ, and προσκόμα all indicate the use of architectural, perhaps even temple, imagery.[17] Rather than becoming a "stumbling" block to the weak and destroying them, the strong must build them up. If we hear the echo of Psalm 68:9–10, the strong in Rome must have a zeal for this house, or church. For Paul, they must even be willing to endure insults for the building up of the church as Jesus did in his crucifixion.

The most jarring feature of the echoes from Psalm 68 in Romans 15:1–6 is that Paul likens the pain of the "strong" in Rome to Jesus being insulted at his crucifixion. Some significant implications arise from this hermeneutical move. First, the fact that Paul chooses the psalmist's line "the reproaches of those who reproach you fell upon me" implies that the strong are being insulted within the church, presumably by the weak. Paul does not provide any verbatim insults, but we can infer from the discussion in Romans 14 that the slurs are related to diet and the observance of holy days. Moreover, Paul's commands to avoid judging one another within the community indicate the insults might have included statements about how God would deal with the strong in judgment. This would explain, at least in part, why Paul links the experience of the strong to the crucifixion. As I outlined earlier, the specific insults leveled against Jesus revolved around God's apparent judgment against him. We can hear this in the assertion, "He has trusted in God, let him deliver him now if God wants him" (Matt 27:43). Second, the echoes of Psalm 68, and particularly the citation, imply that the insults by the weak against the strong are tantamount to insults against God. The insults against Jesus were actually against God. Therefore, the insults against the strong are actually against God as well. Nevertheless, like Jesus, the strong must endure these verbal assaults for the sake of the very ones that launch them.

THE DIDACTIC NATURE OF OT LAMENT

We cannot ignore that fact that Paul makes a sweeping statement about the didactic nature of γραφή immediately after citing a psalm of lament. He writes, "For as much as was written beforehand, it was written for our instruction (διδασκαλίαν), in order that through the endurance and through the encouragement of the scriptures (γραφῶν) we might have hope" (Rom 15:4). Paul's observation has a gnomic quality, but in the immediate context it further explains (γάρ) the preceding citation of Psalm 68:10. To be sure, Paul has in mind more than OT lament. Both Romans and the larger Pauline

---

17. Cf. Rom 12:1–2.

corpus contain citations, allusions, and echoes from all kinds of OT texts.[18] Paul regards all of the OT to be didactic in nature and a great source of hope and encouragement for the Christians in Rome and beyond.[19] However, given the extensive use of OT lament throughout Romans, and the lament echoes in the immediate context of 15:1–6, there is a distinct emphasis here on what Paul believes lament can teach his recipients.

If Paul believes that Psalm 68 and other OT lament texts are didactic in nature, what does he believe they teach those who are in Christ? The answer requires us to look beyond the immediate context to the specific uses of lament throughout the letter. That is in large part what the final chapter entails. There we will consider how reading Romans as lament impacts the way we understand Paul's theology of suffering. What I want to do here, particularly in light of Romans 15:1–13, is to lay some of the groundwork for that discussion. There are several things to note.

First, OT lament teaches the righteous in Rome how to endure suffering without relinquishing the prior promise of the gospel. Throughout the letter, Paul appeals to figures such as Habakkuk, the psalmist, Moses, Elijah, Isaiah, and others. They all experience a tension between God's prior promise and the pain they actually experience. Nevertheless, they do not capitulate and abandon the prior promise. Instead, they cry out to God for deliverance, and they often find that deliverance through a renewed hope in the prior promise. For Paul, those in Christ must do something similar. He does not expect them to have a Stoic like response to pain.[20] That will not lead to hope. Instead, the righteous in Rome are to be encouraged by how OT lamenters respond to suffering. They cry out, they groan, and they question. This is by no means a reserved or Stoic response, but it truly engenders hope. That is because the permanent salve to pain and what the righteous truly hope for is the resurrection of the dead inaugurated in Christ and to be completed at his return.[21] Yet, without the tension between the promise of the gospel and the pain of the righteous there will be no cry for that return, for that hope. In Paul's theology, particularly in Romans, ἐλπίς is ultimately a theological abbreviation for the resurrection of the dead at the return of Christ. OT lament instructs the righteous how to endure in that hope until the promise is realized.

---

18. See Seifrid, *Romans*, 607–94.

19. Cf. 1 Macc 12:9.

20. On Paul, Stoicism, and the letter to the Romans, see Engberg-Pedersen, *Paul and the Stoics*, 179–292; Thorsteinsson, *Roman Christianity & Roman Stoicism*, 89–102.

21. See Rom 8:23–25.

Next, OT lament teaches the righteous in Rome about the kind of faith that justifies them before God. We saw in chapter 3 how the echoes of OT lament impact our reading of Paul's thesis statement in Romans 1:16–17 including his partial citation of Habakkuk 2:4, "But the righteous will live by faith." In its original context, this is God's response to Habakkuk's cry in which he questions how God plans to judge Israel.[22] Paul and those in Rome have similar questions about the revelation of God's wrath against humanity, Israel, and even the church. The divine response to those questions is the same one Habakkuk received. The righteous in Rome must live by faith. It is the kind of faith that believes there is salvation beyond present and eschatological judgment. That is the kind of faith that justifies.

Third, OT lament teaches the righteous in Rome how to deal with their enemies. We have seen throughout the letter that both sin and cosmic powers oppose the righteous. The characterizations of these enemies often echo OT lament. Consequently, the lamenters' response to these oppressive enemies is also echoed. What we find is that OT lamenters do not quietly endure the oppression nor do they attempt to muster the intestinal fortitude to overcome their opponents. Instead, they see their weakness and cry out to God for deliverance. Even when their pain seems to indicate that God is pouring out his wrath upon them, they cling to what God promised. They are not driven to look inside themselves but outwardly to the prior promise. This is the kind of response to enemies that Paul encourages. Whether the enemy is sin, cosmic powers, or even lingering doubts about God's wrath, Paul constantly points the Romans to the promise of the gospel.

Fourth, Paul uses OT lament to teach the righteous in Rome that sin's use of the Mosaic Law should always drive them to a cry of distress that requests deliverance from sin and judgment. We saw this in Romans 3:1–20. Paul's catena of lament identifies the Jew and Gentile as enemies like those bemoaned in OT lament. The echo of Psalm 142:2, "no flesh will be justified before him," in Romans 3:20, is the cry towards which the catena of lament pushes them. Similarly, the echoes and pattern of lament in Romans 7:7—8:4 indicates that sin always use the law against the "I." Such a combination compels the "I" to cry out for deliverance from sin, death, and ultimately judgment.

Fifth, in light of the citation from Psalm 68:10 in Romans 15:3, OT lament teaches the righteous in Rome that they must endure insults from within the believing community for the sake of that community. Just as the lamenter in Psalm 68 and Jesus at his crucifixion did not hurl insults at their opponents, attempt to defend themselves, or seek vengeance, the righteous

---

22 See Hab 1:12–17.

in Rome must do the same. Paul uses OT lament to push the Roman community towards a unified voice that praises God together rather than a divided one that insults one another. This is the sense of Paul's prayer in Romans 15:5-6, "Now may the God of endurance and encouragement give to you to think the same thing with another according to Christ Jesus, in order that together with one mouth you might glorify (ἐνὶ στόματι δοξάητε) the God and father of our Lord Jesus Christ."

Finally, Paul uses OT lament to teach the recipients in Rome that the δικαιοσύνη τοῦ θεοῦ has a hidden and mysterious quality that ultimately leads to hope and praise among the nations. We saw this already through the echoes of lament in Romans 1:16-17, 8:31-39, and Romans 9-11. OT lamenters acknowledge that they cannot always discern how God is acting in righteousness. God's ways often strike lamenters as inexplicable, but the experience still engenders hope and praise. The same dynamic shapes much of Paul's argument in the letter. The hiddenness, mystery, or inexplicability of God's righteousness leads to lament which leads to hope and praise. We can also see this in Romans 15:1-6. Paul does not explain why the strong in faith must bear the reproaches of God, as the psalmist suggests. Nevertheless, through the encouragement of lament texts such as Psalm 68, they can have hope. He wishes for his recipients to be in harmony with another, and the purpose of that harmony is "in order that together with one mouth you might (δοξάζητε) glorify the God and father of our Lord Jesus Christ" (Rom 15:6). Paul continues his exhortation in 15:7-13 where he further explains that hope (ἐλπίς/ἐλπίζω) and praise (δόξα/δοξάζω) are the intended outcomes of scripture's teaching to the weak and strong, especially OT lament (Rom 15:3-4). It is an explanation teeming with OT texts in which Israel and the Gentiles praise God for his salvation through the "root of Jesse" (Rom 15:12).[23] Paul exhorts:

> Receive one another, just as Christ also received you for the glory of God (εἰς δόξαν τοῦ θεοῦ). For I say Christ has become a servant (διάκονον) to the circumcision (περιτομῆς) for the truth of God, in order to confirm the promises of the fathers, and for the Gentiles (ἔθνη) to glorify (δοξάσαι) God for his mercy, just as it is written, "On account this I will praise (ἐξομολογήσομαί) you among the nations and I will sing (ψαλῶ) to your name."

Christ the διάκονος confirms God's prior promises to Israel and engenders Gentile praise for his mercy. This is all in accordance with scripture.[24] Paul

---

23 On the importance of Rom 15:7-13 to the entire letter, Keck notes that it "states the grand horizon of Paul's theology in the letter." Keck, *Romans*, 353.

24 Paul specifically cites Ps 17:50; Deut 32:43; Ps 117:1; Isa 11:10.

ends this section with the request, "Now may the God of hope (ἐλπίδος) fill you with all joy and peace in believing, so as for you to abound in hope (ἐλπίδι) in the power of the Holy Spirit" (Rom 15:13). Once again, ἐλπίς is one of the main hook words in Romans 15:1–13. The hope that Paul wants his recipients to have is found in Israel's γραφή, especially OT lament. Yet, γραφή only leads to hope in as much as it is understood that Jesus Christ is the fulfillment of the very promises that elicit both cries of distress and praise from Jew and Gentile. In this way, the request in 15:13 forms an *inclusio* with the letter's opening where Paul describes the gospel of God as that "which he promised beforehand (προεπηγγείλατο) through his prophets in the holy scriptures" (Rom 1:2).

SUMMARY

When Romans 15:1–6 is read in light of its OT lament echoes, we find that the gospel answers the church's lament. The verbal insults endured by some believers in Rome must have been quite intense given the fact that Paul likens their experience to Jesus being reproached at his crucifixion. Although Paul does not explicitly portray the "strong in faith" as crying out to God in the way he portrays Christ doing, it stands to reason that they were uttering a similar complaint. Such a complaint would be understandable given the nature of the reproach they were facing. The specifics of the reproach are also not explicitly provided, but when can hear them through the echoes of Psalm 68 and the narrative of the crucifixion. In short, just as onlookers at the crucifixion mockingly denied that God was pleased with Jesus given his predicament, the strong in faith were probably facing a similar insult. It is really an insult directed against God. Nevertheless, it "falls upon" the strong.

Paul's answer to this situation, or lament, within the church is that the strong must not please (ἀρέσκω) themselves by returning insult for insult. Instead, they must bear the insults as Christ did at his crucifixion for the sake of the weak. Furthermore, Paul explains that OT texts such as Psalm 68 are instructive for the believing community in the midst of all kinds of suffering. We briefly summarized the didactic nature of lament as it is contained in the letter. One characteristic that emerges from Romans 15:1–13 is that God's righteousness is mysterious but ultimately leads to hope and praise among the nations. Israel's γραφή, especially lament, produces hope and shifts cries of distress to praise. This shift only transpires when it is understood that Christ fulfills the prior promises to Israel and the nations.

9

Lament and Paul's Theology of Suffering in Romans

LAMENT IS THE QUINTESSENTIAL language of suffering. We have seen firsthand that in Romans lament is both an indicator and interpreter of pain. It indicates the severity of the lamenter's suffering and interprets the cause, expectation, and divine response surrounding it. We have spent a considerable amount of time analyzing this phenomenon at various points in Romans. What I want to do in this final chapter is bring that analysis to bear on Paul's theology of suffering.

A number of questions will guide us here. What does Paul's use of OT lament in Romans tell us about the way he understands pain in humanity, creation, the church, and Israel? Why do these various entities/figures suffer? How should they respond to their suffering? What is the divine answer to their pain, to their lament? Before answering these questions, it is necessary to briefly survey how Paul and suffering are usually discussed within scholarship.

PAUL AND SUFFERING WITHIN THE HISTORY OF RESEARCH

In a monograph that addresses suffering in 2 Corinthians, Lim divides the landscape of critical scholarship involving Paul and suffering into three categories: (1) exegetical studies; (2) historical and background studies; and

(3) topical or thematic studies.¹ Obviously, my interest in the first category is specifically related to exegetical studies on suffering in Romans.² However, there are a few exegetical works related to other Pauline letters that are worth considering. The second and third categories are much broader than Romans, but they still belong in this conversation. The following is not exhaustive but rather representative of the trajectories that suffering in Romans tends to follow.

Exegetical Studies on Suffering in Romans

There are two scholars who stand out here. First, J. C. Beker examines Romans in order to articulate how Paul integrates hope and suffering.³ Beker, like many, acknowledges that letters such as 2 Corinthians and Philippians strike a more personal tone as it relates to suffering.⁴ Yet, he recognizes that the integration of hope and suffering has a more comprehensive and cosmic scope in Romans than other letters.⁵ He explains why this letter is foundational for understanding Paul's theology of suffering: (1) Romans indicates that "hope" is apocalyptic in nature; (2) Romans shows that hope and suffering do not "instill a passive quietism" but "an active missionary force in the word"; and (3) Romans helpfully distinguishes "several forms of suffering."⁶ It is the latter point that really drives Beker's study. He is concerned with broader works on the theology of suffering that "tend to fuse all levels of suffering and tend to decry all forms of suffering as a visitation by cruel fate on innocent people."⁷ Beker combats this tendency by comparing the way Paul discusses suffering in Romans 1:18—3:20 to his argument in 8:17-30. The former deals with "suffering at the hands of human injustice" while the latter deals with "suffering at the hands of the power of death."⁸ In Romans 1:18—3:20, suffering arises from human idolatry and God's punishment of it. God allows human idolatry to run its course, and the result is not only "the perversion of the human relation to God" but also a perversion in how

---

1 See Lim, *The Sufferings of Christ Are Abundant in Us*, 1–27.

2 For a review of the research on Romans as it relates to evil, suffering, and the righteousness of God, see Ochsenmeier, *Mal, souffrance et justice de Dieu selon Romains 1–3*, 17–36.

3 See Beker, "Suffering and Triumph," 105–19.

4 See e.g., Hafemann, *Suffering and Ministry in the Spirit*.

5 Beker, "Suffering and Triumph," 107.

6 Ibid., 107–8.

7 Ibid., 108. He notes specifically the works of Kushner and Sölle.

8 Ibid., 108.

the "self" relates to itself, to the social order, and the natural world.[9] Beker concludes from his exegetical analysis of 1:18—3:20 that "Paul here pinpoints the source of the de-orientation of the human condition: that source is idolatry and its consequences are 'man's inhumanity to man,' that is, suffering at the hands of human injustice."[10] Humanity is "caught in the bondage of the will to do evil and so cause immense suffering in God's world."[11] Contrastively, in Romans 8:18–30, Beker argues that Paul juxtaposes the church "against and separated from the world" with a "picture of the church for the world."[12] The whole experience is set within the context of hope, the hope of God's triumph.

Based on his exegetical observations in these two sections of Romans, Beker suggests how suffering and hope are integrated as well as theological implications of that integration for Paul's theology of suffering. The two different causes of suffering call for two different responses by the church. The suffering described in Romans 1:18—3:20 calls for reversing "structures of idolatry and their immoral and hurtful consequences by establishing orders of justice in the world."[13] However, suffering caused by the power of death (8:17–30) is "by and large not open to strategies of planning and hope."[14] This kind of suffering raises issues of meaninglessness and theodicy. In this way, Beker observes that Paul is realistic about the power of death in the world. He notes:

> Paul is not an idealist when it comes to the reality of suffering; neither he is a spiritualist who comforts people with the thought that because of Christ's cross suffering can and should be spiritualized, interiorized, or neglected if only we take a properly heavenly perspective and look with Platonic eyes away from this transient and corrupted world. Moreover, Paul is not a person who counsels mature resignation in the face of suffering as if it is a necessary and endemic ingredient of created life.[15]

For Beker, Paul's theology of suffering allows for "the mystery of meaningless suffering" so that everything is not explained away by sin and human guilt.[16] Nevertheless, Paul sees "the mystery of meaningless suffering" within

---

9 Ibid., 109.
10 Ibid.
11 Ibid.
12 Ibid., 110.
13 Ibid., 111.
14 Ibid., 112.
15 Ibid., 112–13.
16 In other words, the cause of suffering cannot be reduced to Rom 5:12.

the horizon of the "forthcoming apocalyptic triumph of God." Hope then is not a human disposition but a gift from God found in apocalyptic triumph. That gift is guaranteed in Jesus' death and resurrection (Rom 8:32).

The theological implications in all of this are that Paul leaves some issues of suffering unanswered. Beker recognizes the objections that Paul's theology of suffering in Romans might raise. He asks, "Can the unjust present suffering of one child of God be righted and compensated for by his/her future restoration in the Kingdom of God?" Additionally, with an eye towards God's sovereignty in Romans, Beker questions "How can God with his redemptive plan for the creation continue in apathy? How can he continue to tolerate the present power of death in his creation?" Additionally, reflecting on the work of Macquarrie, Beker questions the eschatological expectation within Romans and the charge that "it directs hope toward an Utopian project, the actualization of which continues to be nothing but a history of disappointment and frustration."[17] Beker's answer, in light of Romans, is that Paul's theology of hope remains the most adequate response to these questions. If God does not ultimately triumph as Paul believes he does and will, "his purpose in creation will have been defeated."[18]

Erwin Ochsenmeier is another scholar who engages the topic of Paul and suffering in Romans on an exegetical basis.[19] He examines Romans 1–3 from the perspective of what these chapters reveal about Paul's view of God, suffering, and evil in the world.[20] Ochsenmeier asks a number of interpretive questions such as, "Is there a link between evil and suffering in Romans and the issue of the righteousness of God? Is the Epistle meant to encourage the Roman Christians in adverse circumstances? If so, how can the whole Epistle be used today in talking about evil and suffering?"[21] Among other things, Ochsenmeier argues that the language of evil, suffering, and righteousness provide "lexical and thematic continuity" between Romans 1–3. He pays close attention to the impact of the OT on Paul's argumentation in this section of the letter noting, "In line with the passage of the OT used, it shows that even in Romans 1–3 a righteous God is a God who punishes the evildoer who does not practise what is known by revelation and saves those

---

17 Ibid., 117. See also, Macquaire, "Eschatology and Time," 115.

18 Ibid., 117–18.

19. See Ochsenmeier, *Mal, souffrance et justice de Dieu selon Romains 1–3*.

20. Ochsenmeier notes that interpreters such have Augustine, Leibnitz, Moltmann, Ricoeur have interacted with the issue of evil and suffering in Romans. However, they generally limit the conversation to parts of the letter after Romans 4. See Ochsenmeier, *Evil, Suffering, and the Righteousness of God*, 153.

21. Ibid.

who believe in him."[22] Ochsenmeier, similar to what I have suggested about the figure of lamenters throughout this work, argues:

> One of Paul's purposes is to demonstrate that those who can say that God is their God and who can claim the Christian hope are those who, like Habakkuk, David, and Abraham, believe by faith that God is powerful enough to give life even when death seems unavoidable and to suggest avenues of personal and communal application.[23]

Ochsenmeier brings his exegetical findings to bear on the issue of whether or not one can use Romans today in order to talk about God. In this discussion, he interacts with Jürgen Moltmann. He concludes, "The challenge is to read Romans as the good news to believers of the twenty-first century and to show that God fulfills his promises and can thus still be called a God of hope."[24]

The works of Beker and Ochsenmeier draw their conclusions about Paul and suffering based on their exegesis of key sections in Romans, particularly chapters 1–3 and 8. This is commendable. However, their exegesis, and thereby their conclusions on Paul and suffering, can be enhanced by reading other portions of Romans in light of its OT lament.[25] My own conclusions about Paul and suffering, which I will articulate in a moment, are based on such a reading.

Historical and Background Studies on Paul and Suffering in Romans

Historical study related to Paul and suffering tends to involve either the catalogue of hardships described in Romans 8:35–39 or particular historical purposes for the letter. For the former, we must consider works that are not solely dedicated to Romans. Rudolf Bultmann referred to the catalogues of hardships found in Paul's letters as *Peristasenkataloge*.[26] He defined these catalogues as passages "where the speaker enumerates the different strokes

---

22. Ibid., 155.

23. Ibid.

24. Ibid.

25 Ochsenmeier dedicates a short chapter to suffering and evil in Rom 4, 5:1–11, 8:17–39, 12: 9–13:7, and 15:1–13. However, the treatments are limited, and there is no consideration of Rom 7:7–25. Ibid., 255–86.

26 See Bultmann, *Der Stil der paulinischen Predigt*, 17–19. As noted in Fitzgerald, *Cracks in an Earthen Vessel*, 11.

of fate (*Fügungen des Geschicks*), the περιστάσεις, over which he boasts as victor."[27] He compared Romans 8:35 to the *Peristasenkataloge* found in Epictetus, Musonius Rufus, Horace, and Seneca. One similarity he detected between these writers and Paul was that "As the Greek wise man, so also Paul enumerates the strokes of Fate or of the powers to which man is subjected, and he enthusiastically proclaims his superiority to joys and sorrows, to fears and terrors."[28] Although Bultmann saw some differences between Paul's catalogue in Romans 8:35–39 and the Greek preacher, he found the pairings of "death" and "life," as well as "things present" and "things to come," in Romans 8:38 as "quite comparable to the diatribe in expression and tone."[29]

Fitzgerald has more recently examined the so called *Peristasenkataloge*, focusing his attention on the catalogues of hardship in 1–2 Corinthians.[30] His basic thesis is that Paul depicts himself as an ideal philosopher, and his *peristasis* catalogues function in a way similar to those found in the writings of a Greek sage. For example, in 2 Corinthians 4 and 6, Fitzgerald asserts that Paul enumerates his sufferings like a sage in order to "magnify and prove the greatness of his endurance."[31] Fitzgerald also asserts that Paul uses the catalogues for the following: (1) admonish young converts; (2) show that suffering is part of the divine will; and (3) model how one should respond to adversaries. Overall, like a sage, Paul uses the catalogues to rehearse "the hardships over which he triumphed and the forces against which he was invincible."[32] In this way, Fitzgerald argues that the catalogues in 2 Corinthians 4:8–9 and Romans 8:35 are followed with "triumphant certainty."[33] What enables Paul's victory is God's power. Fitzgerald explains, "The hardships and forces that are powerless to separate him from 'the love of Christ' and 'the love of God in Christ' (Rom 8:35, 39) are thus, more fundamentally, catalogues of the evils over which divine love triumphs and against which the divine provides protection."[34] Therefore, at least according to Fitzgerald, Paul's catalogues, including Romans 8:35–39, "are thus, more fundamentally, catalogues of the evils over which divine love triumphs and

---

27 Ibid.

28 Ibid.

29 Ibid., 12.

30 Fitzgerald identifies seven different kinds of catalogues, but identifies the "hardships of various types" as the kinds which best defines the lists in 2 Corinthians. Ibid., 203.

31 Ibid., 204.

32 Ibid., 205.

33 See Rom 8:37.

34 Ibid.

against which the divine provides protection."[35] He then concludes that Paul's catalogues are like those which "celebrate the power of philosophy in regard to suffering" even noting that "What Seneca affirms of philosophy, Paul thus affirms of God."[36]

Thematic or Topical Approaches to Paul and Suffering

Most biographies and theologies of Paul emphasize the role of suffering in the apostle's life and thought.[37] However, fewer writings attempt to synthesize the various strands of suffering in Paul's thought other than to discuss his pain as an apostle who shares in the sufferings of Christ.[38] Nevertheless, there are a few notable Pauline scholars who do speak about the issue from a thematic or topical perspective.[39] Three of them are briefly reviewed here, because their views either represent, or even influence, those of many others.

Albert Schweitzer categorizes all suffering in Paul as "dying with Christ."[40] He argues that suffering per se is not as pronounced in Paul as it is in other NT writings.[41] Instead, Paul often replaces suffering with "dying." Schweitzer explains, "The dying which the believer experiences with Christ is made manifest in suffering which destroys, or tends to destroy, his life. The resurrection state which is in process of formation is manifested by the presence of the Spirit as supernatural life-principle."[42] In Schweitzer's reading of Paul, suffering, or dying, with Christ secures atonement for post-baptismal transgressions. Schweitzer explains, "According to this view of Paul, as of primitive Christianity in general, the atoning death of Christ does not procure continuous forgiveness of sins, but only the release obtained in baptism from previously committed sins. For subsequent transgressions atonement

---

35. Ibid.

36 Ibid., 205. For other studies on the catalogues in Paul, see e.g., Schrage, "Leid, Kruz, und Eschaton," 141–75; Willert, "The Catalogues of Hardships," 217–43.

37 See e.g., Bruce, *Paul Apostle of the Heart Set Free*, 139–40; Schreiner, *Paul*, 87–102.

38 See e.g., Dunn, *The Theology of Paul*, 482–87.

39 For a more synthetic presentation of Paul and suffering, see e.g. Smith, *Paul's Seven Explanations of the Suffering of the Righteous*.

40 See Albert Schweitzer, *The Mysticism of Paul the Apostle*, 141–59.

41 Schweitzer argues, "'In the First Epistle of Peter—from whatever pen and from whatever time it may have originated—there is found more about suffering, and suffering with Christ, than in all the Pauline Epistles put together." Ibid., 141.

42. Ibid., 141.

is secured by suffering with Christ."[43] This experience, and not his conversion, is what Paul sees as paradigmatic for others. Schweitzer posits that Paul reached this perception of suffering/dying through his own "excessive sufferings." He reviews the various sufferings of Paul at the hands of various opponents, including Jews and the Jerusalem church, as they are relayed in Acts and the Pauline Epistles. Schweitzer believes that Paul understood the meaning of his physical, spiritual, and mental pain. He notes, "It is because he alone dares to speak out the full truth about the significance of the Cross that he has to suffer the greatest persecution."[44] Paul, at least according to Schweitzer, knows suffering secures atonement for his post-baptismal sins and the same is true for others who suffer. There stands behind the sufferings "Angel-powers who have directed their enmity against him because he is endeavouring to prevent men from falling again under their dominion owing to false ideas about the Law and circumcision."[45] It is this recognition that leads Paul to value his sufferings more than trips to the third heaven and paradise.

L. Ann Jervis does not attempt a full synthesis of Paul's views on suffering. Yet, her treatment is broader than the exegetical study of a single letter. She examines 1 Thessalonians, Philippians, and Romans in a self-described "novel way."[46] The novelty to her approach, as she sees it, is to read these three letters for the sole purpose of discovering how Paul viewed the suffering of the believer and the nonbeliever. Some of her conclusions vary according to each letter. In Romans specifically, Jervis draws a number of conclusions. First, based on her reading of Romans 1–3, Jervis concludes that Paul portrays everyone as a "victim" of pain and at the same time a "perpetrator" of it.[47] Second, pointing to verses such as Romans 5:17, she posits that "humanity shares in common a horrifying fear of physical death."[48] These first two conclusions apply to the suffering of nonbelievers and believers alike. With respect to the latter, Jervis argues that Paul thinks of the believer's suffering as being both "in Christ" and "with Christ." Suffering "in Christ" means that "Paul regards believers as having the possibility of a believing-specific experience of the inescapable sufferings."[49] Both unbelievers and believers suffer because of sin, but those who are "in

---

43 Ibid., 147.
44 Ibid., 158–59.
45 Ibid., 159.
46 See Jervis, *At the Heart of the Gospel*, 11.
47 Ibid., 83.
48 Ibid., 91.
49 Ibid., 92.

Christ" have a different experience. The latter live in a unique context of suffering, because it takes place in God's love. There is a death to sin and an expectation of sharing in God's glory. Moreover, those who live "with Christ" take on unavoidable suffering not experienced by those outside of Christ. Specifically, in light of Romans 8:29, Jervis argues that conformity to Christ requires suffering with him. Suffering "with Christ" conforms believers to Christ in the sense that suffering is "experienced on behalf of God's creation."[50] Suffering "with Christ" takes place on the "horizon of hope for the end of sufferings." Third, Jervis observes that hope-filled suffering "in" and "with" Christ creates an experiential tension. Pointing to Romans 8:10, she notes "This creates the tension intrinsic to our present hope: we suffer at sin's hands at the same time as we know the opposite experience—life, which is the result of righteousness."[51] The tension produces both hope and suffering, "We are pulled between our firm knowledge (given to us by the Spirit) that there will be an end to pain—the redemption of our bodies, and our acute awareness and experience of the sufferings of the present time."[52]

N. T. Wright's thoughts on Paul are scattered across his many works. I have chosen to base my summary on his latest tome on Paul, because it is here that he provides a more systematic and prolonged treatment of the issue. In short, Wright argues that Paul ultimately suffers because of his monotheistic beliefs in the midst of a pluralistic Roman world. He points to Romans 8:31–39 as an example explaining "It is a glorious expression of second-temple monotheism in the face of all the powers of the pagan world."[53] He likens Paul's willingness to suffer for his monotheism in the face of pagan opposition to the Maccabean martyrs and even Akiba.[54] Wright interprets Paul's citation of Psalm 43:23 as a kind of monotheistic prayer. Of course, for Wright, Paul's monotheism has been "reworked" around "Jesus the Messiah" and the "Spirit."[55] While looking to a number of other passages in 2 Corinthians, Philippians, and 1 Thessalonians, Wright interprets Paul's suffering in light of this reworked monotheism and other Jewish martyrs.

Two other points from Wright's reflection on suffering are worth noting. First, he argues that Paul viewed suffering as a "sign" of the times. Specifically, it was an indication of living between the times. Wright explains, "Suffering was itself a sign, for Paul in his Jewish context, that one

---

50 Ibid., 105.
51 Ibid., 108.
52 Ibid.
53 Wright, *Paul and the Faithfulness of God*, 635.
54 Ibid., 634.
55 Ibid.

was living between the times, caught between promise and fulfillment, between the passing of sentence on the old world and the final disappearance of evil."[56] Second, Wright also considers the relationship between sin and suffering in Paul's thought. He sees in Paul's writings sin working on two levels. On the one hand, the problem of sin is "personal." Sin has infected the heart, corrupted the mind "into idolatry and the person into dehumanized behaviour."[57] Yet, sin in Paul's view, as Wright sees it, is also "cosmic." That is because:

> The worship of idols allows the demons who masquerade behind them to gain power not rightly theirs. Thus both "Sin" with a capital S and "the powers," variously described, and also Death itself, have replaced, in Paul's mind, the wicked, idolatrous pagans as seen from within his pre-Christian Pharisaism.[58]

SUFFERING IN ROMANS IN LIGHT OF LAMENT

The preceding survey indicates that suffering in Romans has received treatments from varying perspectives. My purpose here is to treat suffering from the perspective of the letter's echoes of lament. This naturally involves exegetical, historical, and topical considerations such as those outlined above. However, much of the exegetical work has been carried out in the preceding chapters; therefore, I will not rehash those conversations here. Instead, I want to consider how these lament echoes, which work in concert with the letter's rhetorical argument, inform our understanding of Paul's theology of suffering. Although a number of approaches could be employed at this point, the following discussion is shaped by the idea that lament is an event. I want to focus especially on the lamenter's experience with God and enemies as Paul presents it in Romans. As we have seen, Paul often describes believers according to the experiences of lamenters. He sees something in the latter that is instructive for the former. What follows is an attempt to articulate Paul's perception of that experience based on the echoes of lament within Romans.

---

56 Ibid., 1117.
57 Ibid., 756.
58 Ibid.

The Prior Promise of γραφή and τὸ εὐαγγέλιον

At its core, the prior promise of OT lament is that God will deliver those who cry out to him. He delivers by judging the lamenter's enemies while also forgiving the lamenter's sins. In this way, God saves in truth, mercy, and righteousness.[59] God assures those who hope in him that they will not be ashamed or disappointed for looking to him for deliverance. In this way, Israel's γραφή, particularly lament, provides the framework for the prior promise in Romans, but the details are filled in by the gospel of God. Those who cry out to Jesus are saved from their enemies, because in Christ's death and resurrection God has judged those enemies and forgiven those who cry out to him. While OT lament describes this kind of deliverance in terms of truth, mercy, and righteousness, Paul abbreviates all of that as the revelation of the δικαιοσύνη θεοῦ. Faith in this promise justifies both Jew and Gentile. They will not be disappointed (ἐπαισχύνομαι) presently or eschatologically. It is the promise that Paul and his recipients live by, but their trust in the promise of the gospel is not without its difficulties.

Suffering and the Promise

Paul discusses multiple causes of suffering in Romans that, in some way or another, challenge the prior promise of the gospel. In the preceding chapters, by listening to the echoes of OT lament, I discussed the following causes: sin, cosmic forces, inexplicable rejection, Israel's unbelief, and ecclesiastical unrest. These are many of the things that afflict Paul and his recipients. Not coincidentally, the description of that affliction often echoes OT lament. Paul portrays sin as an enemy like those often bemoaned in OT lament. We saw this especially in our discussion of Romans 7:7—8:4. Sin's work within the body of believer and unbeliever alike, though only recognized by the former, is deceitful, unceasing, overbearing, and of course deadly. In Romans 8:31–39, Paul describes suffering at the hands of cosmic forces. There is a strong implication here that either Paul, his recipients, or both attributed this pain to some inexplicable divine cause. What also perplexes and pains Paul is Israel's unbelief. The lament echoes in Romans 9:1–5 indicate the severity of Paul's distress caused by his kinsmen's rejection of their Messiah. There are also echoes of lament in Romans 15:1–6 that signal suffering among believers in Rome stemming from the friction between the strong and weak in faith.

---

59 On this point, see chapter 2.

However, the suffering caused by sin, cosmic forces, Israel's unbelief, and ecclesiastical unrest all feed into a larger source of pain, namely the wrath of God. The ultimate cause of suffering in Romans is a concern with divine judgment. Fear of the ὀργὴ θεοῦ both now and on the last day is the common thread in all of the lament echoes we examined in this work. For example, the cluster of lament echoes in Romans 1:16–17, which themselves have in view divine judgment (e.g. Habakkuk), is followed by Paul's observation that the "The wrath of God is being revealed from heaven" (Rom 1:18). Similarly, the lament echoes in Romans 3:1–20 evoke the certainty of divine judgment against God's enemies and then culminate in 3:19–20 with an echo of a plea for mercy. After all, the entire world is accountable (ὑπόδικος) to God. The underlying cause of pain in the struggle of the "I" (Rom 7:7–24) is divine condemnation, as indicated in Paul's announcement that there is no κατάκριμα for those who are in Christ Jesus (Rom 8:1). The echoes of lament in Romans 9–11 evoke concerns with God's wrath. This can be seen in Paul's prayer that he could be ἀνάθεμα from Christ in place of his fellow kinsmen. Finally, with respect to the echoes of Psalm 68 in Romans 15:1–6, the preceding context of chapter 14 includes a staunch warning about appearing before the judgment seat of God (Rom 14:10). Even sections of the letter that do not have strong echoes of lament indicate a concern with God's wrath. There is of course Paul's entire argument in Romans 1:18—2:29 that revolves around present and eschatological judgment. Far from a mere tractate on human sinfulness, Paul's instruction about divine wrath and judgment is applicable to both unbelievers and believers alike. Additionally, in Romans 5:1–10, Paul assures the reader of peace with God, both now and on the last day, over against his wrath. The conclusion to Paul's argument about death to sin and life in Christ is "For the wages of sin is death but the gift of God is eternal life in Christ Jesus our Lord" (Rom 6:23). Clearly, divine wrath is a key motif in the letter. Moreover, especially in light of the letter's echoes of lament, God's wrath and judgment is the all-encompassing source of suffering.

Ultimately, the tension that exists between the prior promise of the gospel and suffering is the threat of divine wrath. To be sure, Paul assures his recipients "Therefore how much more having been justified now by his blood we will be saved through him from the wrath" (Rom 5:9).[60] Yet, that Paul even has to make this statement only serves to confirm what I am asserting about suffering in Romans. Ongoing problems with sin, inexplicable pain, Israel's unbelief, and ecclesiastical unrest are painful in and of themselves. However, more troubling than these varied forms of suffering

---

60. See also Rom 5:10.

are what they might indicate, namely that God will condemn us, or God is against us. On the one hand, Paul and his recipients have the promise of the gospel. God's righteousness has been revealed. He has judged their enemies, had mercy upon them, and thereby delivered them. On the other hand, there is the multifaceted suffering that collectively could spell divine wrath. If God does not bring an end to this pain, then Paul and his recipients are indeed lost to his judgment. It is in this tension that the suffering of Romans is truly felt, and it is here that cries of distress are elicited. This is the warp and woof of OT lament where the ultimate cause of suffering is also linked to divine wrath which lamenters express in complaints about God's rejection, hiddenness, and the like.

The Cry of Distress

The cries of distress in Romans arise from various forms of suffering and the larger concern with divine wrath. Some of them can be heard in the echoes of lament, and others are explicitly stated. I have discussed these cries at length in previous chapters. Here I simply want to note that the cries of distress in Romans are all associated with divine wrath.

The immediate catalyst for cries of distress in Romans are sin's work within the "I," inexplicable suffering, Israel's unbelief, and ecclesiastical unrest. Yet, the underlying catalyst is divine judgment. The immediate and underlying causes behind these cries of distress echo OT lament. When the "I" of Romans 7 cries out "Miserable man that I am who will deliver me from this body of death," it echoes Psalms of Lament such as Psalm 37 where the lamenter is afflicted by his own guilt before God and enemies. The "I" of Romans 7 suffers from a similar situation, though his enemy is sin.

Romans 8 contains echoes and a citation of cries of distress. The tripartite groaning (στενάζω) of creation, God's children, and the Holy Spirit echoes a unified cry of distress (Rom 8:18–27). They long for Christ to return and raise the dead, because resurrection will bring an end to creation's futility and the children's bodily affliction. Until that time, both creation and the children of God continue to suffer from the effects of divine wrath. In Romans 8:36, Paul cites a cry of distress from Psalm 43 "On account of you we face death all day long, we were reckoned as sheep for the slaughter." The cry originally functioned as part of the psalmist's complaint about God's inexplicable rejection and wrath towards his people. It is wrath manifested in God's refusal to go out with Israel's armies in battle.[61] Similarly, the confident, poetic, and doxological nature of Romans 8:31–39 notwithstand-

---

61 See Ps 43:10.

ing, God does not bring an end to the afflictions of Paul and his recipients. Inexplicably, he treats them as enemies, like sheep for the slaughter.

The cry of distress in Romans 9:3 and 15:3 also echoes concerns with divine wrath. In the former, Paul cries out "For I myself was wishing to be accursed from Christ for my brethren my fellow kinsmen according to the flesh." This prayer echoes Moses' cry from Exodus 32 in which God threatens to wipe out Israel. Paul, like Moses, is worried about Israel's judgment before God. Once again in the letter, we see that divine wrath is the ultimate cause of suffering. Additionally, Paul cites a cry of distress from Psalm 68 "The reproaches of those who reproach you fell upon me" (Rom 15:3). The citation is part of Paul's larger argument about ecclesiastical unrest between the weak and strong in faith. The larger context of Psalm 68 reveals a lamenter who, although he asks for wrath to be poured out on his enemies, appears as one who is under God's judgment. For Paul, the strong in faith must appear as those under God's wrath, even enduring reproach about it, for the sake of the weak.

Deliverance from Suffering

Paul follows every cry of distress in Romans by reflecting on the gospel. He highlights a certain aspect of the gospel that corresponds with the nature of the cry. In this way, the gospel answers the plea for deliverance. Paul follows the cry in Romans 7:24 by explaining that God condemned sin, that pernicious enemy that afflicts the "I" in 7:7–25, through Jesus' death and resurrection. God brings an end to the death and condemnation that the "I" feared by condemning sin in the "flesh" of Jesus (Rom 8:3). The cries in Romans 8 are also answered through reflection on the gospel. The children of God, who groan with creation and the Spirit, were saved in hope (ἐλπίδι) (Rom 8:24). In their hearing of the gospel, the children of God were made to hope in the redemption of their bodies (Rom 8:23).[62] Paul also answers the cry in Romans 8:36 with reflection on Christ's work at the cross and at the right hand of the Father. The elect may suffer inexplicably, but they will not ultimately be handed over to God's wrath (or separated from him). That is because God handed over (παρέδωκεν) his own son on behalf of the elect (Rom 8:32). He also raised him from the dead. Jesus' intercession foils the efforts of enemies who accuse or condemn the elect in order to have them suffer under God's wrath.

The cries in Romans 9:3 and 15:3 are also answered by the gospel. Paul's reflection on how the gospel answers his intercessory cry is extensive

62 This hope puts Paul miles apart from Stoic views of suffering. See Acts 17:16–34.

spanning Romans 9–11. In short, God is sovereign over Israel's salvation from his own wrath. Yet, Israel is also without excuse for its unbelief in the gospel that incurs that same wrath. Thus, God answers Paul's cry in two ways. He answers Paul in the same way he answered the lamenting Elijah, namely that a remnant has been preserved. Yet, since Israel is responsible for its unbelief, God also answers Paul by calling him to preach the gospel to the Gentiles. Paul must "glory" in his ministry to the Gentiles, in order to make his Israelite kinsmen jealous. In this way, Paul hopes to save some through preaching the gospel. All of this, both God's sovereignty and Israel's responsibility to believe, will culminate in the return of Jesus from the heavenly Zion. That appearance will save an eschatological remnant of Israel from its sins and the divine wrath that ensues from those sins. With respect to the cry in Romans 15:3, the answer of the gospel is heard in Israel's scriptures that contain promises now confirmed by Christ (Rom 15:8). The "strong" in Rome may have to bear the accusation (reproach) that they are under God's wrath. Yet, the people of God, both Jew and Gentile, both weak and strong, have a sure hope in the "root of Jesse" just as God had promised (Rom 15:9–13).

Praise for Deliverance from Suffering

One distinguishing feature of OT lament is the shift from a cry of distress to praise. That shift signals the hope lamenters have in the midst of their ongoing pain. There is never a permanent shift to praise, because the suffering is ongoing. This holds true in Romans as well. Each cry of distress in Romans also has a corresponding shift to praise, though not a permanent one. The cry in Romans 7:24 is immediately followed by "I give thanks to my God through Jesus Christ our Lord. So then I myself in my mind am serving God but in my flesh the law of sin." The praise for deliverance, which Paul goes on to explain in Romans 8, is tempered with the reality that sin will continue to cause pain. Similarly, the most doxologically charged portion of the letter, Romans 8:31–39, is immediately followed by the shift to Paul's intercessory cry in Romans 9:1–5. Praise for God's inseparable love in Christ does not mute the apostle's concern that Israel is separated from him. Yet, even here, there is a shift to praise in Romans 11:33–36. Paul, in praise that echoes more OT lament, extols God's mysterious ways and wisdom of deliverance. He confines both Jew and Gentile to disobedience in order to have mercy upon them (Rom 11:32). In other words, suffering from God's wrath has a salvific value. This is something Paul praises as truly inscrutable.

CONCLUSION

We have only scratched the surface with respect to how reading Romans as lament informs our understanding of Paul's theology of suffering. There is much more that could be said based on the exegetical findings presented in the preceding chapters. Nevertheless, I want to close by focusing on the connection between OT lamenters, Paul, and his Roman recipients. In short, Paul uses the polyvalent figures of OT lament to articulate the believer's experience of the δικαιοσύνη θεοῦ revealed in the gospel. These figures include Habakkuk, David (or the psalmist), Abraham, Moses, Isaiah, Elijah, Israel, and Jesus.[63] Even more, creation and the Holy Spirit join in the lament. Their laments shape Paul's perception and discussion of how believers experience the interplay between suffering and God's righteousness that is revealed in the gospel.

While each figure suffers and cries out to God, they do so in unique ways. Their experiences are instructive for how we read Romans and understand the letter's theology of suffering. There are echoes of lamenters in Romans who cry out because of sin, both their own and that of others. David and or the psalmist can be heard here. The letter also echoes lamenters who cry out because the promise of protection and an inheritance are presently not experienced. Abraham, the key figure in Romans 4, can be heard here. Additionally, echoes of Moses, Isaiah, and Elijah who lament Israel's unbelief can be heard in the letter. Creation and the Holy Spirit join in the groaning of God's children eagerly awaiting the resurrection of the dead. The church takes up one of Israel's ancient cries bemoaning the seemingly inexplicable rejection by God. We even hear Jesus from the cross. His cries speak to the pain caused by bearing insults for the sake of those who perpetrate them.

When we listen to the cries of these figures, a full picture of hope and suffering in Romans emerges. Paul and his recipients suffer from concerns with sin, protection from inimical forces, inexplicable rejection by God, Israel's unbelief, and insults within the ecclesiastical community. Once again, the common thread in all these various sources of suffering is a concern with divine wrath. Ongoing problems with sin, inimical forces, the apparent and inexplicable rejection by God, Israel's ongoing unbelief, and ecclesiastical judgmentalism raise questions about God's condemnation of the righteous. Consequently, Paul and his recipients, like the lamenters before them, and in conjunction with creation and the Holy Spirit, cry out to God for deliverance from these various sources of pain.

---

63. For explicit references, allusions, and echoes of these figures in the letter, see Rom 1:16–17; 3:4, 10–20 ; 4:1–25; 7:7—8:4; 8:18–39; 9:1–5, 27; 10:13; 11:2–6; 15:3.

God's answer to them is in the gospel that reveals his righteousness. Just as in the theology of OT lament, particularly the Psalms of Lament, God's righteousness is the only remedy to the pain that Paul and his recipients experience. God must simultaneously judge the unrighteous while protecting, forgiving, and being present with the righteous. Otherwise, God's prior promise is left unfulfilled and the hope of the lamenting community is in vain. For Paul, such righteousness is only located in the gospel of the crucified and risen Jesus. In Christ's death and resurrection, the unrighteous, a group that includes everyone to some degree, are condemned. Yet, the righteous are protected and forgiven. Faith in the gospel signals God's victory in both judging and saving those who cry out to him. However, for Paul, the promise of the gospel paradoxically intensifies the pain and cry of the righteous. That is because the gospel ultimately promises God's presence in the crucified and risen Christ at the parousia. It is then that the dead shall be made alive by the same Spirit that raised Jesus from the dead. In this way, the righteous will ultimately be conformed to the image of the son. It is only then that cries of distress about divine wrath stemming from ongoing suffering will finally cease. Only then will lament permanently shift to praise. It is a permanent shift grounded in both Jews and Gentiles finally seeing the righteousness of God which the gospel promises them and which they hope for, namely the crucified and risen Jesus Christ. Christ is the righteousness of God, because his death, resurrection, exaltation, and return answer every kind of cry caused by every kind of pain, especially any and all fears of divine condemnation.

Bibliography

Abasciano, Brian J. *Paul's Use of the Old Testament in Romans 9.1–9: An Intertextual and Theological Exegesis.* Library of New Testament Studies 301. London: T. & T. Clark, 2005.
Ahearne-Kroll, Stephen. *The Psalms of Lament in Mark's Passion: Jesus' Davidic Suffering.* Cambridge: Cambridge University Press, 2007.
Anderson, Bernhard W. *Out of the Depths: The Psalms Speak for Us Today.* Philadelphia: Westminster, 1983.
Arnold, Clinton E. *Ephesians.* Grand Rapids: Zondervan, 2010.
Balentine, Samuel. *The Hidden God: The Hiding of the Face of God in the Old Testament.* Oxford: Oxford University Press, 1983.
Barclay, J. M. G. "'Do We Undermine the Law?': A Study of Romans 14.1—15.6." In *Paul and the Mosaic Law: The Third Durham-Tübingen Research Symposium on Earliest Christianity and Judaism,* edited by James D. G. Dunn, 287–308. Grand Rapids: Eerdmans, 2001.
Barrett, C. K. *I Corinthians.* London: Black, 1968.
Basson, Alec. *Divine Metaphors in Selected Hebrew Psalms of Lamentation.* Forschungen zum Alten Testament 2. Reihe 15. Tübingen: Mohr Siebeck, 2006.
Bauckham, Richard. *Jesus and the God of Israel: God Crucified and Other Studies on the New Testament's Christology of Divine Identity.* Grand Rapids: Eerdmans, 2008.
Bauer, Jonas. "Enquiring into the Absence of Lament: A Study of the Entwining of Suffering and Guilt in Lament." In *Evoking Lament: A Theological Discussion,* edited by Eva Harasta and Briand Brock, 26–27. London: T. & T. Clark, 2009.
Bauer, Walter, Frederick W. Dankder, W. F. Arndt, and F. W. Gingrich. *Greek-English Lexicon of the New Testament and Other Early Christian Literature.* 3rd ed. Chicago: University of Chicago Press, 2000.
Baumgartner, Walter. *Jeremiah's Poems of Lament.* Decatur, GA: Almond, 1988.
Bayer, Oswald. *Living by Faith: Justification and Sanctification.* Grand Rapids: Eerdmans, 2003.
———. "Toward a Theology of Lament." In *Caritas et Reformatio: Essays on Church and Society in Honor of Carter Lindberg,* edited by David M. Whitford and George W. Forell, 211–20. St. Louis: Concordia, 2002.
Beker, J. C. "Suffering and Triumph in Paul's Letter to the Romans." *Horizons in Biblical Theology* 7 (1985) 105–19.
Bekken, Per Jarle. *The Word is Near You: A Study of Deuteronomy 30:12–14 in Paul's Letter to the Romans in a Jewish Context.* Berlin: de Gruyter, 2007.

Bell, Richard H. *Provoked to Jealousy: The Origin and Purpose of the Jealousy Motif in Romans 9–11*. Wissenschaftliche Untersuchungen Zum Neuen Testament 2. Reihe 63. Tübingen: Mohr Siebeck, 1994.

Berkley, Timothy W. *From a Broken Covenant to Circumcision of the Heart: A Pauline Intertextual Exegesis in Romans 2:17–29*. Atlanta: Society of Biblical Literature, 2000.

Berlin, Adele. "Psalms and the Literature of Exile: Psalms 137, 44, 69, and 78." In *The Book of Psalms: Composition and Reception*, edited by Peter W. Flint and Patrick Miller Jr., 65–86. Leiden: Brill, 2005.

Betz, Hans Dieter. *Galatians*. Minneapolis: Fortress, 1980.

Black, Clifton. "Pauline Perspectives on Death in Romans 5–8." *Journal of Biblical Literature* 103 (1984) 413–33.

Boyce, Richard Nelson. *The Cry to God in the Old Testament*. Society of Biblical Literature Dissertation Series 103. Atlanta: Scholars, 1985.

Bratsiotis, Panagiotis. "Eine Exegetische Notiz zu Rom. IX 3 und X.1." *Novum Testamentum* 5 (1962) 299–300.

Braaten, Laurie J. "All Creation Groans: Romans 8:22 in Light of the Biblical Sources." *Horizons in Biblical Theology* 28 (2006) 131–59.

Broyles, Craig. *The Conflict of Faith and Experience in the Psalms: A Form-Critical and Theological Study*. Sheffield, UK: Sheffield Academic Press, 1989.

———. "Psalms concerning the Liturgies of Temple Entry." In *The Book of Psalms: Composition and Reception*, edited by Peter W. Flint and Patrick D. Miller Jr., 248–87. Leiden: Brill, 2005.

Bruce, F. F. *Paul: Apostle of the Heart Set Free*. Grand Rapids: Eerdmans, 1977.

Brueggemann, Walter. "The Costly Loss of Lament." In *The Psalms and the Life of Faith*, edited by Patrick D. Miller, 98–111. Minneapolis: Fortress, 1995.

———. "Psalms and the Life of Faith: A Suggested Typology of Function." In *The Psalms of Life and Faith*, edited by Patrick Miller, 3–32. Minneapolis: Fortress, 1995.

Bruno, Christopher R. "Readers, Authors, and the Divine Author: An Evangelical Proposal for Identifying Paul's Old Testament Citations." *Westminster Theological Journal* 71 (2009) 311–21.

Bultmann, Rudolf. *Der Stil der paulinischen Predigt und die kynisch-stoische Diatribe*. Göttingen: Vandenhoeck & Ruprecht, 1910.

Calvin, John. *Romans*. Grand Rapids: Baker, 2003.

Campbell, Keith D. "NT Scholarship's Use of Old Testament Lament Terminology and Its Theological and Interdisciplinary Implications." *Bulletin for Biblical Research* 21 (2011) 213–25.

Caragounis, Chrys C. *The Development of Greek and the New Testament: Morphology, Syntax, Phonology, and Textual Transmission*. Grand Rapids: Baker, 2006.

Carraway, George. *Christ is God Over All: Romans 9:5 in the Context of Romans 9–11*. Library of New Testament Studies 489. London: T. & T. Clark, 2015.

Carr, Wesley. *Angels and Principalities: The Background, Meaning and Development of the Phrase hai archai kai hai exousiai*. Cambridge: Cambridge University Press, 1981.

Christoffersson, Olle. *The Earnest Expectation of the Creature: The Flood-Tradition as Matrix of Romans 8:18–27*. Stockholm: Almqvist & Wiksell, 1990.

Ciampa, Roy E. "Deuteronomy in Galatians and Romans." In *Deuteronomy in the New Testament*, edited by Steve Moyise and Maarten J. J. Menken, 99–117. London: T. & T. Clark, 2007.

Collins, Raymond F. *The Power of Images in Paul*. Collegeville, MN: Liturgical, 2008.

Coetzee, J. H. "A Survey of Research on the Psalms of Lamentation." *Old Testament Essays* 5 (1992) 151–74.

Crisler, Channing L. "Locative Language in Romans." *Anderson Journal of Christian Studies* 2 (2014) 6–21.

Crump, David. *Knocking on Heaven's Door: A New Testament Theology of Petitionary Prayer*. Grand Rapids: Baker, 2006.

Davidson, Robert. *The Courage to Doubt: Exploring an Old Testament Theme*. London: SCM, 1983.

DeSilva, David A. *Galatians: A Handbook on the Greek Text*. Waco, TX: Baylor University Press, 2014.

DeVos, Christiane. *Klage als Gotteslob aus der Tiefe*. Forschungen zum Alten Testament 2. Reihe 11. Tübingen: Mohr Siebeck, 2005.

Dillard, Raymond Bryan. "Joel." In *The Minor Prophets: An Exegetical and Expository Commentary*, edited by Thomas Edward McComiskey, 239–313. Grand Rapids: Baker, 2009.

Dodd, C. H. *According to the Scriptures: The Sub-Structure of New Testament Theology*. London: Fontana, 1965.

———. *The Epistle of Paul to the Romans*. London: Fontana, 1959.

Dodson, Joseph R. *The Powers of Personification: Rhetorical Purposes in the Book of Wisdom and the Letter to the Romans*. Berlin: de Gruyter, 2008.

Dunn, James D. G. "Formal and Theological Coherence of Romans." In *The Romans Debate*, edited by Karl P. Donfried, 245–50. Peabody, MA: Hendrickson, 1991.

———. *Romans 1–8*. Word Biblical Commentary. Dallas: Word, 1988.

———. *Romans 9–16*. Word Biblical Commentary. Dallas: Word, 1988.

———. *The Theology of Paul the Apostle*. Grand Rapids: Eerdmans, 1997.

———. "What's Right about the Old Perspective on Paul?" In *Studies in the Pauline Epistles: Essays in Honor of Douglas J. Moo*, edited by Matthew S. Harmon and Jay E. Smith, 214–29. Grand Rapids: Zondervan, 2014.

Eklund, Rebekah. *Jesus Weeps: The Significance of Jesus' Lament in the New Testament*. Library of New Testament Studies 515. London: Bloomsbury T. & T. Clark, 2015.

Ellington, Scott A. *Risking Truth: Reshaping the World through Prayers of Lament*. Eugene, OR: Pickwick, 2008.

Elliott, Neil. *The Arrogance of the Nations: Reading Romans in the Shadow of Empire*. Minneapolis: Fortress, 2008.

Engberg-Pedersen, Troels. *Paul and the Stoics*. Louisville: Westminster, 2000.

Ferris, Paul Wayne Jr. *The Genre of Communal Lament in the Bible and the Ancient Near East*. Atlanta: Scholars, 1992.

Fitzgerald, John T. *Cracks in an Earthen Vessel: An Examination of the Catalogues of Hardships in the Corinthian Correspondence*. Atlanta: Scholars, 1988.

Floysvik, Ingvar. *When God Becomes My Enemy: The Theology of the Complaint Psalms*. St. Louis: Concordia, 1997.

Freithem, Terrence E. *Jeremiah*. Macon, GA: Smyth & Helwys, 2002.

Futato, Mark D. *Interpreting the Psalms: An Exegetical Handbook*. Grand Rapids: Kregel, 2007.

Gaventa, Beverly Roberts. "The Shape of the 'I': The Psalter, the Gospel, and the Speaker in Romans 7." In *Apocalyptic Paul: Cosmos and Anthropos in Romans 5–8*, edited by Beverly Roberts Gaventa, 77–92. Waco, TX: Baylor University Press, 2013.

Gieniusz, Andrzej. *Romans 8:18–30: Suffering Does Not Thwart the Future Glory.* Atlanta: Scholars, 1999.

Goldingay, John. "Psalm 51:16a (English 51:4a)." *Catholic Biblical Quarterly* 40 (1978) 388–90.

Grogan, Geoffrey W. *Psalms.* Grand Rapids: Eerdmans, 2008.

Gunkel, Hermann. *Introduction to the Psalms: The Genres of the Religious Lyric of Israel.* Macon, GA: Mercer University Press, 1988.

Hafemann, Scott J. *Suffering and Ministry in the Spirit: Paul's Defense of his Ministry in 2 Corinthians 2:14—3:3.* Grand Rapids: Eerdmans, 1991.

Hahne, Harry Alan. *The Corruption and Redemption of Creation: Nature in Romans 8.19-22 and Jewish Apocalyptic Literature.* Library of New Testament Studies 336. London: T. & T. Clark, 2006.

Hanson, Anthony Tyrell. *Studies in Paul's Technique and Theology.* London: SPCK, 1974.

Harrisville, Roy A. "Paul and the Psalms: A Formal Study." *Word & World* 5 (1985) 168–79.

Hartley, John E. *The Book of Job.* Grand Rapids: Eerdmans, 1988.

Havemann, J. C. T. "Cultivated Olive—Wild Olive: The Olive Tree Metaphor in Romans 11:16–24." *Neotestamentica* 31 (1997) 87–106.

Hayes, Katherine M. "When None Repents, Earth Laments: The Chorus of Lament in Jeremiah and Joel." In *Seeking The Favor of God, Vol. 1: The Origins of Penitential Prayer in Second Temple Judaism*, edited by Mark J. Boda et al., 119–43. Atlanta: Society of Biblical Literature, 2006.

Hays, Richard B. *Conversion of the Imagination: Paul as Interpreter of Israel's Scripture.* Grand Rapids: Eerdmans, 2005.

———. *Echoes of Scripture in the Letters of Paul.* New Haven: Yale University Press, 1989.

———. *The Faith of Jesus Christ: The Narrative Substructure of Galatians 3:1—4:11.* 2nd ed. Grand Rapids: Eerdmans, 2002.

———. *Reading Backwards: Figural Christology and the Fourfold Gospel Witness.* Waco, TX: Baylor University Press, 2014.

Hengel, Martin. *The Pre-Christian Paul.* London: SCM, 1991.

Herold, Gerhart. *Zorn und Gerechtigkeit Gottes bei Paulus: Eine Untersuchung zu Rom. 1,16–18.* Frankfurt: Lang, 1973.

Horsley, Richard A., ed. *Paul and Politics: Ekklesia, Israel, Imperium, Interpretation: Essays in Honor of Krister Stendahl.* Harrisburg, PA: Trinity, 2000.

Hübner, Hans. *Gottes Ich und Israel: Zum Schriftgebrauch des Paulus in Römer 9–11.* Göttingen: Vandenhoeck & Ruprecht, 1984.

Huttunen, Niko. *Paul and Epictetus on Law: A Comparison.* Library of New Testament Studies 405. London: T. & T. Clark, 2009.

Jewett, Paul. *Romans: A Commentary.* Minneapolis: Fortress, 2007.

Janowski, Bernd. "Das verbogende Angesicht Gottes. Psalm 13 als Muster eines Klagelieds des Einzelnen." *Jahrbuch für Biblische Theologie* 16 (2001) 25–53.

———. "Klage." In *Religion in Geschichte und Gegenwart*, edited by Hans Dieter Betz et al., 4:1390. Tübingen: Mohr Siebeck, 1998.

Jervis, L. Ann. *At the Heart of the Gospel: Suffering in the Earliest Christian Message.* Grand Rapids: Eerdmans, 2007.
Johnson, E. Elizabeth. *The Function of Apocalyptic and Wisdom Traditions in Romans 9-11.* Atlanta: Scholars, 1989.
Karris, Robert J. "Romans 14:1—15: 13 and the Occasion of Romans." In *The Romans Debate*, edited by Karl P. Donfried, 65-85. Peabody, MA: Hendrickson, 1991.
Käsemann, Ernst. *Commentary on Romans.* Translated by Geoffrey Bromiley. Grand Rapids: Eerdmans, 1980.
———. *Perspectives on Paul.* London: SCM, 1971.
Keck, Leander E. *Romans.* Nashville: Abingdon, 2005.
Keel, Othmar. *The Symbolism of the Biblical World: An Ancient Near East Iconography and the Book of Psalms.* New York: Seabury, 1978.
Keener, Craig S. *Romans.* Eugene, OR: Cascade, 2009.
Keesmaat, Sylvia C. *Paul and His Story: (Re)-Interpreting the Exodus Tradition.* Sheffield, UK: Sheffield Academic Press, 1999.
———. "The Psalms in Romans and Galatians." In *The Psalms in the New Testament*, edited by Steve Moyise and Maarten J. J. Menken, 139-61. London: T. & T. Clark, 2004.
Kittel, Gerhard, and Gerhard Friedrich, eds. *Theological Dictionary of the New Testament.* 10 vols. Reprint. Grand Rapids: Eerdmans, 2006.
Koch, Dietrich-Alex. *Die Schrift als Zeuge des Euangeliums: Untersuchungen zur Verwendungund zum Verständis der Schrift bei Paulus.* Tübingen: Mor Siebeck, 1986.
Kraus, Hans-Joachim. *Psalms 1-59: A Commentary.* Translated by Hilton C. Oswald. Minneapolis: Fortress, 1988.
Kuntz, J. Kenneth. "Growling Dogs and Thirsty Deer: Uses of Animal Imagery in Psalmic Rhetoric." In *My Words Are Lovely: Studies in the Rhetoric of the Psalms*, edited by Robert L. Foster and David M. Howard, Jr., 46-62. London: T. & T. Clark, 2008.
Kushner, Harold S. *When Bad Things Happen to Good People.* New York: Schocken, 1989.
Levy, Ian Christopher, et al. *The Bible in Medieval Tradition: The Letter to the Romans.* Grand Rapids: Eerdmans, 2013.
Lichtenberger, Hermann. *Das Ich Adams und das Ich der Menschheit: Studiem zum Menschenbild in Römer 7.* Wissenschaftliche Untersuchungen Zum Neuen Testament 164. Tübingen: Mohr Siebeck, 2004.
Lim, Yong Kar. *The Sufferings of Christ Are Abundant in Us: A Narrative Dynamics Investigation of Paul's Sufferings in 2 Corinthians.* London: T. & T. Clark, 2009.
Lohse, Eduard. *Der Brief an die Römer.* Göttingen: Vandenhoeck & Ruprecht, 2003.
Longenecker, Richard N. *Introducing Romans: Critical Issues in Paul's Most Famous Letter.* Grand Rapids: Eerdmans, 2011.
———. "Prayer in the Pauline Letters." In *Into God's Presence: Prayer in the New Testament*, edited by Richard N. Longencker, 203-27. Grand Rapids: Eerdmans, 2002.
Lust, Johan, Erik Eynikel, and Katrin Hauspie, eds. *Greek-English Lexicon of the Septuagint.* Stuttgart: Deutsche Bibelgesellschaft, 2003.

Mandolfo, Carleen. *God in the Dock: Dialogic Tension in the Psalms of Lament*. Journal for the Study of the Old Testament Supplement Series 357. Sheffield, UK: Sheffield Academic Press, 2002.

Meeks, Wayne A. *The First Urban Christians: The Social World of the Apostle Paul*. 2nd ed. New Haven, CT: Yale University Press, 2003.

Melanchthon, Monica. *Rejection by God: The History and Significance of the Rejection Motif in the Hebrew Bible*. Studies in Biblical Literature 22. Frankfurt: Lang, 2001.

Miller, Patrick D. *Interpreting the Psalms*. Minneapolis: Fortress, 1986.

———. *They Cried to the Lord: The Form and Theology of Biblical Prayer*. Minneapolis: Fortress, 1994.

———. *The Way of the Lord: Essays in Old Testament Theology*. Tübingen: Mohr Siebeck, 2004.

Middendorf, Michael Paul. *The "I" in the Storm: A Study of Romans 7*. St. Louis: Concordia, 1997.

Moberly, R. W. L. *At the Mountain of God: Story and Theology in Exodus 32–34*. Sheffield, UK: Journal for the Study of the Old Testament Press, 1983.

Moo, Douglas J. *The Epistle to the Romans*. Grand Rapids: Eerdmans, 1996.

Morris, Leon. *Apostolic Preaching of the Cross*. 3rd ed. Grand Rapids: Eerdmans, 1965.

Mounce, William D. *Pastoral Epistles*. Nashville: Thomas Nelson, 2001.

Mowinckel, Sigmund. *The Psalms in Israel's Worship*. Oxford: Blackwell, 1962.

Ochsenmeier, Erwin. "Evil, Suffering, and the Righteousness of God according to Romans 1–3: An Exegetical and Theological Study." *Tyndale Bulletin* 59 (2008) 153–55.

———. *Mal, souffrance et justice de Dieu selon Romains 1—3: Etude exegetique et theologique*. Berlin: de Guyter, 2007.

Ogden, Graham S. "Joel 4 and Prophetic Responses to National Laments." *Journal for the Study of the Old Testament* 26 (1983) 97–106.

Öhler, Markuks. "To Mourn, Weep, Lament and Groan: On the Heterogeneity of the New Testament's Statements on Lament." In *Evoking Lament: A Theological Discussion*, edited by Eva Harastra and Brian Brock, 150–65. London: T. & T. Clark, 2006.

Oswalt, John N. *The Book of Isaiah: Chapters 40–66*. New International Commentary on the Old Testament. Grand Rapids: Eerdmans, 1988.

Sanday, William, and Arthur C. Headlam. *A Critical and Exegetical Commentary on the Epistle to the Romans*. Edinburgh: T. & T. Clark, 1895.

Sanders, E. P. *Paul, the Law and the Jewish People*. Minneapolis: Fortress, 2009.

———. *Paul: A Very Short Introduction*. Oxford: Oxford University Press, 2007.

Schlier, Heinrich. *Der Römerbrief*. Freiburg: Herder, 1977.

Schreiner, Thomas R. *Romans*. Grand Rapids: Baker, 1998.

Schultz, Richard L. "Form Criticism and the OT." In *Dictionary for Theological Interpretation of the Bible*, edited by Kevin J. Vanhoozer, 232–37. Grand Rapids: Baker, 2005.

Schweitzer, Albert. *The Mysticism of Paul the Apostle*. Translated by William Montgomery. Baltimore: John Hopkins University Press, 1998.

Seifrid, Mark A. *Christ Our Righteousness: Paul's Theology of Justification*. Downers Grove, IL: IVP Academic, 2000.

———. "Paul's Approach to the Old Testament in Rom 10:6–8." *Trinity Journal* 6 (1985) 3–37.

---. "Righteousness Language in the Hebrew Scriptures and Early Judaism." In *Justification and Variegated Nomism, Vol. 1: The Complexities of Second Temple Judaism*, edited by D. A. Carson et al., 415–42. Grand Rapids: Baker Academic, 2004.

---. "Romans." In *Commentary on the New Testament Use of Old Testament*, edited by D. A. Carson and G. K. Beale, 607–94. Grand Rapids: Baker Academic, 2007.

---. "Romans 7: The Voice of the Law, the Cry of Lament, and the Shout of Thanksgiving." In *Perspectives on Our Struggle with Sin: Three Views of Romans 7*. Nashville: B. & H. Academic, 2011.

---. *The Second Letter to the Corinthians*. Grand Rapids: Eerdmans, 2014.

---. "Storylines of Scripture and Footsteps in the Sea." *The Southern Baptist Journal of Theology* 12 (2008) 88–106.

Seybold, Klaus D. "Zur Geschichte des Vierten David Psalters." In *The Book of Psalms: The Composition and Reception*, edited by Peter W. Flint and Patrick D. Miller, Jr., 368–89. Leiden: Brill, 2005.

Shum, Shiu-Lin. *Paul's Use of Isaiah in Romans: A Contemporary Study of Paul's Letter to the Romans and the Sibylline and Qumran Sectarian Texts*. Wissenschaftliche Untersuchungen Zum Neuen Testament 156. Tübingen: Mohr Siebeck, 2002.

Smith, Barry. *Paul's Seven Explanations of the Suffering of the Righteous*. Frankfurt: Lang, 2001.

Sölle, Dorothee. *Suffering*. Philadelphia: Fortress, 1975.

Stendahl, Krister. *Paul Among the Jews and Gentiles and Other Essays*. Philadelphia: Fortress, 1976.

Stowers, Stanley. *A Rereading of Romans: Justice, Jews, and Gentiles*. New Haven, CT: Yale University Press, 1994.

Stuhlmacher, Peter. *Paul's Letter to the Romans: A Commentary*. Translated by Scott J. Hafemann. Louisville: Westminster, 1994.

Sumney, Jerry L. *Reading Paul's Letter to the Romans*. Atlanta: Society of Biblical Literature, 2012.

Thorsteinsson, Runar. *Roman Christianity & Roman Stoicism: A Comparative Study of Ancient Morality*. Oxford: Oxford University Press, 2010.

Terrien, Samuel. "The Metaphor of the Rock in Biblical Theology." In *God in the Fray: A Tribute to Walter Brueggemann*, edited by Tod Linafelt and Timothy K. Beal, 157–71. Minneapolis: Fortress, 1998.

---. *The Psalms: Strophic Structure and Theological Commentary*. Grand Rapids: Eerdmans, 2003.

Villanueva, Federico G. *The Uncertainty of a Hearing: A Study of the Sudden Change of Mood in the Psalms of Lament*. Leiden: Brill, 2008.

Wagner, J. Ross. *Heralds of the Good News: Isaiah and Paul in Concert in the Letter to the Romans*. Leiden: Brill, 2002.

Wallace, Daniel B. *Greek Grammar Beyond the Basics: An Exegetical Syntax of the New Testament*. Grand Rapids: Zondervan, 1996.

Wallace, David R. *Election of the Lesser Son: Paul's Lament-Midrash in Romans 9–11*. Minneapolis: Fortress, 2014.

Waltke, Bruce K., James M. Houston, and Erika Moore. *The Psalms as Christian Lament: A Historical Commentary*. Grand Rapids: Eerdmans 2014.

Watson, Francis. *Paul and the Hermeneutics of Faith*. London: T. & T. Clark, 2004.

Weiss, Bernhard. *Der Brief an die Römer*. Göttingen: Vandenhoeck & Ruprecht, 1899.

Westermann, Claus. *Praise and Lament in the Psalms*. Atlanta: John Knox, 1981.

———. *The Psalms: Structure, Context, & Message*. Minneapolis: Augsburg, 1980.

———. "The Role of Lament in the Theology of the Old Testament." *Interpretation* 28 (1974) 20–38.

Wildmer, Michael. *Moses, God, and the Dynamics of Intercessory Prayer*. Tübingen: Mohr Siebeck, 2004.

Wiles, Gordon P. *Paul's Intercessory Prayers: The Significance of the Intercessory Prayer Passages in the Letters of Paul*. Cambridge: Cambridge University Press, 1974.

Willert, Niels. "The Catalogues of Hardships in the Pauline Correspondence." In *The New Testament and Hellenistic Judaism*, edited by Peder Borgen and Søren Givenson, 217–43. Aarhus: Aarhus University Press, 1995.

Wilson, Todd. "'Under Law' in Galatians: A Pauline Theological Abbreviation." *Journal of Theological Studies* 56 (2005) 362–92.

Witherington, Ben. *Conflict & Community in Corinth: A Socio-Rhetorical Commentary on 1 and 2 Corinthians*. Grand Rapids: Eerdmans, 1995.

Wright, N. T. *Climax of the Covenant: Christ and the Law in Pauline Theology*. Minneapolis: Fortress, 1993.

———. *Paul and the Faithfulness of God*. Vol. 4 of Christian Origins and the Question of God. London: SPCK, 2013.

———. *Pauline Perspectives: Essays on Paul, 1978–2013*. London: SPCK, 2013.

———. *Romans*. In vol. 10 of *The New Interpreter's Bible Commentary*, edited by Leander E. Keck, 395–770. Nashville: Abingdon, 2002.

Ancient Documents Index

OLD TESTAMENT

Genesis

2:16	108, 110
2:16–17	108, 110
2:17	108, 110
2–3	108
3	97, 120, 123, 125
3:4	108
3:6	108
3:13	108
3:16	121
3:17	123, 125
3:17–19	125
3:18–19	125
3:19	125
4	123
4:7	99
4:10	123
12:1–3	41, 121, 157, 163, 164
15:6	164, 165,
15:13	121, 128
17:1–8	163, 164
18:10	167
21:12	167
25:23	167
37:20	30
37:22	30
37:24	30
37:28	30
37:29	30
40:15	30

Exodus

1–15	21
2	148
2:23–24	21, 98, 111, 121, 128
3:7	25
3:7–9	21
3:7	25, 121
3:9	98, 111
4:22	163
6:5	121, 128
9:16	169
12:25–26	164
13:5	164
14	158
14:14	158
14:17	158
14:18	158
16:2	26
16:7	26, 164
16:8	26
18:22	130
23:10–11	123
23:21	52
24:16–17	164
32	11, 215
32–34	12, 152, 156, 159, 161, 162, 166, 168, 171, 176, 187, 188
32:1–6	156
32:4	156
32:10	156, 157
32:11	28
32:11–14	156, 158
32:12	159

Exodus (continued)

32:12–13	158
32:12–23	169
32:14	157, 161, 166
32:15–29	157, 161, 166
32:30	157, 161
32:30–32	166
32:31–35	161
32:32	152, 155, 156, 157, 158, 160, 192
32:33	158
32:33–35	167
32:34–35	158
33:12	158
33:12–13	158
33:13	160, 161
33:14	158
33:15	160
33:15–16	158
33:16	158
33:18	158, 169
33:19	168, 169
33:19–23	158, 176
40:34–35	164

Leviticus

18:5	109, 110, 164
19:19	123

Numbers

11	131
11:11–15	130
11:17	130
11:23	131
14:2	26
25:10–13	162
35:33	123

Deuteronomy

1:17	52
1:27	26
4:1	109
6:24	109
8:1	109
16:20	109
26:5–11	21
27:26	109
28	137, 143
28:15	137
28:48	137
28:53	137
28:55	137
28:57	137
28:69	164
29:4	177
30:6	109
30:12–14	174
30:19	109
31:17	153
31:17–18	85, 88, 140, 191
31:18	30, 38, 153
31:20	153
32:8	146
32:20	85, 88
32:21	175
32:39	146
32:43	200

Joshua

7:6–9	99
9:18	26

Judges

3:7–11	99

1 Samuel

2:6	146

2 Samuel

7:11–13	41, 164

1 Kings

8:11	164
19	177
19:1–9	176
19:10	176
19:11–13	76
19:14	176
19:15–18	177

2 Chronicles

5:14	164

Esther

1:1	137
4:17	156

Ezra

9	21
9:7	99, 111

Job

3:12	28
3:24	31, 122
5:9	184, 185
9	185
9:3	185
9:6–9	185
9:10	184, 185
9:11	185
10:18	28
12:13	182
13:8	52
17:7	32
19:2	27
23:2	31
24	128
24:1–11	128
24:10	128
24:12	31, 128, 129
26:14	184, 185
28:11	182
30	128
30:17	129
30:19–23	129
30:25	31, 128
30:27	32
31:38	123
34:24	185
38–39	186
41:3	186, 187

Psalms (LXX)

1:5–6	39, 84
5	76, 78, 80
5:2–4	76
5:6	76
5:6–7	88
5:7	76
5:8	96
5:9	91
5:9–11	76
5:10	77
5:11	33, 77
5:11–12	77
5:13	34, 77
6:2–3	36
6:4	23
6:5	106
6:7	31, 120, 122
6:11	47
7:2	106
7:3	23, 39, 100
7:11	34
7:16	30
9	88
9:5	33
9:9	33, 35, 43, 48
9:10	32
9:18	39
9:22	30, 37, 80, 148
9:22–39	79
9:23	79
9:25	79
9:27	79, 88
9:28	79
9:29–32	79
9:30	39
9:32	24, 80, 88
9:34	79
9:35	80
9:36	79
9:37	39
9:37–39	80
10:5	76
11:2	106
11:6	31, 37, 82, 120, 122
12	20, 26, 27, 96, 152, 153, 154, 162
12:1	23, 24
12:1–2	26
12:2	153
12:2–3	26, 96, 153, 154
12:3	153, 155
12:3–5	153
12:5	155
12:6	43, 96, 153, 155
13	73, 74, 75, 76, 88

Psalms (LXX) *(continued)*

13:1	70, 74, 75, 88
13:1–2	74
13:1–5	75
13:2	73, 74
13:4	73, 74 88
13:4–5	74, 76
13:5	34
13:6	47
13:7	74, 75
16:8–9	103
16:9	31
16:12	100
16:13	106
17:3	32
17:5	103
17:18	100, 106
17:20	106
17:28	34
17:31	32
17:50	200
18:1–4	175
18:5	175
18:15	32
19:7	34, 55
20:9	55
21	20, 136
21:1	30, 40
21:2	27, 148
21:5–6	47
21:6	47
21:8	193
21:12–14	136
21:13	39, 103
21:13–14	24
21:15	32
21:17	39, 96, 103
21:21	39, 106
22:3	37
24:1	23
24:2	47
24:10	37
24:11	37
24:16	96
24:20	106
25:1	23
25:11	96
26:1	32
26:2	24
26:3	24
26:7	23
26:7–8	34
26:9	32, 38
26:14	52
27:1	30, 103
27:7	32
27:8	32
29:4	30
29:11	32
30:2	36, 43, 47, 48, 55, 60, 106
30:3	32
30:4	37
30:5	24, 32, 97
30:7	76
30:9	48
30:10	31
30:11	31, 120, 122
30:12	48
30:16	48, 106
30:18	47
30:19	135, 142
30:20	48
31	104
31:3	100
31:4	31, 104
31:7	32
32:20	32
33:8	106
33:15	74
33:16	34
33:17	42
33:19	34
33:20	34, 106
34:4	47
34:7	24, 31, 97
34:22	147
34:24	33
34:26	47
34:28	43
35	70, 71, 72, 73, 76, 88
35:1	88
35:1–5	183
35:2	71, 72, 76
35:3–5	72
35:4–5	97
35:6–12	72

Ancient Documents Index 231

35:7	48, 72, 91, 183	42:1	106
35:11–12	72	42:2	28
36:14	40	43	6, 23, 38, 42, 120, 134, 139, 144, 149, 214
36:27	74		
36:17	34	43:1–9	139, 144
36:32–33	135, 143	43:2	144
36:34	52	43:4	35, 52, 55
36:19	34	43:8	139
36:27	74	43:10	6, 43, 139, 214
36:39	32	43:10–17	144
36:39–40	34	43:11	139
36:40	106	43:12	29, 140, 141, 144
37	100, 102, 104, 113, 214	43:13	139
37:2	23	43:16	139
37:2–4	102	43:17–22	144
37:4	101, 112	43:18	38, 140
37:4–6	113	43:22	140
37:5	24, 25	43:23	5, 6, 29, 40, 134, 139, 140, 141, 144, 149, 210
37:5–6	102		
37:5–7	104	43:24	141
37:7	40, 100, 101, 104, 113	43:24–25	28
37:8	101	43:25	140, 153
37:9	122	43:27	23, 37
37:9–10	120	44:5	55
37:10	31, 122	44:8	76
37:11	101	45:2	32
37:13	40	47:12	183
37:13–22	102	49:15	144
37:14	96	50	67, 69, 87, 91, 92
37:18–19	96	50:3	33, 68
37:20	102	50:3–4	67
37:22	30, 148	50:4	68, 69
37:23	106	50:5	67, 68
38	106	50:5–6	68
38:9	34, 35, 106	50:5–8	67
38:9–11	25	50:6	33, 67, 68, 69
39	103, 104	50:7	68, 69
39:2–3	30	50:7–15	68
39:3	30, 31, 103	50:9–14	67
39:11	34, 35	50:11	68
39:13	24, 104	50:11–14	35
39:13–14	35	50:15–21	68
39:14	52	50:16	68, 91, 106
39:17	34	50:19	34
39:18	31, 32, 96	51:9	32
40:2	106	53:3	33
40:5	36	54	96
41:10	28, 38	54:13–14	25

Psalms (LXX) *(continued)*

54:17	96
54:22	97
55:2	40, 135
55:3	100
55:5	134
55:6	135
55:6–7	100
55:7	97, 135
55:9	135
55:10	135
55:12	134
56:7	104
57:2	33
57:5	39
57:11	33
57:12	33
57:13	79
58:3	34, 106
58:3–4	100
58:7	39
58:8	40
58:12	32
58:15	39
58:17	32
58:18	32
59:7	55
59:17	96
61:9	32
62:8	32
62:9	55
62:12	90
63:4	40
63:4–5	24
63:11	34
65:4	48
65:12	24
67:21	146
67:31	24
68	136, 178, 190, 192, 194, 195, 197, 200, 213, 215
68:2	22, 39
68:2–5	190
68:4	191
68:5	24, 136
68:6–7	196
68:7	23, 34, 47, 191
68:8	193
68:8–9	191
68:9	136
68:9–10	196, 197
68:10	8, 16, 189, 190, 192, 194, 199
68:11–12	191
68:12	193
68:13	191
68:14	36
68:14–15	191
68:15	30
68:16	39, 191
68:18	191
68:19	106, 191
68:20	191
68:21	82, 191
68:22	191, 192
68:22–23	177
68:23	191
68:23–24	191
68:28–29	191
68:29	178
68:31–32	195
68:31–37	192
68:32	192
68:34	192
68:35	192
68:36–37	192
69:3	47
69:4	47
69:5	34
69:6	32
70:1–2	47
70:2	36, 48, 55, 60, 106
70:3	32
70:4	106
70:7	32
70:10	48
70:13	47
70:24	47
71:2	33
71:12	32, 34
72:14	40
73:1	28, 29
73:10	27, 37
73:11	55
73:22	100
73:23	55

Ancient Documents Index 233

74:1	144	93:15	34
75:4	24	93:21	135, 142
76	183	93:22	32
76:1–4	184	94:7	29
76:8–10	184	95:7	144
76:11	55	95:13	33
76:12	184	96:8	183
76:13	184	96:10	106
76:14–16	184	97	55, 56, 63, 64
76:17–19	184	97:1	54, 55
76:21	184	97:2	41, 54, 55, 63
77:21	144	97:2–3	54
77:35	32	97:3	37, 41, 55
77:36	97, 110	97:4–8	54
77:61	99	97:9	33, 41, 54, 63
77:62	40	100:3	144
78:5	27	101:6	31, 120, 122
78:9	106	101:9	100
78:11	31, 120, 122	101:21	120, 122
78:52	144	102	147
79:13	144	102:20	31
79:19	148	102:20–21	147
80:2	32, 144	103	183
81:2	27	103:18	32
81:3	33, 34	103:24	182
81:8	33	103:35	183
82:18	47	104:5	183
83:10	32	105	99
84:8	106	105:8	37
84:10–11	35	105:40	76
85:2	106	105:40–45	99, 111
85:17	47	105:42	99
87:7	30	106	87
87:15	28	106:6	87
87:18	40, 100, 111	106:10–16	87
87:19	31, 82	106:11	87
88:6	37	106:13	87
88:47	27	106:18	76
88:49	106, 113	106:19	87
88:50	37	106:28	87
89:1	32	106:42	90
90	106	107:41	144
90:2	32	108:2	135, 142
90:3	106	108:6	55
90:9	32	108:22	106
90:13	39	108:28	47
93:3	27	113:17	32
93:7	24, 40	113:18	32

Psalms (LXX) *(continued)*

113:19	32
114:4	144
114:6	144
117:1	200
118:6	47
118:43	37
118:46	47
118:62	183
118:78	47
118:80	47
118:160	37
118:176	34
118:155	30
118:164	183
128:5	47
129:1	30
131:11	37
136:8	31
137:6	34
137:7	55
137:8	92
138:8	148
138:10	55
139	80
139:2	78
139:2–4	78
139:3	24, 88, 100
139:3–4	78
139:4	39, 78
139:5	78
139:5–6	24, 78
139:7–9	78
139:10	24, 78
139:11	78
139:12	78
139:13	78
139:14	34
142	36, 42, 84, 85, 86, 89, 90, 92
142:1	91
142:1–3	36
142:1–4	84
142:1–6	84
142:2	33, 84, 85, 90, 91, 199
142:4	84
142:6	84
142:7	30
142:7–9	85
142:7–12	84
142:8–9	85
142:10	85
142:11	85, 91
142:11–12	90
142:12	36, 85
143:2	32
143:7	39
143:10	40
145:6	37
148	147
148:2	147

Psalms (MT)

4:2	79
5:6	79
5:9–10	79
7:12–16	79
10:7–9	79
27:12	79
38	101
44	139
44:10	6
44:23	5, 10
51:6	42, 68
58:13	79
69	8, 9
69:9	8, 9

Ecclesiastes

1	125
1:2–11	125
1:4	125
7	70, 73
7:1–12	70
7:1–22	70, 71
7:2–4	70
7:9–10	70
7:15	71
7:15–18	70
7:16–17	71
7:18	71
7:19–22	71
7:21–22	71
7:20	70, 71, 88
7:21–22	71
7:27–29	71
12:13	71

Isaiah

1:9	172
5:1–7	82
6:1	164
7:11	182
8	137
8:14	173
8:21	137
8:22	137
10:5	172
10:21	172
10:22	172
11:10	200
15:5	82
24	125, 126
24:3	125
24:4–6	124, 125
24:5–6	125, 126
24:7	31
24:22	129
26	122
26:5–6	122
26:17–18	122
26:18	122
26:19	123
26:20	122
27:9	155, 180
28:16	173
28:22	172
29:10	177
29:16	170
30:6	137
30:14	82
33:1	31
40:10–15	186
40:13	186, 187
45:9	170
47:11	31
51:10	182
51:11	31
51:19	82
53:1	174
55	185
55:5	185
55:8–9	185
55:10–11	186
59	81, 83, 86, 181
59:1	81
59:1–8	180
59:2	81
59:3	81, 82
59:4	81
59:5–6	82
59:6	82
59:7	82
59:7–8	81, 83
59:8	82
59:9–15	82, 180
59:10	31, 82
59:12	82
59:13	83
59:13–14	83
59:16	83
59:16–20	180
59:16–21	83
59:17	83
59:19–20	83
59:20	83, 155, 180
65:1	175
65:2	175

Jeremiah

3:21	29
4	126
4:13	31
4:20	31, 82
4:21	27
4:28	124, 126
4:31	31
5:12	138
5:26	31
6:26	82
9:18	31
11:16	74
11:22	138
12	138
12:4	27
14:9	28
14:12	138
14:16	138
15:8	31, 105
16:4	138
18:6	170
18:21	138
20:18	28
24:10	138

Jeremiah (continued)

29:10	177
31:19	31
31:31–34	41
31:33	155
38:31	180
38:33	164
44:16	30
45:6	30
45:7	30
45:10	30
45:11	30
45:13	30
50:6	29
50:17	29
50:25	170
51:33	31

Ezekiel

11:19–20	41
16:1–14	163
16:8	163
21:11	31
21:12	31
26:15	31
26:16	31
26:20	182
31:14	182
31:18	182
32:24	182
34:5	29
34:6	29
34:8	29
34:10	29
34:11	29
34:15	29
34:17	29
43:2	164
43:4	164
43:5	164

Lamentations

1:8	31
1:21	31
1:22	31
2:11	31
2:21	138
3:53	30
3:55	30
4:14	82
5:20	28

Daniel

4:14	74
6:9	30
6:13	30
6:15	30
6:18	30
6:20	30
6:23	30
9	21
10:20–21	146

Hosea

2:25	172

Joel

1:10	31
1:15	104
3:5	174

Amos

5:9	82
8:8–10	124
9:3	182

Jonah

2:2–9	30
2:4	182

Micah

2:12	29
5:7	29
7:14	29
7:19	182

Habakkuk

1:1–4	50
1:2	27
1:2–4	53
1:3	28, 82
1:4	52
1:5	50

1:5–11	53
1:6–11	50
1:12–13	50
1:12–17	53, 199
1:13	51, 52
1:13–17	51
2:2	51, 52
2:2–3	53, 62
2:2–4	51, 52, 53
2:4	7, 13, 49, 52, 53, 61, 62, 65, 199
2:5	53
2:5—3:19	51, 53
3	83
3:2	51, 84
3:3	52
3:4–6	52
3:10	52
3:13	52
3:18–19	51

Haggai

1:10	52

Zechariah

10:11	182

Malachi

1:2	167
2:13	31

APOCRYPHA

1 Maccabees

2:6	21
12:9	198

2 Maccabees

6:9	105
6:23	164

3 Maccabees

6:1–15	21

4 Maccabees

5:35	164
17:16	164

Odes

12:6	185

Psalms of Solomon

12:1	135

Sirach

4:11–19	71

Wisdom

6:7	52

PSEUDEPIGRAPHA

1 Enoch

20:2	146
40:9	146
60:12–22	146
61:10	146
66:1–2	146
89:59—90:19	146

2 Enoch

19:3–4	146

Jubilees

2:2	146
15:30–32	146

NEW TESTAMENT

Matthew

27:34	192
27:37	193
27:39	193
27:40	193
27:42–43	193
27:43	197
27:54	193, 194

Mark

8:38	46
15:23	192
15:29	193
15:39	193, 194

Luke

23:47	193, 194

John

1:13	168

Acts

7:34	121
17:16–34	215

Romans

1–3	205, 206, 209
1:1	133
1:2	201
1:3	69
1:3–4	143
1:5	133
1:6–7	133
1:15	57
1:16	46, 173
1:16–17	4, 7, 10, 15, 45, 46, 48, 53, 55, 56, 57, 58, 60, 61, 63, 64, 65, 90, 199, 200, 213, 217
1:17	7, 52, 53, 54, 58, 60, 61, 62, 64
1:18	62
1:18–32	62
1:18—2:29	66, 213
1:18—3:20	203, 204
1:25	116
1:32	75
2:1–11	114
2:1–16	62
2:3	75
2:9	136
2:17	89
2:28	86
3:1	86
3:1–2	86
3:1–8	67, 69, 87
3:1–18	86
3:1–20	15, 66, 67, 69, 75, 80, 85, 86, 87, 88, 89, 90, 91, 110, 199, 213
3:2	86
3:4	48, 79, 87, 91, 217
3:5	66, 170
3:8	64
3:9	70, 87
3:9–20	57, 66, 80, 83, 213
3:10	48, 70, 73
3:10–18	40, 67, 70, 73, 77, 88, 89, 91, 92
3:10–20	10, 217
3:11	73
3:11–12	73
3:13	48, 78
3:13–14	76
3:14	48, 79
3:15–17	81, 83, 86
3:18	48, 73
3:19	89, 90, 92
3:19–20	73, 89, 90, 91
3:20	84, 85, 86, 91, 110, 199
3:20–21	64
3:21	60, 90
3:21–22	91
3:21–26	62, 66, 90, 91
3:25	92
3:25–26	92
4	61, 217
4:1–25	217
4:3	164
4:6	69
4:7	48
4:8	48
4:9	164
4:22	14
4:23	164
4:25	62
5	48
5:1–10	213
5:5	48
5:6–10	62
5:8	145
5:9	213
5:10	213
5:12	204
5:12–21	110
5:17	209

Ancient Documents Index 239

6:23	213
7	12, 69, 90, 98, 99, 105, 108, 109, 110, 114, 115, 116, 117, 214
7–8	117
7:7	109, 110
7:7–25	14, 22, 25, 32, 40, 57, 89, 90, 94, 95, 97, 100, 101, 102, 105, 107, 111, 114, 116, 117, 127, 206, 215
7:7—8:4	4, 15, 199, 212, 217
7:7–11	107, 110
7:7–12	108
7:8	96, 100, 110
7:8–11	111
7:9	96
7:10	96, 111
7:10–11	110
7:11	96, 97, 98, 100, 108
7:13	96, 111
7:13–23	111, 112
7:14	69, 96, 100, 111
7:17	96, 112
7:18	96, 112
7:20	96, 112
7:21	96, 112
7:23	96, 100, 111, 112
7:24	2, 6, 31, 96, 102, 103, 105, 106, 107, 111, 112, 113, 114, 115, 116, 215, 216
7:24–25	23
7:25	96, 114, 115, 116
8	114, 115, 120, 129, 131, 206, 214
8–9	30
8:1	112, 114, 115
8:1–4	114
8:2	114
8:3	114, 215
8:4	115
8:7–18	132
8:9	115
8:9–17	131
8:10	117, 210
8:10–11	115
8:11	127
8:12–17	127
8:15	129
8:17	127
8:17–18	132
8:17–30	203, 204
8:17–39	206
8:18–27	119, 129, 132, 149, 214
8:18–30	119, 120, 121, 124, 127, 128, 133, 134, 204
8:18–39	57, 116, 119, 128, 149, 217
8:19	126, 127, 129
8:19–22	124, 125, 126, 149
8:19–23	122
8:19–25	123
8:19–27	31, 132, 133, 179
8:20	125, 126
8:20–21	126
8:21	126, 129
8:22	120, 126, 127
8:23	120, 127, 129, 215
8:23–25	127, 128, 129, 130, 198
8:24	116, 127, 129, 215
8:26	120, 130
8:26–27	129, 131
8:27	131
8:28	132
8:28–30	132, 134, 141, 149
8:29	132, 133, 210
8:29–30	133
8:30	133
8:31	134, 142
8:31–35	138
8:31–36	141, 142
8:31–39	6, 10, 25, 29, 119, 127, 129, 131, 132, 134, 136, 139, 141, 149, 151, 152, 200, 210, 212, 214, 216
8:32	142, 144, 205, 215
8:33	143
8:33–34	135, 136
8:34	143
8:35	136, 137, 138, 143
8:35–36	143, 144
8:35–39	6, 206
8:36	2, 5, 10, 23, 48, 134, 139, 144, 214, 215
8:37	145
8:37–39	144, 145, 147
8:38	146, 147
8:38–39	148
9	48

Romans *(continued)*

9–11	12, 13, 151, 154, 161, 162, 165, 166, 167, 180, 182, 183, 185, 187, 188, 200, 213, 216
9:1–3	61, 151, 152, 162, 173
9:1–5	4, 11, 12, 14, 23, 27, 57, 151, 152, 153, 154, 159, 162, 163, 166, 176, 180, 187, 188, 212, 216, 217
9:1–13	166
9:1—11:33	11
9:1—11:36	11
9:3	6, 152, 155, 156, 159, 162, 169, 179, 192, 215
9:4	86, 129
9:4–5	163, 165, 166
9:5	23, 116, 160, 162, 165
9:6	159, 167, 170
9:6–13	167, 168, 170, 188
9:6—11:32	151, 152, 161, 165, 182, 187, 188
9:6—11:36	162, 165, 166
9:7	14, 167
9:8	167
9:9	167
9:10–13	167
9:11	167
9:12	133, 168
9:13	168
9:14	154, 168, 169
9:14–23	170, 173
9:14–29	168, 188
9:14—10:21	166, 173
9:15	168, 169
9:16	169, 170
9:18	169
9:19	169
9:19–23	170
9:21	171
9:21–23	170
9:22	170
9:22–23	171
9:24	170, 171
9:24–29	171
9:24—10:21	171
9:25	172
9:26	172
9:27	172, 217
9:30—10:21	173, 188
9:30–31	173
9:31	177
9:32	173
9:33	48, 173
9:33—10:21	175
10	173
10:1	155, 159, 179
10:2	173
10:3	60, 64
10:4	174
10:5	109
10:9	174
10:11	48
10:13	14, 173, 174, 217
10:14	174
10:14–18	161
10:14–21	174
10:15	174
10:16	174
10:18	10, 14, 48, 175
10:19	175
11	48
11:1	139, 153, 154, 176, 177, 181, 184
11:1–2	10, 176
11:1–6	61, 176
11:1–32	176, 181, 188
11:1–36	166
11:2–4	176
11:2–5	23
11:2–6	217
11:3	177, 183
11:5	178
11:6	177
11:6–7	177
11:7–11	177, 181
11:7–8	177
11:8	177
11:9	48, 69, 191
11:9–10	10, 177
11:11	178
11:11–12	178
11:13–14	161, 179
11:14	180
11:15	159
11:16	179
11:16–24	179
11:20	179

11:23	179
11:24	179
11:25	155, 179
11:25-32	179
11:26	83, 179
11:26-27	155, 180
11:28	180
11:29	155, 180
11:30-31	180, 181
11:32	181, 216
11:33	181, 182, 185
11:33-36	11, 12, 13, 116, 151, 152, 162, 181, 182, 188, 216
11:34	14, 186
11:34-35	186
11:35	186, 187
11:36	187
12:1-2	197
12:9—13:7	206
13:1-6	146
14	189, 195, 213
14-15	196
14:1-9	195
14:1-18	62
14:1—15:13	189
14:4	195
14:10	213
14:10-23	57
14:13	195
14:15	195
14:19	196
14:19-20	196
14:20	196
14:23	196
15:1-3	194
15:1-6	4, 57, 189, 190, 194, 195, 196, 197, 198, 200, 201, 212, 213
15:1-13	198, 201, 206
15:3	9, 10, 48, 189, 190, 199, 215, 216, 217
15:3-4	200
15:4	16, 189, 190
15:4-6	8
15:5-6	200
15:7-13	200
15:8	216
15:9-13	216
15:10	14
15:11	14
15:12	200
15:13	201

1 Corinthians

1:18-31	46
1:23	46
1:24	133
2:6-8	146
2:6-9	185
2:10	182
3:22-23	147
6:14	127
13:9-10	185
15:8-10	177
15:45	127
15:54-57	146
16:22	160

2 Corinthians

1:20	165
11:13	146
12:17	146

Galatians

1:8	146, 160
1:9	160
1:13-14	162
1:22-23	177
2:16	85
2:20	145
3:6	164
3:8	164
3:11	53
3:12	109
3:19	146
3:21	110
4:5	129
4:14	146

Ephesians

1:5	129
3:10	146
3:18	148, 182
5:2	145
6:12	146

Colossians

1:16	146
1:18	134, 146
2:15	146

2 Timothy

2:20–21	170

Hebrews

1:3	143
10:37–38	52

1 Peter

2:12	129
2:23	194
4:11	87

DEAD SEA SCROLLS

1QM

10:11–12	146
14:15–16	146
15:13–14	146

RABBINIC WRITINGS

Mek. Shir.

2:112	146

www.ingramcontent.com/pod-product-compliance
Lightning Source LLC
Chambersburg PA
CBHW051052230426
43667CB00013B/2262